WHAT IS IT LIKE TO FLY THE FASTEST AIRPLANE IN THE WORLD?

Even before you reach Mach 1 you're flying faster than anyone else has ever flown. From .8 Mach you leave the limits of the known, enter a region of speed, sensation, and experience where no other living man has ever been. No matter how small the variance is from something that's happened before, you know it has never happened to anyone else. And you're tempted to go on from there, to go a step further—a hundredth, a twenty-fifth, a tenth.

The figure is meaningless, the change sometimes unnoticeable. It is not the risk you're after, the mere sensation of greater speed, the pull at your guts or the strange new feeling of being suspended in time and space, of floating in motion on top of the ball that moves in every direction at once and never rests. It is the simple, direct, and pointed challenge that lies in doing what no one else has ever done, in the fact that you're pitted alone against some ultimate force.

ACROSS THE HIGH FRONTIER

The Story of a Test Pilot—
Major Charles E. Yeager, USAF

William R. Lundgren

Foreword by J. H. Doolittle

BANTAM BOOKS

TORONTO • NEW YORK • LONDON • SYDNEY • AUCKLAND

ACROSS THE HIGH FRONTIER
A Bantam Book / published by arrangement with
William Morrow & Company, Inc.

PRINTING HISTORY
William Morrow edition published November 1955
Bantam Edition / March 1987

Bantam Books are published by Bantam Books, Inc. Its trademark, consisting of the words "Bantam Books" and the por-
trayal of a rooster, is Registered in U.S. Patent and Trademark
Office and in other countries. Marca Registrada. Bantam
Books, Inc., 666 Fifth Avenue, New York, New York 10103.

Contents

Foreword

The modern airplane has a long and complex pedigree. It is the end-product of the technical ingenuity and skills of a large number of people. Inventors, research men, designers, builders, and many others have contributed their imagination and talent to the airplane's development and fabrication. Yet, as history relates it, the airplane is the product of much more; it is made up as well of the dreams and faith of pioneering men who shared a belief in and a devotion to aviation. Indeed, the spark of air progress was often kept alive only by their vision and determination.

The story of the men who conceived the Bell X-1 research airplane and of Charles "Chuck" Yeager symbolizes the foresight and resourcefulness of these air pioneers. It is the story of men of courage who looked beyond the horizons of their day to see a new era of exploration and promise where others saw only a barrier in the sky, a sonic barrier.

Chuck Yeager and the X-1 proved that the sonic barrier, like so many other "insurmountable" barriers, existed only in the minds of men. But Chuck and the airplane represented more than a man and a flying machine. They were symbols of man's faith in himself and in the science and technology he had created—a faith upon which air progress is built.

In *Across the High Frontier*, William R. Lundgren has paid proper tribute to Chuck Yeager, the test pilot and the man. While people of varied skills work together to conceive, develop and construct an airplane, it is the test pilot who alone must prove that their theories and handicraft are sound. As such, a test pilot is the loneliest man in the sky. And during his test flights, his wife is the loneliest person on the ground.

The task of a test pilot of an ultra high-speed research airplane is an especially hazardous one. Research airplanes like the X-1 and X-1A are essentially flying laboratories designed to probe the unknown, to study the basic problems of flight. By the very nature of the test vehicle and its environment, its performance is not entirely predictable. The man who tests it must give it a good part of his life. He must live with it, understand it, and have confidence in the airplane and in the men whose ideas it embodies. In the air, he must become a part of it. Together, man and machine must yield the new aeronautical knowledge from which advanced, operational aircraft and missiles are evolved. It was so with Chuck Yeager.

A double ace of World War II, skilled in the precision art of aerial combat, Chuck Yeager was more than a name when Air Force test pilot ranks were screened for the man to penetrate beyond the knowledge of aeronautical science. To his fellow workers and flying partners Chuck Yeager was synonymous with stability, reliability, precision, alertness, enthusiasm and a deep appreciation of and respect for the known and unknown. In flyers' parlance, Chuck was "solid as a rock."

His story is a typical American story: a small town boy sparked with a determined yen to fly. World War II gave him the chance and Chuck became a skilled fighter pilot. His combat experiences, including bail-out and escape from German occupied France, laced adventure into a brilliant career which led Chuck to an envied place in aeronautical history.

I know Chuck as a friend, as a family man and as a test pilot. His quiet and unassuming manner gives no hint of the world acclaim he has received from being the first to break through the sound barrier, and later, to fly two and one-half times the speed of sound. In his own modest perspective, he was simply a test pilot who had a job to do. In the light of aeronautical achievement, however, he is one of the dedicated air pioneers who have repeatedly

risked their lives to extend man's knowledge and the
horizons of flight.

J. H. DOOLITTLE

Washington, D . C .
24 August 1955

Prologue, September, 1953

There are three small offices and a big, square lounge on the second floor of one of the hangars at Edwards Air Force Base. The walls of the lounge and of the offices are covered with maps, with photographs of men and planes, with posters and with charts. Clipboards of Air Force bulletins hang haphazardly from hooks.

The lounge itself, the first room you enter from the stairs, is a scuffed and battered square littered with furniture and gear. A black- and orange-checkered helmet lies like a big bright gourd on the leather cushion of one chair. A parachute and its harness lie on another. In one corner there are shelves carelessly stacked with magazines, the journals of a trade. You can read, if you're interested, about the human factor in jet accidents. Posters advise you that if something doesn't work, report it now. Later might be too late. From this your eye slips past two sets of dusty windows and falls on the detailed map covering one wall from floor to ceiling and from door to door, a map of the desert area above which the pilots fly.

In the small office immediately beyond this lounge there are three desks. Above each desk hang blown-up photographs of complicated instrument panels in the ships these pilots test. The desks and photographs shrink the room to closet size, drawing its walls together into a crowded rectangle. The windows of this office too are glazed with dust.

Walking away from the lounge, through the small hallway leading past this first office, you come into an even smaller room with even dustier windows. Here there are

1

three more desks, two of them face to face, the third jammed into a corner near the door. On the first desk there is a stack of papers and reports, a half-empty box of ten-cent cigars, an ash tray full of butts. The second desk holds more papers, another ash tray, the switch box for an intercom system and its speaker with a built-in microphone. When you want to use the intercom you talk back into the speaker facing you.

One of the windows of this small office looks down into the big hangar. But its size is diminished too by the planes that are scattered across its floor. Immediately below the window men are working on a jet whose fuselage has been disassembled in three sections. Two men work on the ejecting mechanism that will throw the pilot clear of the ship if he has to bail out, if the mechanism works. Their movements are slow and studied. Beyond them, almost in the center of the hangar, three men slowly wheel another plane in a circle to face the open doors. And beyond that ship, in the far corner, there is a fat little fighter, its nose painted in a bright, distracting spiral of red and white.

Turning from there you can see through the tall doors of the hangar, folded open now and reaching from the ground below you to a distance above your head. You can see more hangars in the background, a big four-motored, propeller-driven bomber warming up, and the long, sandy stretch of desert, the dry lake on which the runway lies. The dry shore climbs into bare, dry hills and these rise into bare, dry mountains in the distance, mountains themselves dwarfed by the desert's spread, mountains that fade from purple to copper-red to gray as the sun and the sand and the wind move through the bright blue sky.

But you're not here to see this landscape or to watch the mountains fade. You turn away, your interest drawn back to the working men below you, men who are working even on this hot summer Saturday afternoon. They will work on Sunday too and without complaint. They like their work. They do it well.

Then, turning away from them, you face the open door that was behind your back. Through this you enter the colonel's office, largest of the three, another room jammed with desks, its walls also plastered with pictures of men and planes. Half-hidden by the open door, a pilots' performance-rating chart is painted on one big blackboard covering the wall. Its blanks and squares are partially filled in with colored numbers, yellow, red and blue. But you have the feeling it is probably not up to date. You begin to suspect that the men who work in here are not good clerks, that they're not very likely to keep records with much concern or to fill in the proper blanks on every chart. You have the feeling they're too busy thinking about the planes they've flown or the planes they're going to fly.

For these casual rooms are the offices of the Flight Test Section of the United States Air Force Air Research and Development Command at Edwards Air Force Base near Muroc, California. And the casual pilots reporting for duty here are the men who fly the fastest aircraft in the world.

Jammed usually with pilots, alive with the excitement of their work, sometimes these offices are completely empty, quiet even in the surrounding noise—the blast of engines and of planes high in the distant air, the noise of trucks and scooters and the sounds of working mechanics down on the floor below. They are empty now and quiet. But not for long. A scheduled flight is called on the intercom. The pilot comes in then, dressed in a sports shirt and a pair of slacks, wearing old tennis shoes, calmly at ease. With him and tightly holding his hand is the pilot's seven-year-old son.

A lieutenant colonel comes wandering in behind them, one of the colonels—there are a lot of them working around the base. This one is slight and thin, stooped almost, with an Oklahoma farmer's weathered face and leathery neck. His drawled hello is nasal. "You flyin' one-fifty-one?" he asks the pilot. And the pilot nods. "Hell," says the colonel, "here I was hopin' you'd take that thing I got to fly."

"That's too bad, Jack," the pilot answers in a West Virginia drawl, and you're struck for a moment by a sudden likeness between the two men. It is not a physical likeness and it isn't marked, although each has the weather-lined eyes and the sun-and-wind-burned hands all pilots seem to have. It is perhaps a common attitude you sense, a shared familiarity with risk, that makes for the moment these two dissimilar men seem to resemble one another.

But then the pilot grins and the moment is gone. He helps his young son climb from a chair up to a radiator and from there to a window ledge on which the boy stands impatiently watching all the activity on the big apron thirty or forty feet below his perch.

There is activity now in the small office next door as well. A man in faded denim slacks and a jacket stands at the desk, a schedule in his hand. "Who in the hell flew one-five-three?" he wants to know. There is complaint in the sound of his voice.

"Hare had it," the colonel calls laconically from the other room.

"Well, I'd like to have some of his hair," the man in faded denim says. "You seen him around?"

"No," answers the colonel, idly paging through a copy of an aviation magazine. "Guess he's gone home."

The man in denim picks up a phone and begins to call. He calls the pilot's home, the officers' club, the pool, a friend's house. Hare has disappeared. "Oh well." He cradles the telephone. The complaint in his voice has faded now. "You ready, Chuck?"

The pilot nods and calls to his son. "Be right back, Don," he tells the boy. "I'm going out that way." He points to the west, smiles briefly at his son and leaves the room.

"Clearance," the man in faded denim, who is the dispatching engineer, says into the microphone. He gives the number of the ship, the pilot's name, the time at the moment he's speaking, 1526, and the length of time the ship will be in the air. This done, he sits for a moment on his desk, lights a fresh cigarette and quietly swears to himself. "Dammit, Colonel," he tells the man in the other office, "I've got to get two more pilots somewhere. Where are they all?"

"Gone into town," the colonel answers, idly turning

the pages of his magazine. Then glancing at the pilot's son, he asks him kindly, "You all right up there, Don?"

The boy, still perched on the window ledge, turns to the colonel and grins his father's grin. "I'm all right, Jack," he answers and looks through the window again. "There goes my dad!" he shouts.

Looking over the small boy's shoulder, you too look down on the width of concrete apron, seeing what the boy sees, even more. You see his father, bareheaded, wearing his working clothes—a blue flying suit that looks like a mechanic's coverall—chute and harness hanging from his left arm and shoulder, straps swinging loosely as he walks. In his right hand he holds his bright gold helmet, stuffed with its rubber oxygen mask. You watch as he walks that distance to his ship. And without sentiment you see the man himself, a solitary pilot, experienced and skilled, walking alone from his son to the ship he is going to fly, one man alone on whom this flight depends.

There are others, too, a long succession of draftsmen, mechanics, designers and engineers whose combined intelligence and skill have brought this particular aircraft to its place on the line at Edwards in this moment of this day. The whole base sprawling beneath the desert sun supports the pilot as he walks. And the whole base will stand by watching as he flies, with its intelligence alerted, reaching through complex ganglia of technical electronics to the pilot's brain, to centers of speech and hearing, to the perimeter of thought. But there it stops. From that point on it is the pilot's ship. And as you watch him cross the glaring concrete apron to his waiting plane, your understanding of this pilot, your appreciation of his essential calm and quality, increases as you consider the odds against him and his skill. His nine-year record of testing high-speed military aircraft has never been matched.

Then the pilot disappears into the long belly of the plane. Servicing trucks drive off. The ground crew wheels the last of its equipment to one side. A man runs from the tail of the ship up to one wing and runs away. There is a sudden increase in the blasting sound the plane's engines make. Crewmen duck down behind their orange-painted carts as the big ship moves slowly forward, wheels in a quarter-turn and taxis out onto the runway.

It is a curious-looking plane, long and cigar-shaped with short, stubby wings set at a vertical angle of almost 45 degrees to its fuselage. Its rudder stands high above its tail on a complicated open superstructure. The pilot sits far forward in a big teardrop high on the slender nose. This much you see before the plane rolls out of sight. Then there is silence and the pilot's son squirms on the window ledge and catches his breath. Sudden static on the intercom precedes a statement of which you can hear only the last word, ". . . clear."

From off to the left you hear the rising crescendo of the big jet and it comes suddenly into view again, its landing gear just touching and then leaving the runway as you watch the plane rise gradually into the west. "He's off the ground," the pilot's son says proudly. Even the colonel has left his chair and is watching now from the window behind his desk. "Can't get up the forward gear," he drawls. But the gear goes up and the plane banks through a lazy S that slowly becomes a figure 8. Then it comes back again, just window-high above the runway, and you feel the tight constriction of that small boy's chest, the lump in his throat as he and his father communicate through time and space. Then the big bomber disappears. The boy jumps from his radiator perch, runs to the window in the other office, climbs on a chair and sees through the open hangar door one last glimpse of his father's plane as it climbs into the east and out of sight.

For the boy there follows now a restless, long half-hour in which he wanders from one attraction to another. From a glass jar filled with pencils used to mark out squares on the pilots' performance-rating chart he takes a red grease pencil. "Can I have this, Jack?" he asks the colonel.

"Why, I guess so, Don," the colonel tells him and lights a fresh cigarette. The colonel is restless, too. He wanders down into the hangar to check on the plane he's waiting to fly.

Now the boy moves from room to room, from photograph to photograph. He picks up the black- and orange-checkered crash helmet lying on the chair in the lounge and tries to fit it on his own small head. He snaps the Polaroid sun visor down, squeezes the rubber mask and its accordion-pleated tube. "My dad has one of these," he says. He puts down the helmet then, walks back through the corridor into the other office, climbs into the chair in there and for a long time watches the mechanics working on planes in the hangar below. From time to time he looks through the open door at the empty sky. He runs to the washroom and runs back again, taking his old place on the radiator, his eyes fixed on the sky.

The colonel comes back into the room, sits in his chair, lights up another cigarette and turns to his magazine again.

"How long has my dad been gone?" the boy asks.

"Not so long," the colonel says. "He'll be back soon," he reassures the boy, "It won't be very long."

"It never takes long," the boy replies, "when my dad flies." And he turns back again to watch the sky. But his glance is distracted then. He sees another pilot ride out to a small jet plane. He watches the pilot climb into his cockpit, watches the ground crew wheel the plane around, watches the plane as it taxis out onto the runway, watches it gather speed and climb. "There goes a fighter," the boy says quietly. He opens the window so that he can hear. He leaves the radiator then, runs into the other room and opens its window, too. He climbs into a chair and from there climbs up to the window ledge. Fidgeting, awkward, careless of himself, he examines the sky and stands waiting to hear the sound.

"Careful, Don," the colonel cautions him.

Then after a while there is the sound he's been waiting to hear. His father's plane rolls suddenly into sight, its speed decreasing as it pounds across the runway. From heading west, it turns to the right and taxis carefully back to its place, waved slowly into position by the directing arms and signaling hands of the crew chief standing on the ramp. The crew collects under the belly of the ship. But nothing happens.

"When is he coming out?" the boy wants to know.

"Pretty soon, Don," the colonel answers without looking up from his magazine.

Then, finally, the boy says, "There comes my daddy now." And over his shoulder you watch with him as his father walks slowly back from the plane to his waiting son.

A few minutes later he's back in the office, dressed as before in casual slacks and sports shirt and the casual tennis shoes. "You ready, Don?" he asks.

"I'm ready," the boys says quietly.

They leave, walking together down the stairs, the boy taking again his father's hand. "I'm thirsty, Dad," he says. His father holds him over the fountain while he drinks. The pilot drinks, too, still holding the boy tucked underneath one arm. Then placing him gently on his feet, he follows his son out to their car, an old Model A coupé the pilot has rebuilt himself.

"It's cooler than the other car," he explains.

The short ride home through midafternoon heat is quiet. "Can I drive?" the boy asks his father.

"No, son," the pilot says.

At four o'clock they're home. Dinner is on the table. The children are sent out to play. The pilot sits down to eat. At five he has to fly again, and again at five in the morning. It is a matter-of-fact routine to which his wife has calmly adjusted her life, his life, the lives of their children and their life together.

"Everything go all right?" she asks him.

"Yup," he says, and begins to eat his dinner.

The pilot is Major Charles E. Yeager, USAF, who on the fourteenth of October, 1947, first smashed the sound barrier. Alone in the Bell X-1, he was the first pilot ever to fly at the speed of sound. He flew with calmness and, he says, with certainty. That this was so in no way can detract from his accomplishment, nor does it reduce the hazard with which he flew.

At ten o'clock on the morning of October 14, 1947, preliminary investigation and research had led a few men to suppose that given certain conditions, a given pilot could fly a given plane at the speed of sound at a given altitude.

At eleven o'clock on that morning their supposition had been verified.

Yeager, alone, at half-past ten had proved it. It had taken him four months of hard work and the whole of his experience.

Part One

1

You know how fighter pilots are, not exclusive but separated somehow from the man who walks or rides or drives to his job in a plant or an office on the ground. Pilots work with risk, sometimes with the unknown and always subject to laws of chance, of mechanical failure and of gravity. Flying, they'll tell you, is just another job. But you can be killed in your plane. "You can be killed a lot deader flying than in any other line of work."

There aren't many fighter pilots in the world, a few thousand among the millions of men who live and who work on the ground. There are even fewer fighter test pilots, men who fly and accept as reliable or reject new fighter aircraft never flown before—a few hundred, perhaps, among the few thousand fighter pilots, who have the skill, the nerve and the intelligence to rate as fighter test pilots. These work with greater risk against the same unalterable laws of chance, of mechanical failure and of gravity. These have a greater familiarity with abrupt and violent death.

But among these few hundred fighter test pilots there is an even smaller, even more separated group of experimental flight test pilots who work with even larger risk against those same unchanging laws. These few men live in almost daily intimacy with death.

They don't particularly like to discuss this, though not because of any occupational superstition or because of fear. There is a fundamental need among them not to let it become an issue. These few pilots share an experience common only to them. It is extremely personal, something

13

in which, they feel, no others should intrude, something to be disposed of only among themselves and with a minimum of talk. But the world does intrude, forcing each pilot to step aside and to walk around the subject with a kind of quiet dignity.

He seems in a way to defy the obvious, if only in that he continues to fly and continues to like to fly. Yet it is not bravado or recklessness, although it may seem to be, that pushes him on from risk to risk. It is not simply the heady taste of success that brings one pilot back from each experimental flight dogfighting with another all the way down. It is not competition with each other that produces the drive to excellence with which each pilot lives. It is not the thrill of fear or of overcoming fear that has brought him into this business and that keeps him there.

It's simply that each of these pilots likes to fly. And this is flying at its best. Your pilot is impatient with any other theory. You don't, says Yeager, go into this business because you like the risk. You begin simply by wondering what it's like to fly. And then you fly. Once you've flown, you never grow tired of flying. That's what you want to do. You don't know why. You don't get a sense of freedom or of emotional release. You don't put it that way. You do get away from everything. You get up high to where you can see everywhere and you like that. But you don't feel that you're free of your bonds and you can go flitting off through the wild blue yonder. That's for the birds.

When you're flying a plane you have the same sensation you feel when you're driving alone in a car on a lonely road. It's just the idea that you've got control of it and you're alone. You never get tired of flying, really. No matter how much work you do in these planes, you don't get much of a chance to look around while you're on the job. So you really enjoy getting an airplane out when you're on your own. It's fun to fly for an hour or so, to be up doing rolls and loops and the rest. You like it. You like to know that you can do those things. When you've learned to do something like that it's fun just to get up in the air and do it.

You don't take off in a plane just simply to place

yourself in jeopardy. It's only that flying's your job. It's all you've done and it's all you know how to do for a living. The risk is something you have to accept. It's there. You can't afford to spend too much time considering this. When you do, you call it something else. You don't crack up and kill yourself. You "prang" your airplane or you "auger in." You might be "clobbered." But you might not. It's always the other guy who's killed. It's never you. And it never has to be you. You can be careful.

It slips into your mind only when you're alone, this idea that you might be killed—when you're alone and hunting or fishing by yourself. Then almost immediately you think of your family. You think of the children, your friends' and your own. It's the worst thing that can happen to any of them. You're always losing pilots in this business. Whenever a pilot is killed the worst thing about it is the effect it has on his children. It has an awful effect on all of them.

They know what it means. Whenever a pilot augers in, your children know it. They actually saw one pilot crash in a B-47 from the base. They were playing outside. They saw this plane come down, saw it go off across the road. They heard the explosion and saw the fire and smoke. They'd known the pilot well. He used to come over and play with them. It affected them roughly. They have a respect for airplanes. They knows planes can kill.

Even the little girls know this. The father of one of their friends got clobbered awhile ago. They wanted to know what happened. "Lennie's daddy's dead," they tell you when you come home that night. "What happened?" they ask you then. You tell them, "Well, he was taking off in an F-84 and the airplane caught on fire. He went into the ground, dove in. He couldn't get out of the plane." "Did they find anything?" they ask you. Yes, you tell them, pieces. They pick them up. "What did they find there, Daddy?" Arms, you tell them, everything. "Does he know it?" No, you say, he doesn't know it. It happens too fast. If you hit the ground going 400 miles an hour, there wouldn't be very much left of you.

You have to be factual. You can't tell them pretty

stories. You can't fool yourself. You just have to realize that for you to auger in yourself would be the worst thing that could ever happen to them. It makes you more careful. It makes you think. You don't want that to happen to your children, not if you can avoid it. And you think you can.

But sometimes, on a cross-country flight when you don't have anything else to do, you begin to worry. It would sure be a hell of a note, you tell yourself, if you augered in now. Not for yourself. You've lived a full, rich life. You've got the most envied job in the Air Force. And you remember then how you enlisted, how you were trained, the months of practice, the months of combat, too. You've had a taste of everything. You've been shot down. And you've shot German pilots down. You came out with a whole skin, came back home, got married, fell into this flight-test job. And here you are on a project that's really hot, one that looks as if it's going to be successful. You think you're pretty lucky. You wouldn't have it any other way, not for yourself.

But for the children—they'd have no father. It would be a low blow, too, on Glennis, who's had a rough time all these years, the two years you were overseas, the years you've been testing planes. You talk about this sometimes, you and your wife, the other pilots and you. But it's nothing you like to talk about with people who don't know what it is. It's too damned personal.

Sometimes you go down to the School of Aviation Medicine and talk to the doctors stationed there. They talk to you. Not the psychologists, though, and a good thing, too. They never bother you. You'd buck it if they tried. You think you're pretty normal in the circumstances with which you have to live. People may think the doctors should be with you all the time, sticking their needles into your arms and their noses into your private life. Well, hell, if they want to know what high-speed flight does to your heart, your liver and your nerves, they can get that from monkeys.

As far as the rest of it goes, your feeling about these things, that's your own business. You're not freaks; you're just pilots doing a routine job. You don't ride the sled. You don't eat special foods. You live with your family. You eat at home. You drink when you're thirsty. You'll probably go on living until you die. And if sometimes you think that maybe you shouldn't fly any more, you always think, No. That's what you've been doing almost all of your life. And if you're just careful you can go right on flying and living, too.

But it isn't only up to you. You develop the attitude that someone is watching over you. That's the way you come to feel. Somebody must be taking care of you. You don't have to make it on your own.

2

If you were a fighter pilot in 1943, you flew with certain normal risks. These were the hazards of enemy action, of pilot error and of defective equipment or mechanical failure in your plane. These risks accounted for almost all planes lost or pilots killed, but they were greatly increased for fighter pilots by the speeds at which their aircraft traveled and by the fact that fighter pilots fly alone.

Then, in the spring of that year, you began to hear talk about a new risk in high-speed flight, the risk of a power dive at speeds approaching the speed of sound. Flight at these dangerous transonic speeds is characterized by serious shock or vibration which pilots began to refer to as buffeting. One Army pilot who survived a power dive from 35,000 feet in a Republic P-47 Thunderbolt reported that his control stick froze at 30,000 feet. He used the crank controlling the elevator trim tabs to bring his ship out of its dive. When the plane leveled off, it shuddered, he said, "as though it had been hit by a truck."

Pilots who first experienced this were often lost. Some planes nosed under and couldn't be leveled off. Others came out abruptly. Pilots blacked out; planes came apart in mid-air.

What happened no one really knew. The strange behavior of aircraft flying at transonic speeds could be investigated only in the air. These speeds, if they could be reached at all, could be reached only in dangerous power dives. The risks were obvious but they were taken. One pilot returned from a power dive in his North American

18

P-51 Mustang to report he had seen shock lines, "rising like heat waves from a radiator." On a second flight these shock waves were photographed. Then instrumented models were fixed to the wings of fighter planes and tested in other deliberate power dives through different densities of atmosphere. These wing-flow model tests, as they were called, gave only a rough idea of the stick force reversals to be expected in the transonic range. Buffeting remained an unknown quantity.

If little could be learned in the air, less could be learned on the ground. Laboratory wind tunnels then in use were not vented and suffered a "choking effect" at speeds approaching the speed of sound. Back in the air again, experiments were made with falling bodies and with rocket-propelled models. But since there were then no electronic telemetering devices with which to record or to transmit to ground observers the strange phenomena of shock or buffeting at transonic speeds, little was learned from these experiments.

Meanwhile the risk of high-speed flight continued. Operational fighter aircraft achieved speeds as high as .75 Mach number, approximately 527 miles an hour at 20,000 feet. But if the speed of sound could be approached and measured in 1943, few men thought Mach 1 would ever be reached by a pilot-operated plane.

A Mach number represents the ratio of the speed of an airplane to the speed of sound in the surrounding atmosphere. But the speed of sound varies with temperature and temperature varies with altitude. The higher you go, the colder it is. At sea level with a temperature of 59 degrees Fahrenheit, sound travels at roughly 750 miles an hour. But 40,000 feet in the air, where the temperature drops to 70 degrees below zero, the speed of sound also drops, to about 660 miles an hour. The speed of sound is therefore expressed in terms of temperature.

To most pilots and to many scientists and engineers, however, this seemed an academic exercise so far as the flight of an aircraft was concerned in 1943. Missiles might move as fast as sound, but no airplane ever would. Mach 1 seemed unattainable then if only because of what happened

to planes that reached .75 Mach number in power dives.
You couldn't build an airplane, they said, that would fly at
the speed of sound. And if you did, your plane wouldn't
stand the stress of buffeting in the transonic range. And if
it did, the pilot might not survive.

A tremendous amount of power would be required to
propel any airplane faster than our best fighters would go
in 1943. You would need more than 16,000 horsepower, it
was argued, to fly at the speed of sound. The best piston
engine then available produced only 5,000 horses and
propelled our fastest fighters at only 450 miles an hour.
This did not mean you could put three or four of these
piston engines into a single air frame and reach Mach
number 1. Other factors, additional weight, for example,
would cut down speed.

And if you could build an engine or a combination of
engines capable of producing the power needed, what
about buffeting? Planes flying at less than the speed of
sound send signals ahead to warn air molecules that
something is on the way and to prepare the air. These
signals travel at the speed of sound. An airplane flying
faster than sound, however, piles up unprepared air into
shock waves and other disturbances creating turbulence.
But the most dangerous area is the transonic range where
the airflow around the plane is mixed, part slower than
sound, part faster. At these transonic speeds, 600 to 800
miles an hour, the turbulence is greatest, buffeting is at its
worst.

Not all of this was known then. Some pilots knew
what buffeting was. Others who had experienced it were
dead. Whether the pilots had been more vulnerable than
their planes was an open question. But there seemed to
be some sort of barrier in the air, a speed beyond which
men would never fly. It was in this year, however, in 1943,
that the first jet aircraft engines were developed. A part of
the problem was therefore solved.

Turbojet and rocket engines not only produce more
power than conventional piston engines do; they become
more effective as speed is increased. Rated in pounds of
thrust, at 375 miles an hour one pound of thrust equals

one horsepower. But at 750 miles an hour one pound of thrust is equal to two horsepower. The same pound of thrust is equal to three horsepower at 1,025 miles an hour. The power problem seemed to be licked.

It was in December of 1943, therefore, that Dr. George W. Lewis, then director of the National Advisory Committee for Aeronautics, called a meeting at NACA headquarters in Washington, D. C. At this meeting Lewis brought together representatives of the Army, the Navy and the aircraft industry. Among those present was a young engineer named Robert Wolf, assistant chief design engineer of the Bell Aircraft Corporation.

Bell had already built and flown the first jet airplane made in the United States, the XP-59. "Now that we have jet propulsion," Wolf told the others, "and since jet propulsion greatly increases the speed at which we can fly, a high-speed research airplane should be built. With such a plane, an airplane capable of flying at even subsonic speeds, we could at least explore the transonic range, find out what causes buffeting. Perhaps we can fly even beyond these speeds."

Why not? The conclusion had been reached independently by other men who had asked the question of themselves. But Wolf went back to Buffalo, New York, and put the question to Larry Bell. Bell acted almost at once. From that moment on the project began to grow.

On the twenty-ninth of December Larry Bell, president of Bell Aircraft Corporation, wrote to Dr. Lewis at NACA suggesting again the value of a high-speed flying laboratory to everyone concerned with the future of aviation. Lewis replied immediately, expressing specific interest in a gas-turbine jet. He asked Bell for details. A three-view drawing of the proposed airplane was prepared by Bell design engineers and delivered to Lewis in April of 1944. Meanwhile, the Army Air Corps had been busy, too.

Major, then Captain, Ezra Kotcher, an Air Corps officer assigned to the Engineering Division at Wright Field in Dayton, Ohio, had independently reached the conclusion Robert Wolf had reached and had asked the same question Wolf had asked at the NACA conference in December of 1943. He had sold the idea of building a high-speed research airplane to General F. O. Carroll, chief of the engineering division to which Kotcher was assigned. A preliminary project had been set up under Kotcher's direction. A 6,000-pound-thrust rocket engine was being developed as the next step to the 2,000-pound-thrust rocket engine being built for an experimental airplane, the XP-79. This larger rocket engine was being considered, early in 1944, for possible application in a superperformance research aircraft. The problem facing Kotcher was who could be found to take the responsibility and the risk of building such an experimental plane. For the country was still at war and all the emphasis in the aircraft industry was still being placed on turning out quantities of operational fighters, bombers and transport planes. It was Kotcher's difficult job to convince production-minded men that time and money spent on the project would not be time and money lost. The job seemed almost hopeless. But the inevitable happened. Robert Woods, chief design engineer of the Bell Aircraft Corporation, visited Wright Field. He met Kotcher there.

"We are anxious," Woods told Kotcher, "to get an Army contract to design and build a high-speed research aircraft, a flying laboratory with which to explore the transonic range. We think this has to be done because until it is done, there's nothing else we can do. We want to do it. Do you think the Air Corps would be interested?"

Kotcher was completely surprised. Kotcher, who had been offering just such a contract to one representative after another of almost every major aircraft company in the country, was also delighted. Wolf was as much surprised and delighted as Kotcher had been when he learned of the work that was already under way. The two sat down to talk it over. It was not, of course, as simple as that, nor would it be quite as easy as it first seemed.

Having gone roughly over the questions of what should be done and why and how, Kotcher and Woods reached an equally rough agreement. But the project now had to be geared to the needs and demands of three entirely different kinds of men in as many distinctly different organizations. To the scientists and engineers of the National Advisory Committee for Aeronautics, design of the plane would pose a problem in pure research and theory. To the accountants, designers and engineers of the company which would go on to build the plane, the problem would be a more practical question of ways and means. To the military personnel of the Army Air Corps who would ultimately accept or reject the plane, the problem would be even more specialized, the problem of adapting the product resulting from theory to their specific purposes. The men concerned would not always see eye to eye.

But tentative plans were made in Kotcher's office on November 30, 1944. Then Woods left Kotcher to telephone Larry Bell. "How are you, Larry?" he asked. Bell said he was feeling fine and asked Woods what he wanted. "Do you feel like taking a chance?" Woods asked him then. What sort of a chance, Bell wanted to know. "You'd better sit down and relax," Woods said. "I've got some news. I've just committed you to the production of an 800-mile-an-hour plane."

There was no answer to that from Larry Bell in Buffalo. 800 miles an hour is faster than sound. Woods said, "Of course, if you think it can't be done—" Bell interrupted him. "Come back to Buffalo," he said, "and tell me what it's all about. We'll let the commitment stand." Bob Woods laughed and put down the phone. Returning to Kotcher's office he formally gave the Army his company's verbal agreement to build the plane. Then he returned to Buffalo. Four days later Woods and Robert Stanley, the company's chief engineer, took an oath of allegiance and secrecy and went to work. The Air Technical Services Command at Wright Field was notified that afternoon in writing that Bell Aircraft would design and build the X-1. The project was numbered MX-524.

The final preliminary meetings were held in Kotcher's Wright Field office on the twentieth and twenty-first of December, 1944. Kotcher, as Air Corps project officer, spoke for the Army. Bell was represented by Robert

Woods; Paul Emmons, chief aerodynamacist; Benson Hamlin, their own project engineer; and Dr. Vladimir Morkovin. They sat around Kotcher's table and for two full days they talked and argued about what the airplane ought to be.

It should be a practical airplane, they agreed. If the war went on, the X-1 might have to serve as a prototype for later production models for combat flight. At least, the performance of a practical plane could be more easily related to operational aircraft then in use. It was agreed also that the plane should carry a pilot who should be seated and not prone.

The plane should also be designed to carry 500 to 1,000 pounds of recording instrumentation in 20 cubic feet of space. This instrumentation would include cameras, recorders, telemetering devices necessary to obtain research data for different air speeds—airfoil pressure distribution readings, for example, strain gauge readings, accelerations, stick forces, control surface displacements and angular velocities. These would report phenomena no pilot could observe. But the pilot's experience would prove as valuable to future research and development as would the performance of the plane. And whatever might be learned from recording instruments would have more meaning if it could be associated with a pilot's report, with a pilot's interpretation of whatever might happen in the air. That is, if the pilot survived. It was thought possible that he might not.

The specific requirement would be for transonic speed study only. But the plane was to fly at supersonic speeds, if possible. If the airplane did go through the sonic barrier, this would be done only at the pilot's discretion and with the agreement of everyone concerned, of the engineers assigned to and responsible for the project.

It was also decided that the speed of the plane should be controllable. It should be designed for use on a 7,000-foot runway, should be capable of taking off within 5,000 feet at 150 miles an hour, of climbing to 35,000 feet for ten minutes of powered flight and of landing then at a speed of 90 miles an hour.

The plane, it was finally agreed, should be completed within a year.

"Do you think you can do it?" Kotcher asked Woods.

"I think we can," Woods answered. "We'll build the plane. But who's going to fly the thing? Have you thought about that?"

3

If you were a working pilot assigned to the Flight Test Division of the Air Matériel Command at Wright-Patterson Air Force Base in the spring of 1947, you'd have heard rumors about the X-1. You might even have seen it once, hanging under the wing of the B-29 that ferried it through. You were sure to have heard some talk.

You knew the X-1 was a rocket airplane expected to go twice the speed of sound, more than 1,700 miles an hour. You couldn't see how it could ever do it. You didn't know what a rocket was or how it worked. But granted the fact that a rocket motor could produce the necessary power, you didn't see how any plane could fly at that speed. Most of the pilots had flown F-80's or F-84's in acceptance tests or in accelerated service tests and in air shows around the country. You were all familiar with buffeting or compressibility, with the effects of shock waves passing over the control system, over the ailerons and over the elevators of these planes.

If you went over eight-tenths of Mach 1 in the F-80, you knew, the whole aircraft began to shake and the ailerons fluttered. If was impossible to fly it any faster than that. It just wouldn't go. It would only hit that much speed in a power dive.

So any plane that would fly at the speed of eight-tenths *over* Mach 1 would be a tremendous plane to fly. You didn't believe the X-1 would do it. But everyone talked about flying the airplane, wondering what it would feel like, how it would handle. It had been flown, you knew. Civilian pilots had flown the airplane while you'd wondered how.

Then in June of that year it was rumored that the Air Force would take the project and that a military pilot would be assigned to fly the plane. It had been flown up to a speed of .8 Mach number. The pilot who had been flying the plane wanted more money, thirty or forty thousand dollars to crash the sound barrier. The Air Force was dissatisfied. The program was being delayed. These were the rumors but few of the pilots believed they were true.

It had always been an Air Force policy to hire civilian pilots for extremely hazardous missions. You could pay the civilians a bonus for taking the risk you couldn't expect an Air Force pilot to take in peacetime for just his pay. So no matter how anxious the Air Force might be now to fly this plane, to go through the sonic barrier, to get it done, none of the flight test pilots thought it would ever happen. They'd never assign an Air Force pilot. And if they did, it wouldn't be you.

You didn't stand a chance. If you were an AUS officer with a temporary captain's commission, you didn't rate very high on the list of men assigned to the Fighter Test Section. In fact, you ranked fairly low. It was something to moan about. When you came into the Fighter Test Section you thought you were getting in with pilots who were really hot, who could fly anything, wax anyone. But the fighter pilots with whom you'd flown in combat made these test pilots look like junior birdmen. They were nice guys, sure, the flight test pilots at Wright Field in 1946. They had rank and reputation. But they just didn't know how to fly fighters the way fighters should be flown. There were plenty of combat pilots who could wax your fanny, really make you cut tail. But these test pilots just didn't know how to dogfight.

That's all you'd done since 1943, dogfighting. You could take care of yourself in almost anything that would fly. You could wax almost every one of the flight test pilots with whom you worked. You had a rough idea of what you could do. You'd been in some air shows in the last two years. You'd kept your nose clean, hadn't had any accidents. You'd flown F-80's, F-84's, 59's and 83's. You'd shot gunnery and put on acrobatics. And you'd done all right.

But to be picked to fly the X-1—you didn't think you had a chance, if only because you were new to Fighter Test.

And you can't really say for yourself how well you fly. No pilot can. You like to fly. You get a feeling of satisfaction whenever you do a good job in any airplane. You try to do the best you can. But if you ever achieve perfection, you never know it. You never can see yourself while you're in the air. There'd been shows you thought were pretty sad because you hadn't been able to do just what you wanted to. You were always surprised when the others said you'd done pretty well or that you'd put on the prettiest show they'd ever seen. It's pleasant to have some other pilots tell you that about your work because they can judge. But it always seemed to you as if you hadn't done point rolls or acrobatics just the way you should have. So discounting what other pilots said, you were never quite sure how good you were. Whenever a chance came along to measure yourself against some other pilot or in some other plane, you grabbed it. That's why you always raised your hand when they asked for volunteers.

That's why it was nice to hear those rumors finally verified. They called a meeting of all the pilots assigned to the Fighter Test Section early in June of 1947. It was at this meeting that Major Ken Chilstrom, chief of the section, walked into the room and abruptly announced that the Air Force had taken the X-1 and would assign a military pilot to fly the plane. He wanted to know how many would like to be considered for the job. Most of the pilots raised their hands.

You raise yours, too. But you're certain you don't have a chance. There are too many guys ahead of you. They want a single man. You've got a wife and a couple of boys. They won't get down to your name. But you can't help talking about it. You talk it over with Ridley. Ridley knows. He's a pilot and he's a graduate engineer. "Jack," you ask him, "how does the damn thing fly?"

"It must have a rocket motor," Ridley says, "to go that fast. It's the same principle as a jet. But with a rocket, all the elements of combustion are contained in the plane. Jets take oxygen from the air as they fly."

"I wonder," you say, "what it's like to fly."

"Same as a jet, I suppose. Just faster."

"Do you think it will go through the sound barrier, Jack?"

"I doubt if there's any barrier."

"But they say—"

"I know what these armchair pilots say. They may be right. But an ordinary rifle bullet travels as fast as sound or faster. Of course, there are other factors involved in the flight of a plane. A .50 caliber bullet is perfectly symmetrical and the forces acting on it are in symmetry. It has no wings or tail. And a bullet doesn't lose weight as it moves along. It carries no fuel. And its speed decreases from the muzzle velocity with which it leaves the rifle. But the important thing is that bullets do travel at supersonic speeds. And nothing happens to alter their shape or to change the pattern of their flight until their final impact on the target. There is no sonic barrier. The problem is something else. The factor of just going faster than sound isn't dangerous. The trouble with airplanes is they're not symmetrical and they have wings and tails. Maybe with this new plane they've got that licked."

You talk some more. But meanwhile there are other planes to fly. And then one day the major sends for you. "The old man," he tells you bluntly, "wants to see you in his office right away."

"Now?" you ask uneasily, wondering why.

"Right now," the major tells you. He says nothing more.

There's nothing more to say. The old man, Colonel Albert Boyd, chief of the Flight Test Division, is not known for his friendly familiarity with the pilots under his command. He's tough, a disciplinarian. He's not in the habit of asking you into his office unless you've committed some God-awful breach of the discipline he's imposed. You haven't buzzed anyone's property lately. You've broken no rules that you can recall. But you move unwillingly away and your mind runs through all you can remember of everything you've done or might have done or might be thought to have done to earn a reprimand. With a sudden start you recall the one thing Colonel Boyd would want to discuss with you. It makes you feel somewhat sick.

It happened not long ago, the night you came back from the Cleveland air show. You'd flown an F-80. You'd done all right. The old man had been there himself to see you fly. Precise and neat for once, you thought you'd made some points. You were feeling good as you set up your pattern and came in to land. The colonel was right behind you as you made the final turn. At the end of the runway you turned your plane and taxied back to park on the ramp. Just as you parked you saw the colonel's plane touch down. Filled with good humor, pleased with yourself, aware of a sudden sense of the casual brotherhood of flight, you disregarded all the military courtesy and discipline demanded of you by this officer who was landing now. It was like stealing jam from the kitchen at home as you flipped on the switch for your microphone.

"Pretty good," you said, commenting on the colonel's handling of his plane. "Pretty good for an old man." Then grinning into your cockpit's solitude, you cut off the microphone switch and waited. There was a moment of absolute silence, no word from the tower, nothing, just for the space of time it must have taken the colonel to put himself on the air. But then it came.

"Who said that?" The colonel's voice cracked like static in the quiet air. "Get that pilot's name!" He'd known it was something only another pilot would say with a motive only another pilot could understand. But the air remained silent. There was no answer from the tower, nothing.

It would have been all right, too, you tell yourself as you walk heavily on to headquarters now. They'd never have found out who it was. The colonel would never have guessed. But you'd seen him in Operations a few moments later. Unable to suppress a grin, you might just as well have admitted it then and there. You'd known by the look in his eyes that the colonel had understood. It was one of those things. He'd known and you'd known he did. You were two of a kind who'd suddenly found each other out as you'd brushed each other in the hall with polite formality. But you'd been a fool to think you were going to get away with it. The old man had investigated first. Now he had proved his case. You'd hear about it now.

And you didn't particularly like to think of what you'd hear. You knew some of the pilots who had been called to the old man's office in the past. It had changed them somehow, sobered them all.

You've reached the door to his office now. But you don't really care to go in.

You have to go in. There is nothing else you can do. You give your name to the colonel's secretary, admitting, "The colonel sent for me." It's almost like telling her good-by.

"I know," she says. "He's waiting now." Your uneasiness grows as she tells you to go in.

You walk in as briskly as you can, salute and stand at attention, very much aware of where you are but wishing to God you were anywhere else.

"Sit down," the colonel tells you. He flips a button on the squawk box on his desk as you sink nervously into a chair. "Fred?" he says to someone in another room. "Come on in. I've got Yeager here." There's an awful moment then until the colonel's deputy, Colonel Fred Ascani, comes quietly into the office. You can't tell whether he knows you're there or not.

"Yeager," Colonel Boyd suddenly begins. He leans back in his chair, resting his elbows on its arms and bringing the tips of his index fingers together against his stubborn chin. "I suppose you know . . ." he continues.

Why you're here? Of course you know. You can't wait to get it over with and to get out.

"The Air Force has taken over the X-1 project," the colonel is saying now. You have to go back in your mind to remember his words. You begin to relax for a moment, finding a pleasant relief in the fact that you're not in a jam. Then your mind comes back into focus and you can hear again as the colonel talks on, his finger tips still together at his chin, his eyes fixed steadily on yours.

"As you may know, this aircraft was designed to fly at twice the speed of sound. It has a load factor of about 18. Bell Aircraft Company has had responsibility for developing the aircraft and for the flight-test program.

"The plane has been flown by two civilian pilots in both glide and powered flight. The pilot most recently assigned has not been making the progress we had anticipated in that he's only flown up to the speed of .8 Mach number. He has, ah—indicated—" The colonel's hands come down from his chin to rest for a moment on top of his desk—"that he would like to be paid a substantial sum for flight at higher speeds. That is the background."

You're aware of his eyes on yours and of Colonel Ascani's eyes on yours as you answer briefly, "Yes, sir."

"I have been approached," Colonel Boyd continues, "by Colonel George F. Smith, the Air Force project officer assigned to this program. Colonel Smith asked me whether we would like to take the project. I have assured him we would very much like to take the project and that we have many pilots who would enjoy flying the airplane. He then conferred with the chief of the engineering division and with the deputy for development. The project has now been transferred to the Flight Test Division." Colonel Boyd leans back again in his chair and his finger tips come together again beneath his chin.

"It is now our very responsible job to select the pilot who will make the first supersonic flight. Have you any idea, Yeager, of what this project means to the Air Force? I'm sure you have. But I want to say something about it anyway." He stops for a moment and turns to the window behind his desk. Out on the field an engine roars and then settles down to a steady drone. The colonel turns back to face you now, fixing his eyes again on yours. His voice, as he begins to talk, is strong with his determination, rich with the intensity of the thing he feels. It is as if you knew he wanted you to understand much more than he can say to you.

4

"The world has changed considerably since I came into aviation twenty years ago." There's a trace of the South in the colonel's accent. His words are precise, clipped almost, but he drops an occasional g. "In those days flying was still new and a man could feel, no matter who he was or what he might be, that there was something he might contribute or something important he might help to do. It was a wonderful period, really wonderful.

"Then things were diminished suddenly. We saw barriers everywhere we looked. It may have been something widespread in the world at that time, something everyone felt. It was pretty bad. Oh, there were things to be done. You could fly faster by just a few miles an hour than someone else had flown, or farther without refueling, or push up the ceiling a couple of hundred feet. That's all you could do.

"I don't know what flying may mean to you, Yeager. It has always been more than a job to me. I was only twenty when I began to fly. But the minute I got in the air I knew what I wanted to do. I have never changed my mind.

"Well, then," the colonel says, "the war began." His eyes are still fixed on yours but they seem to see something back in the past, or something within his mind. "War gave us a strange new set of circumstances with which to work. There was, as they used to say, the impossible to be done. We did the impossible then. I do not like war. The last one taught us a lesson we should have been able to learn for ourselves and demanded a terrible price. There is much to regret in the role that

33

aviation is forced to play in war. There is, of course, no alternative choice. And there is in war an adventure, too.

"We were made immediately aware of the limits we'd set for ourselves in years of depression and of fear. If someone had told us in 1935 that we'd soon be flying operational planes at better than 400 miles an hour, we'd have said no. When General Arnold demanded that 400-miles-an-hour from the 1,000-horsepower engines we had available in 1941, there were some who still said no. And when that goal had been reached they said we had reached the limit, this was the end. But the jet engine came along and we moved ahead. Now they have said there's a limit to that. There's a brick wall in the sky." The colonel leans forward in his chair and touches his desk for emphasis. "Son," he says, forgetting a moment to be precise, "just as surely as you and I and Colonel Ascani are sitting here, we are going to fly supersonic. There are, fortunately—" He leans back in his chair again—"a number of others who agree with me." The colonel's finger tips return to his chin.

"It seems not only proper, therefore," he says with even more emphasis than before, "but absolutely necessary that an Air Force pilot should make this flight, that we take the lead in the air and hold it. We should be the first to fly in a region where danger lies. That is our mission in time of peace as well as in war. We have a tradition. We have, I believe, the finest pilots in the world. It seems a good time to demonstrate the fact. We should ourselves say no to the people who still say no. This is, if you follow me, not the time for fear. Do you understand?"

"Yes, sir," you answer him eagerly, "I understand."

"Few men," the colonel continues, speaking now almost as if to himself, "few men, indeed, are given an opportunity to accomplish something no other man has ever done, to go where no one has ever been. There are no more voyages of discovery to be made on earth. Even the first flight was made more than forty years ago. This flight, I believe, will rank with that. This flight—" His eyes meet yours again—"must therefore be made by an

Air Force pilot. This flight must be a successful'flight. Do you understand?"

"Yes, sir." It's perfectly clear. "Whoever flies the plane is going to be entirely on his own," you say. "He'll have some decisions to make." It is hard to put into words the thing you believe the colonel wants you to understand. "The decisions the pilot makes will have an effect far into the future. He'll be alone in the plane. If he's right, the pilot will have accomplished something for aviation, for the Air Force and for himself. I believe we have pilots, sir, who can do this as well as any civilian pilot can."

"Are you aware of the hazards, Yeager? Do you know that a great many responsible scientists and engineers anticipate that complete loss of control will be experienced by the pilot at speeds approaching that of sound? Some say we will never fly the plane at sonic speeds because of this shockwave effect. Are you fully aware of the hazards involved?"

"Sir, of course." You speak very slowly, trying to form the proper answer. "I've flown F-80's and F-84's here, as you know. I've experienced buffeting at high Mach number—"

"What would you do," Colonel Ascani interrupts suddenly from across the room, "if you were the pilot assigned to fly the X-1?"

It seems to you now for the first time that you have a chance, that you might be picked to fly the airplane. And for a moment, you don't know what to say. "Sir," you begin, "I'd start with a great deal of care. With so much at stake, I'd proceed very cautiously."

"Do you think," Colonel Boyd asks then, "that an aircraft can fly at sonic speeds?"

"Yes, sir," you answer, with Ridley's conviction supporting your own.

"Why do you think so?" Colonel Ascani wants to know.

"Sir," you answer, not knowing what to say, "I've fired many a rifle, Colonel. Even a .22-caliber bullet travels at faster than the speed of sound. You can fire into the water, which is much denser than air, and the bullet is not distorted by speed alone. There may be other factors involved in the flight of an airplane. But that speed itself is no insurmountable obstacle. If you take it a little bit at a time—" You stop then, suddenly hearing your voice in the room, suddenly conscious of yourself.

"And if we established a schedule," Colonel Boyd asks, his eyes still fixed on yours, "could we depend on you? If you were selected as the pilot assigned to this project, could you follow a rigid schedule increasing the speed in very small increments?"

"Yes, sir. You could depend on me to follow a schedule."

"You don't feel you'd be tempted—"

"No, sir." It has suddenly come alive for you, the idea that you might really fly the plane. "I wouldn't be tempted," you insist, not even aware of the fact that you've interrupted him. Because you're eager to get that chance, you're eager to fly the plane. And you're anxious to say whatever it is the colonel wants you to say.

"Of course," the colonel is saying now, "we recognize your ability. If we did not, you wouldn't be in here now. You have shown outstanding pilot ability, Yeager, in local flight demonstrations here at the field, in the test projects to which you've been assigned, in ferrying aircraft and even—" The colonel's voice softens for just a moment—"in those air shows to which you've been sent from time to time." He clears his throat and continues, "You have always performed your assigned duty in what I may say is an outstanding manner. Your flying is generally done just absolutely in accordance with the schedule and with a great deal of precision. Except for one or two incidents—

"Are you quite certain," the colonel underlines his words, "that you can stick to a schedule at all times? No matter how great the temptation may be to go just a little beyond the limits set for you?"

"Yes, sir," you answer, feeling suddenly flushed, "I'm sure I could stick to the schedule, sir."

"Then you would be interested," the colonel asks, "in being assigned to such a project?"

"Interested!" For a moment you almost forget your rank. "Yes, sir," you say, collecting yourself. "I would very much like to be assigned to such a project. I'd be very much interested in the project, sir."

"Do you realize, Yeager, the significance of this project for the pilot who will be assigned to fly the plane?" Colonel Ascani asks.

"Yes," Colonel Boyd continues, "do you understand the role the pilot will play in the history of aviation? Do you realize the tremendous amount of personal publicity to which he will be exposed? If you were assigned," he continues above your formal assent, "do you think it would have a negative effect on you as an Air Force officer? Would this publicity interfere with your performance as a pilot? Would you be able to go on with your routine duty? Would you go right on flying as a regularly assigned pilot? Would you continue to be stable under the pressure imposed by fame?"

"Yes, sir," you interpose between each of the colonel's questions.

"And you are quite certain," Colonel Ascani asks again, "that you understand the significance of this program, not only to the Air Force and to you, but to the future of aviation?"

"Yes, sir, I think I do."

There is a moment of silence now in which the colonels exchange brief, questioning glances and then carefully study their hands. "And who would you select," Colonel Boyd asks suddenly, "if the choice were yours? Who in your opinion is the best pilot we could assign to this project, excluding, of course, yourself?"

"Bob Hoover," you answer, without hesitation.

"Why?"

"Sir, because in my opinion Hoover is the best stick-and-rudder pilot we have."

"And if you had to select a pilot who is also an engineer? Who has an engineering education?"

"Ridley, sir, beyond a doubt. As far as I know he's the best practical engineer-pilot in the Air Force today." Your answers are honest. If you can't have the flight, then Hoover should have it. As for Ridley, you know him well. You went out to Muroc together in 1945 for the F-80 accelerated service tests. You've flown a lot together. You've talked and argued and drunk beer together. Ridley is much like you. He's from somewhere down in Oklahoma, from a family like your own. You get along with Ridley. You talk with him about almost everything and he looks at it all from your own point of view. "Yes, sir," you say again, "I think Ridley would be your best bet there."

"All right, Yeager." For a moment Colonel Boyd studies your face with a steady look, a look that measures and weighs and probes under the surface of what he can see. "That's all," he says then with blunt formality.

"Yes, sir." You stand, come stiffly to attention, salute and leave. You don't know any more than you did when you walked into the office an hour ago. You know that you're not in any trouble. But that's all you know.

5

Colonel Albert Boyd sits pensively at his desk. He must be absolutely certain. He must be sure that the pilot assigned to this project will be the best pilot he can select.

More than the million dollars the plane has cost will be at stake, much more than the plane or the project itself. It is in a way the whole of the future the colonel now weighs with his choice, the future not only of flight and of men who fly, but the future of men.

For this pilot's life, it seems to him, will stand as a firm example to all who will follow him into the air. It is there that the future will be tried. This pilot's past, his present, his future performance both in the plane and on the ground, will all become standards for the rest. In his mind's eye the colonel can see top-spinning boys who one day may or may not be permitted to fly, depending on how the patterns of their lives conform to the pattern this pilot's life will inevitably set. It will not be planned that way. It will merely happen. This pilot, therefore, must be an exceptional man, selected without bias, with no prejudice for any particular point of view.

The colonel has made his choice. Yet he's unwilling to act on this. He can't say why. The names he has neatly written along the left-hand margin of one clean white sheet of paper are clearly legible. And it is clearly up to him to act now on the decision he has written down. *Pilot*, he's written, *Yeager*. Beneath this he has written, *Engineering Officer*, after which for some reason or another he has carefully printed Ridley's name. Then he has written,

Alternate Pilot, Hoover. It seems to him now the only decision that can be made.

"All things considered," Colonel Ascani has conceded a moment ago, "it's the best decision you can make. Since time is so damned important, why not send them to Buffalo tonight? They can look over the airplane, hear it growl. We needn't commit ourselves with them. We can think it over and see what the old man says."

The colonel has nodded at his deputy. "Thank you, Fred," he has said and Colonel Ascani has gone away, correctly leaving the last decision to him, a decision that seemed to be simple in that it seemed so right. But Colonel Boyd stares at the page, unwilling still to commit himself. Then, not knowing what else to do, yet feeling the pressing necessity to act, he raises his arms, stretching them out and back before he brings his clasped hands together behind his motionless head. Then again in his mind he weighs each scrap of evidence.

The argument repeats itself, and yet, beneath its rational display there runs a deeper statement, one which the colonel feels but cannot articulate, an argument that as strongly supports the colonel's choice as do the acknowledged facts. It is an argument, however, that he mistrusts and one he must therefore reject as soon as it enters his mind.

It is not a question of whether his choice is right or wrong. The decision seems right to him. It is a question of why that choice has been made, or how. Has he relied entirely on facts? If he has, he is free to act. But what if he has relied on something else, on some well-hidden, personal argument, one that has colored the facts to suit his taste? This is the question he forces against himself. Have you selected Yeager only because of his merit both as a pilot and as a man? Or is it because you find in him a number of characteristics you recognize in yourself?

Certain differences admitted, there is a marked resemblance between Yeager and himself. At least, it seems that way. The mere fact that he likes the younger man and can even laugh with him at his own expense makes the selection extremely difficult. It would be proving too many things too easily.

That it is better, for instance, to begin with nothing and to make your own way from ledge to ledge; that too much formalism dulls the edge of a pilot's eagerness to fly, makes him a better officer, perhaps, but less of a pilot; that a farm boy from the hills is a match for anyone or that—It is frankly dangerous to go on. You can skip from one slippery generalization to another and you might find yourself at the end with a dead pilot on one hand and a smashed airplane on the other.

You can't help liking a man who seems as steady as you are in a situation in which he need not be, a capable man with a sense of humor and with absolute confidence in himself, a younger man who speaks your language, who is crazy to fly the fastest, most dangerous airplane in the world, who is sure he can fly it and who makes you feel with him his own deep certainty. But you have to be sure you're right this time. You'd better call Yeager back and talk to him once again.

The colonel's unwillingness to act is still apparent in his unwillingness to move. His hands still clasped behind his head, he stares at the wall beyond him, thinking again that there's more at stake than either the pilot or the plane. It may be only the future of common men, of men like Yeager and himself who are born into the world with nothing and who come of age with nothing to recommend them except their personal courage and their ability. Even that stake is worth the risk. The door is still open now to men like Yeager, and Ridley, too. There are some who might like not necessarily to slam it shut but to close it so far that only a few would squeeze their way in between unpleasant safeguards blocking the way. Would he be right or wrong in risking the project for this?

He can't be sure. And he has to be right this time. He has to select not only the pilot who can and who will take the X-1 through the sonic barrier, he must also select the man who thereafter will carry himself with credit, not just to the service but to himself as well and to all men like him. When it has finally been done, no one must ever be able to say, You see, this type of fellow is wrong. Let's close the door. The door would thereafter be shut. And who would reopen it?

It is at this moment, having reached this point in the argument with himself, that the colonel is interrupted by the ringing of his telephone.

"General Chidlaw is calling you," his secretary says.

"Yes?" he answers, feeling his doubt slip suddenly away.

"Boyd?" The general's voice is crisp in the colonel's ear.

"Good morning, sir."

"I am very anxious," the general says, "to get your project under way, to get the X-1 and the pilot out to Muroc and to get them both in the air. What date can you give me? Have we a pilot? And if we have, is he on his way out there? How does it stand?"

"Sir, we've made a tentative selection."

"Good. Come over and tell me all about it. I will wait."

With the general's brief words still in his mind, the colonel puts down his phone and rings for his deputy. He is pleased to find the decision has been firmly made. "Fred," he says as Colonel Ascani enters the room, "I am going over to see General Chidlaw now. Will you see that Yeager, Hoover and Ridley leave for Buffalo?"

A few minutes later he stands in the general's office, as ill at ease as Yeager had been as he stood before the colonel's own desk. But in place of the younger man's anxiety, the colonel feels only impatience to get back to work, to get on with the project and to see it done. He will not really rest until it is over and this the colonel acknowledges with a wry grin.

"Sit down," the general says informally. Then, when the colonel has seated himself, he asks him, "What's been done?"

"Sir," the colonel begins, "in selecting a pilot for an assignment like this one, there are several factors one considers. You know, of course, what we've been looking for. But let me describe as well as I can the process of selection.

"Colonel Ascani and I sat down together and went through our roster of pilots, all one hundred and twenty-five of them. We first selected twenty-five we thought were qualified to make the flight. We then called in each of these pilots for an interview, having, of course, a good deal of personal knowledge by then of their attitudes and their abilities. In these interviews, General, there were several characteristics for which we particularly looked. Alertness, eagerness, reliability, over-all pilot attitude."

"You must be preparing me," the general comments dryly, "for something unusual."

"No, General, we've made the best possible choice, although it's only tentative. I believe we've chosen one of the finest pilots we have in the Flight Test Division. We've certainly chosen the best pilot for this particular project. Yeager, sir. Charles E. Yeager."

"Yeager." General Chidlaw repeats the name reflectively, his voice noncommittal, his expression bland.

"The pilot assigned to this project must have, as you know, sir, an over-all appreciation of the problem involved. He must have, above all, reliability, must have stability, must have enthusiasm to carry a program like this. Yeager has all these qualities. He is certainly the most stable individual we've interviewed. And there is no doubt about his enthusiasm.

"I think my feeling about his stability has come most from my observation of his ability during the air shows we've been performing, General Chidlaw. In every event in which he's flown, Yeager has performed absolutely as scheduled and with the greatest precision.

"I think Yeager is one of the greatest flyers I've known," the colonel continues as General Chidlaw nods agreement with his argument. "All of his flying is done just absolutely in accordance with the schedule and with this perfect precision. It's just a pleasure to watch him fly. Then, of course, in talking with him, you can't help observing his stability. He's just as solid as the building.

He's unexcitable. I have never seen him excited. He's as stable as a rock.

"Now, it is true, General Chidlaw, that Yeager is not an engineer. He has had no formal engineering education. Here is his record."

The pilot's pink qualification card is formally placed on the general's desk top and the colonel goes on. "Regardless of this, each time we reviewed the several pilots who were considered, we always came back to Yeager because of his stability, particularly, and his reliability. We knew then that we had to have a team, in that Yeager does not have the formal engineering education he should have to carry the project as an engineer and as a pilot. We looked then for the ideal teammate for him among those pilots who are graduate engineers. This turned out to be Ridley, sir. Captain Jack Ridley.

"Needless to say, we have given a great deal of thought to the selection of this team, in that it means so much to the Air Force and to the future of aviation. We have considered everything. Ridley is truly a very capable engineer and a very capable pilot. More than that, he and Yeager are very compatible and will do well together as a team. Each, I am certain, will support the other. Each has a great deal of confidence in the other. Here, sir, is Ridley's record."

Ridley's pink card joins Yeager's on the general's desk. A third card follows. "Captain Hoover's," the colonel explains. "Hoover has been selected by Colonel Ascani and me as alternate pilot. Bob Hoover wanted the project as much as Yeager did." The colonel smiles at a memory. "He is a very good pilot, too, outstanding in his technique particularly. In our final selection we'd have included both Hoover and Yeager, in any event. It was merely a question of who would be pilot and who would be alternate. Our final decision was Yeager, of course."

"On what basis?" the general asks.

"Stability, sir."

"All right," the general answers almost immediately. "No need to leave all these records here. It's your project. If Yeager's the choice you've made, then Yeager it is." The general stands and comes out from behind his desk. "Does he know what the odds against him are?"

"Well—" the colonel grins suddenly—"he doesn't look at it that way, General Chidlaw. That's why he's been assigned to this project. He knows there's a risk. But I'm sure he's convinced that the odds are on his side."

"I see. And he understands his responsibility? The over-all significance of this?"

"I am sure he does."

"All right." The general holds out his hand. "Good luck to all of you. Keep me informed."

"Thank you," the colonel says. "I will."

The lives of three pilots, the future of many more have been unalterably changed. The colonel can now go back to work.

6

The T-11 flies lazily through the air. A slow airplane as modern aircraft go, it is piloted now by Ridley with deceptive, seemingly casual skill. The night is clear. The stars stand brightly in the sky.

It is a short cross-country flight from Dayton, Ohio, to Buffalo, New York, three hundred and some odd miles, less than two hours in this plane. Yet Ridley, Hoover and Yeager are all impatient. Time and distance seem to have gone awry.

But it's a holiday for them, this run to Buffalo. And it is more than that. It is the beginning of something new. Action has picked them up again from where last it let them down. In spite of impatience, their good humor grows as the plane drones through the quiet night. The cockpit gradually fills with easy laughter and with easier talk.

There is more in this than the pleasure of having been chosen above all others for their particular skills. It is more than the fact that they are friends. Thrown suddenly together—and they are used to this—each pilot has begun to find his familiar place in the new group to which he now belongs. From here on they will live and work as a group, moving together into each new experience as the project to which they've been assigned takes form and grows.

Its purpose itself is enough to excite the calmest man: to fly at speeds and altitudes not yet explored. Not just to establish one more record in the conventional scale beginning at Kitty Hawk in December of 1903, but to do or to have a part in the doing of what was yesterday impossible.

To do what many consider impossible even now as these pilots fly through the first hours of a mission set up to accomplish the fact. To fly in level flight at the speed of sound. To shatter a barrier of fear and to bring men closer to whatever may be destiny.

Meanwhile, the pilots laugh at things which hardly matter. "What did he say to you, Bob?" Yeager asks Hoover.

Hoover grins. "The old man? 'Bob,' he says, 'you're the finest pilot in the world. We want you to go along and hold Yeager's hand. Want you to keep him sober, keep him away from girls.'"

"Is that a fact?" says Yeager. "He said the same damn thing to me. He said, 'Yeager, you're the finest pilot we have. But your prime responsibility is to keep Bob Hoover busy.' He told me, 'I hate to say this, Yeager, but I won't be there to handle him and Fred just hasn't got the time.'"

"That's funny," Ridley says. "He told me to run a bed check on you two guys, to make you do all your flying in the air."

"Now, seriously, Ridley, what did he really say to you?"

On through the night the three men fly, speeding above the world, yet moving too slowly for their own sense of time set up as it is beyond the world's by hours of flight in faster and faster planes at altitudes where time itself shrinks into smaller and smaller segments of space traveled at always increasing speeds. So that now to return to this level of lower and slower flight in an older ship is like leaving a train to drive in traffic, like leaving a car to walk a few feet turned suddenly into a mile, a half-second stretched into a long half-hour.

But even as time lags with the T-11, the pilots' impatience dims again, the night around them serving to set them apart for the moment from time itself and to encircle the three of them alone. This unity is not disturbed until they land again, and even then they remain an entity, a unit together, detached from the point at which they were brought together, but still a group. Their first sight of the X-1 on the following day serves only to underline this fact, to draw them even more tightly together, to set them even more firmly apart from everyone else. For no matter who built the airplane or how little they know of its intricate, new and still secret power plant, it stands there now in its steel-and-concrete testing ramp, a small, bright orange little plane blasting its powerful testament to their experience as military pilots and to the rich experience of all men who have ever flown.

The three men stand together, feeling the sound beat into them, feeling it hammer them all together, pounding them into an even tighter pact of anticipation and of will. They will somehow or other fly this plane that stands in its gentle shroud of liquid oxygen and frosting nitrogen gas, this little plane that bursts into a sudden roar, shaking the steel-and-concrete-studded floor and walls and ceiling too as a long, bright blue and blinding flame of standing shock waves skids over the floor, its wild roar bouncing from floor to walls, from walls to ceiling and from ceiling back to the floor again, heating the concrete, jarring it loose and shaking a shower of dust and fragments down on the wide-eyed, listening men.

Ridley can see and hear these strange phenomena as an engineer with an understanding of all the principles involved, knowing what happens when the switch is flipped, guessing at what he doesn't know. Hoover can watch with some impartiality. It's not his, really. He's just the alternate. But Yeager is big-eyed with delight, like a small boy with a new and noisy toy.

"I couldn't quite understand it," he will later admit. "I mean, there sat an airplane, looked to me like there was smoke pouring out of it. How did I know what liquid oxygen looked like? I thought it was smoke or some kind of fog. Gas and liquid oxygen blowing from three or four holes in front and frost all over the thing. Men working around. I didn't understand the plane the way Ridley did. I didn't know what its systems were or anything. All I knew is somebody flipped a switch and boy, all hell broke loose! Fire flew out of the back end. There were a couple of big explosions. It settled down then and this real long flame of standing shock waves—blue they were and pretty but just screeching and making a lot of noise.

"Later, when it was over, I looked in the cockpit. There was nothing that moved in there, just little switches. I didn't know what they were for. They checked them out and asked if I'd like to throw one. 'Hell, yes,' I told them and reached inside. I flipped a switch. Pressures came up. It fired off and the damn thing started all over again! It was quite an experience, really. It was a lot of fun. I was really impressed."

Then Hoover fires a chamber. Ridley, too. Lashed down to the ground, the small plane trembles beneath restraint, struggles to rise against force that holds it down. And it seems for a moment to be a living thing, captive, imprisoned but struggling to be free.

"That's quite an airplane," Ridley comments as the sound of the rocket motor dies. "How did you come to build the damn thing, Mr Bell?"

7

A small, energetic and driving man dressed in a dark-blue, rumpled suit, Larry Bell laughs at the fact that the question should even be asked of him. Back in his office, he takes off his black-rimmed glasses and briefly massages his forehead and his eyes. "I don't really know," he admits. "It wasn't my own idea to begin with. In my opinion, as far as I know, the credit for starting this project belongs to two men, to Ezra Kotcher, who was an Air Force engineering officer at Wright Field in 1943, and to our own chief engineer, Bob Woods, who worked with Kotcher closely from the beginning and who designed the airplane.

"You know, I've played a funny role in this flying business." Bell laughs again as he leans back in his chair. "If I can make a personal digression for a moment, I'd like to tell you something. I went to work for Glenn L. Martin in California back in 1912. I was sixteen years old, fresh out of high school and just a green, green kid. I wasn't even the bicycle mechanic the other beginners were. Maybe it's just because I knew I didn't know anything that I decided we ought to hire an engineer. So I talked Glenn Martin into hiring what I believe was the first honest-to-God engineer ever employed by any aircraft manufacturer. His name was Donald W. Douglas.

"And that," he concludes, "is all I can really take credit for, for introducing an engineer into the aircraft business and for relying on engineers to design the best airplanes that can be designed. This company, for example, is nothing more than an organization built around the genius of our chief engineer, Bob Woods, and around the professional skills of the engineers who work with him. That's what produced the XS-1, or the X-1 as we've come to call it.

"Now, I suppose, you want to know how it was done." Bell stands and gestures toward a door. "You know," he says, coming out from behind his desk, "it's not every day we turn out a million-dollar airplane. When Colonel Boyd wired us you were coming, I decided we'd better get set to brief you gentlemen." He leads the way now from his office into the hall. "There's nothing like getting it right from the horse's mouth," he says as he holds the door for Hoover and Ridley and you. "So I've gotten together the men who designed and who built the airplane. They'll tell you as much as they can and try to answer whatever questions you care to ask."

He opens another door now and stands to one side, inviting you into another room. There is laughter and talking inside and smoke lies heavy in the air. But the talk dies and the laughter trails away as you enter. Six or eight men are seated around a long conference table. On this there is a small scale model of the X-1, painted the same bright orange and mounted nose down, with one wing up, on a metal stand. Scattered around the table top are ash trays, match books, pencils and paper and printed or handwritten notes. Each man sits in a different position in his chair, some slouching, at ease, and others attentively erect. But all of them stand as you follow Bell into the room. They are almost all of them rather young.

"I'd like you to meet one another," Bell says in the silence that follows the last few technical words. "Captain Yeager, who's going to fly the X-1. His alternate, Captain Hoover, and Captain Ridley, the Air Force project engineer." Then in a round of greetings you meet Bob Woods, chief design engineer; Paul Emmons, chief aerodynamicist; Bob Stanley, chief engineer, and Benson Hamlin, Roy Sandstrom and Stanley Smith, who have all been project engineers.

There is one older man, the last to be introduced. "More young men," he says as he takes your hand in his.

"I am van Lonkhuyzen," he tells you. And you all find chairs as Bell begins.

"These boys are in a hurry," he says, lighting now the first of a string of cigarettes. "That's understandable. But there are some things they'll have to know. I think we'll just let someone break the ice and see where we go from there."

"I would like," van Lonkhuyzen says quietly, "to make a very brief opening comment. We all have, I believe, a special affection for the X-1, for this little plane." He nods at the model airplane standing on the table top. "It has given to each of us," he says carefully, "the rare opportunity to step out into the unknown.

"Looking around this room you can see that the engineering of this airplane placed a definite emphasis on youth. It was, I believe, a job that could have been done only by such young engineers. I say this because I believe that all the decisive human qualities which have made the X-1 possible are precisely those qualities characteristic of young men—unhesitating boldness to undertake a venture so few men think will succeed, an exuberant enthusiasm which has so far overcome all obstacles and unknowns, the unprejudiced imagination which has led us so drastically away from familiar paths. I am speaking of the improvisation, of the speculation, of the really original work that has gone into this project.

"When you consider—" He leans forward now and his voice becomes firm with emphasis—"that this airplane has been designed and built to explore temperatures and stresses of which we still know little, if anything at all, when you think that this airplane was born almost four years ago, and when you remember that these young engineers found themselves forced to throw away all their books and references in conceiving this airplane, you can appreciate what a tribute it is to all of them now in this room.

"And you young pilots—" The older man smiles at them—"when you fly this airplane will know how well they have done their work. I believe," he says now to

Larry Bell, "that is all I have to contribute to this discussion, unless any specific technical matters should arise."

"I believe it is true, what you say," Bell says reflectively. "I think you are right." Then crushing out one cigarette as he takes up another and strikes a match, he suddenly grins. "Now let's have a little wisdom from the mouths of the babes. Woods, you designed the air frame. You begin."

"Sure, Larry," Woods says quietly. Then with the slowness of a man forced suddenly to recall the past he cautiously begins. "The project first took definite form in December of 1944. There were meetings at Wright Field. We decided then that the airplane should be a conventional, piloted aircraft capable of carrying 500 pounds of recording instrumentation and of flying at supersonic speeds. Its speed was to be controllable. It was to take off from the ground, have ten minutes of powered flight at 35,000 feet and land at 90 miles an hour.

"This seems simple enough. But we discovered right off that none of us knew anything about specific problems the program began to present. Bob Stanley said recently—" Woods nods at Stanley across the table top—"that structural design criteria were arbitrary, that they were based principally on ignorance. That is true. It has been true of everything we've done.

"We didn't know where to begin. Bob Sandstrom and Benson Hamlin, who sit there not looking any the worse for wear, did much of the original work resulting in the airplane's design. They started from scratch, did the best they could with what little was known. The plane's design has been based on ballistic data, in part, and on highly dubious wind tunnel data."

Facing these engineers, you listen. You listen carefully. You want to know all there is to know about this plane you're going to fly. And listening, you study the faces of those around you, the men who designed and who built the X-1. But always your eyes keep coming back to the plane itself, to that small scale model, bright orange above the dull-green table top.

"We began—" Woods is remembering now—"by applying common sense to what little was known or could be extrapolated. Ben Hamlin and I spent time at the Army's Aberdeen Proving Ground, for example. And we visited several arsenals to study shock-wave patterns of high-speed projectiles. The result of what we learned was to make the airplane, as you can see it is, essentially bullet shaped and symmetrical and to get the horizontal tail at least a wing cord length above the wing plane.

"If you will look at the model—" Woods speaks more incisively now—"you will see that the air frame is of conventional configuration with a mid-wing design. It has, however, many unconventional features, thinner wing sections, for example, and even thinner tail sections set high above the wing wake to reduce buffeting. The tail stabilizer is not a fixed surface but is quickly adjustable. I'll say more about this in just a moment.

"The plane has a wing area of 130 square feet, an aspect ratio of six and a wing loading at the beginning of its flight of 100 pounds a square foot. It is 31 feet long and has a span of 28 feet. Now for its less conventional features. The wing is strong enough to carry the weight of a fully loaded B-36 yet it is smaller than one-seventh of the B-36 tail and at most only three inches thick—three and a half inches thick, I should say. Since this is quite thin, the thickness of its covering is unusual. Machined out of solid aluminum plate, the upper and lower halves of the wing are each more than half an inch thick at the inboard end and tapered to conventional thickness at the tip. This wing, incidentally, is honeycombed with something like 240 pressure orifices, from each of which a tube runs to a recording manometer carried in the plane. A dozen strain gauges are also installed in the left wing and a similar quantity in the empennage.

"Stabilizer construction is similar to that of the wing. We think wing wake interference over the horizontal tail will present one of the greatest difficulties of transonic flight. So we've placed the horizontal stabilizer as high as possible above the wing wake and made it rapidly adjustable to accommodate large changes of trim.

"Finally, the airplane has been designed to a load factor of 18, well above the conventional 11.7. We beefed it up to this extent because, as you may know, a number of people believe that everything, including air loads, will go to infinity at the speed of sound.

"Now the airplane has been flown," Woods says and he speaks with less formality. "I should say airplanes, really. We have three X-1's. There are three air frames involved. There were many variants in the original contract, which called for three. There were to be various thicknesses of wings and tail, and so forth. The first airplane, the one with which we made glide flights at Pinecastle, Florida, has an eight per cent thick wing and a six per cent tail. The second airplane has a ten per cent thick wing and an eight per cent thick tail. This was actually the first airplane to fly with power. Its power plant was installed while the first plane was being glide tested in Florida. But apart from the thickness of tail and wing these two ships are identical. The third air frame was also finished with the ten per cent wing and eight per cent tail. It is presently stored here pending development of a turbine pump to supply fuel to the rocket motor. Bob Stanley will tell you something of that in a moment.

"Now, in these glide tests made in Florida in January of 1946," Woods continues, "the airplane has flown by Jack Woolams, who was then our chief test pilot. We ran through a series of ten glide tests, the plane, minus its power plant, weighing about 4,000 pounds. On the first drop the inboard engines of the B-29 were feathered, the flaps in take-off position. An ejector expelled the X-1 at a speed of about 150 miles an hour. This ejector was simply a converted bomb-bay actuator in the B-29 that expelled the plane vertically, giving it at the same time a slightly nose-down, pitching movement to insure a clean break-away.

"We were afraid, you see, that the X-1 would drag back into the tail section of the B-29. So we had sway braces or yaw braces and drag struts surrounding the X-1 like a picket fence. We painted these practically at the very last moment with bright red paint, the idea being that if any of these were contacted by the X-1, it would leave a wet paint mark on the airplane. The first test was highly successful. No paint marks appeared. In tests that followed the launching speed was therefore progressively increased. I think the second test was made with all four engines of the B-29 running, but with inboard engines at low power to decrease turbulence around the wings of the X-1 from the propeller slip stream from the inboard engines. This was a clean drop, too. We finally moved up to normal power with all four B-29 engines running and with all braces and guards and the ejector strut eliminated. We found that the X-1 will drop cleanly out of the B-29, dropping just about straight down with no rearward movement.

"We had no trouble on the glide test program except during the first landing. Woolams, who was later killed just before the 1946 Thompson Trophy races when the special P-39 he was preparing dove into Lake Ontario— Woolams was having so much fun with the airplane, he found it such a delight to fly because it was small and light and very responsive, that he undershot his landing. We'd picked that airport because it had one of the longest runways in the United States, ten thousand feet. But Jack found he was undershooting so he had to cut in and land cross lots. He just barely made it into the field. But the airplane, he said, flew perfectly. There was no vibration, no noise. It was, he said, the best damned airplane he'd ever flown.

"Later experience bears this out. We have encountered no aerodynamic difficulties with the airplane. I attribute the lack of trouble to the symmetry of the design, to the mid-wing and also to the fact that the airplane was built to withstand so much stress. The plane has made twenty successful powered flights up to a speed of .8 Mach number. But I think Bob Stanley ought to brief you on the power plant before we go into that."

As Woods leans back in his chair, you look up from the notes you've made to find that Hoover is scribbling too and that Ridley is writing as fast as he can.

"I think," Bell says, "that does it, Bob. That covers it pretty well. But maybe you gentlemen have some questions now." And you find Bell looking at you.

"Yes, sir," you say. "There's one thing I've been

wondering about. Looking at this model here, and from what I recall of the plane we saw, isn't that windshield rather high on the nose? How much can you see? Just what is the angle of vision from in the cockpit when you're coming down?"

Smiling wryly, Woods leans out over the table top to look down at you. "The pilot's vision during landing," he admits, "is marginal."

"How about that cockpit door?" Hoover asks. "It's not hinged or anything. How is the door secured? And why is it cut so low in the fuselage?"

"Entry into the X-1 is made from the B-29 during flight," Woods explains. "The door is lowered on a cable and set in place. It is locked from within and the cabin is sealed and pressurized. We haven't had too much trouble with that. We almost lost a door once but that was an accident." Woods pauses and Hoover grins at you.

"On the other matter," Woods then explains, "the door is located so that in case of a bail-out, the pilot is forced to go downward. This will increase his chances of missing the tail."

"I see. Thank you." Hoover seems even more highly amused with this.

"Any more questions?" Bell asks, lighting a fresh cigarette from the butt of another. "If not, I think we'll let Stanley go on with the power plant."

8

"Let me begin," Bob Stanley says with a sudden smile, "by admitting the very worst. We wound up our program two weeks ago with a near disaster.

"We'd finished the twenty powered flights required of us and they'd been very successful. The last ten or fifteen were without incident. Slick Goodlin, who took the plane after Woolam's death, and our chief test pilot, Tex Johnston, had both flown the plane up to .8 Mach number. And Johnston had put the plane through an 8 g pull-out at minimum speed. He had no difficulty. The plane is beautifully designed and it's built, as you may know, to withstand a stress of 18 g's or eighteen times the force of gravity. So to put the X-1 under a stress of 8 g's at minimum speed was no problem at all. We were feeling pretty good.

"Then came the crowning touch. We were asked to take part in a show being put on out at Muroc for aviation news writers. There were a couple of hundred or so who came up to visit the base. We had both planes out there and we decided we'd make a flight in one of them and a ground run in the other. We thought we'd just park the number-two plane in front of the crowd and scare them a little with all that noise and the sight of the flame shooting out from the tail. Well, the flight went off all right but the ground run was almost disastrous.

"Richard Frost, the project engineer we now have at Muroc, had charge of the ground run. He got one cylinder going all right and fired the second, but it blew up. There was an explosion, causing a fire in the engine compartment. No one noticed this in the noise and excitement

58

until the red fire warning light came on in the cockpit of the airplane. Frost, who generally stands on a stepladder leaning into the cockpit, jumped down and ran back toward the tail to see if he could find anything wrong. To his horror and dismay—he was standing there waiting to have the access doors removed—he saw the paint on the fuselage begin to blister right before his eyes.

"He shouted and some of the Bell crew members very bravely hopped onto the wing to take off the largest access doors over the instrumentation compartment so that fire hoses could be brought into play. The Muroc firemen also very bravely came running up and put out the fire. We were very lucky. The airplane might have exploded, killing a number of people in the area. But nothing happened. Alcohol, which was burning, burns with an almost invisible flame and there was no smoke. So none of the spectators even knew there had been a fire until it was over. Incidentally, Frost sent the airplane back here for repairs. It is the plane used in the ground run you witnessed a little while ago. I believe you will ferry it back out to Muroc when you go.

"Well—" Stanley grins as everyone else laughs—"this, as I say, is the only serious trouble we've had with the flight-test program."

"There is," Bell says, shaking his head, "nothing like building confidence in the product. I'm not so sure at the moment that I shouldn't have hired a few less engineers and a few more salesmen. Now go on—" He laughs at Stanley—"give them a few kind words about the power plant."

Stanley, still grinning, settles himself in his chair. "Well, we began with a tremendous problem. The horsepower we needed to take this aircraft into the air and keep it there for ten minutes of powered flight was equivalent to that produced by twenty-five diesel railroad engines. We could get that much power only from a rocket motor. The question was, who could design and build the type of motor we had in mind?

"It wasn't until March of 1945 that Benson Hamlin, who'd been traveling around looking for aerodynamic information, learned that a small company in Pompton Lakes,

New Jersey, was building rocket motors for the Navy's Bureau of Aeronautics. This was Reaction Motors, Incorporated, R.M.I. We went to them right away and after a long period of research and experimentation, of trial and error, they came up with the power plant we now have in the airplane, an assembly of four 1,500-pound-thrust rockets operating at a chamber pressure of 230 pounds per square inch, or 230 psi.

"The rockets can be run separately or in any combination selected by the pilot. Let me show you a rough diagram of how the rocket engine works."

Standing now, Stanley turns to a blackboard fastened to one wall and begins to sketch a perspective drawing of the source and fuel systems leading back to the rocket motor. "We won't have time now to go into all the systems. You'll get that anyway when you meet Frost at Muroc. Now, here in the forward end of this cylinder is the igniter. This fires a stream of fuel and gaseous oxygen, this spark plug. When the chamber pressure reaches a value of approximately 50 psi, the propellant valves open to admit the fuel and liquid oxygen or lox, as we call it. I'll have more to say in a moment about how the fuel and lox are fed to the motor."

"Excuse me," Ridley interrupts, "but are those rockets throttled?"

"No. No provision was made to throttle the individual rockets. The pilot flies with either 25, 50, 75 or 100 per cent of full thrust."

"And the fuel," Ridley asks, "is liquid oxygen and alcohol?"

"Yes. The final selection of a propellant fuel was made in much the same way we did everything else. We considered everything possible, tried everything, ruling out one thing at a time until we found the mixture we wanted. Hydrogen, for example, showed low specific impulses. Acid and aniline are too combustible. Nitromethane is subject to detonation under circumstances we don't understand. Gasoline and liquid oxygen can't be cooled without the addition of a third tank for water, which meant additional weight. We settled for lox and alcohol because they're readily available. They have good specific impulse, are relatively safe and easy to work with. They're not spontaneously combustible and in small amounts they're not injurious to the people who have to handle them.

"Well." Stanley turns back to the blackboard, pointing to his diagram as he goes on. "We had the motor and the fuel. Then we came to the problem of getting the fuel from storage containers or tanks back to the motor. The contract had specified and the plane—horse calculations and everything—had been designed for a turbine-driven pump. No such pump has ever been developed. We found that to design and build this pump would have been as much of a job as we'd had with the rocket motor.

"It seemed to us that the idea was to get the airplane into the air and to fly at the speed of sound as quickly as possible. So we decided to use the brute force technique. We dropped the turbine pump program in favor of a system of pressure-fed propellants. This is a fairly simple system, as you can see. You have spherical tanks pressurized with gas, in this case nitrogen gas, which expands and expels propellants to the motor at the necessary high pressure.

"This was a major decision. It involved dropping back a number of steps, to some people, because you had to go to something new in tanks and the idea of carrying liquid oxygen at minus 300 degrees Fahrenheit in an uninsulated container in an airplane was very disturbing. It meant the tanks had to be much heavier than those we'd have used with the turbine pump.

"The rocket motor develops a chamber pressure of about 220 psi. To force propellants into the chamber against that internal pressure, we use a feed pressure of 300 to 330 psi. The turbine pump would have produced this, if we'd had it. It would have been essentially just a fuel pump driven by a gas generator. You'd have needed only a small amount of pressure on the propellants to prevent cavitation in the pump, 10 or 15 psi. And you'd have had very light tanks, cylindrical in shape.

"With pressures as high as 330 psi, however, we've had to use spherical tanks or the weight would have been prohibitive. Even these spherical tanks increase the weight of the airplane and their shape is inefficient. The fuselage of the X-1, as you can see for yourselves, is essentially cylindrical and for maximum efficiency you should use tanks just fitting its volume. Instead, we've had to put what you might think of as an egg inside a cylinder. This reduced the amount of fuel we can carry and has reduced the duration of powered flight, with all four chambers burning, from a little over four minutes to two minutes. And it gave us some new problems.

"There was the storage of gas, for example. We have a dozen containers scattered all over the plane. There is a sphere in the nose, forward of the cockpit, a ring of seven spheres just after the cockpit around the forward end of the liquid oxygen tank. And there are two spheres in the landing gear well, the main wheel well, and two more tanks, one sphere and one cylinder, behind the fuel tank.

"This is all the storage space we have in the airplane. So in order to carry enough gas to expel all the propellants and also to operate the various other systems, we carry this gas at 4,500 psi. This is," he explains, as Ridley raises his head in surprise, "an unheard-of pressure, commercially speaking. The highest pressure at which you can buy nitrogen gas is 2,200 psi. And the commercial companies get it to that pressure by pumping it.

"We couldn't do that because the pumps you have to use introduce some oil into the gas. Such oil droplets would certainly have been mixed with the liquid oxygen and we'd have had a bad explosion. So we had to develop a method of making nitrogen gas at 4,500 psi. We got the idea of evaporating it, of making it by evaporation from liquid oxygen. One of our engineers, Lloyd Bevan, developed a practical nitrogen evaporator which we are now using.

"Well, all this increased the weight of the airplane and reduced its flying time. So we came back to what was one of the original problems, the problem of getting it up into the air with fuel enough left for a high speed run. Ground take-off had been specified. But as we saw it, the problem wasn't simply to meet each specification established to fly the airplane, but to get the plane up to altitude and fly at the speed of sound. We therefore conceived the idea of the air launch, of dropping the X-1 from the B-29 and, as Woods has told you, we developed this air launch technique in a series of tests.

"These, then, were the major problems: getting the power plant, selecting a fuel, developing a fuel supply system to replace the turbine pump, storing nitrogen gas and getting the airplane up to altitude with sufficient fuel for its high speed run. We solved them as quickly as we could. If we had not, I don't think the X-1 would be flying today. As it is, we're about two years ahead of everyone else. I hope we can keep that lead."

Dusting the chalk from his hands, Stanley walks back to his chair and sits down. "Of course, there were other problems. So if you have any questions to ask while we're all here—"

Ridley begins. "How is the motor cooled?" But you've all got questions, all three of you. For over an hour you question these engineers. And for another hour you sit there talking about the airplane. Some of the talk is over your head. The X-1 is something new to you. But you feel it's a challenge. You're eager to fly the airplane, eager to see what will happen and to know just what you'll do. Then, as you listen, your eagerness becomes impatience. You've got hard work ahead. You'll have to study the X-1, learn each of its systems backward and forward before the old man will let you even sit down in the plane. You want to get out to Muroc and get down to work.

"Well," Ridley says as you finally leave the big Bell plant in Buffalo, "looks like we got ourselves a pretty good deal."

And you agree with him. But back at Wright Field your chance of ever flying the X-1 has begun to slip away. The old man, Colonel Boyd, sits waiting impatiently in his office to tell you why.

9

The colonel's mouth is just a hard, straight line across his face. Something is wrong but you don't know what it is. He studies you closely for almost a minute and you study him. Then he finally says, "Sit down."

For several moments nothing more is said. The colonel leans back in his chair. You settle yourself uncomfortably in another chair facing his desk. And you wait, your eyes on the colonel, his eyes on yours.

"You've seen the airplane?" he asks.

"Yes, sir."

The colonel looks up at the ceiling. "You were all briefed on the airplane?" His eyes come back to yours.

"Yes, sir."

The colonel pushes a button on his desk and a few seconds later Colonel Ascani comes quietly into the room. He closes the door and takes a chair.

Then, in a voice grown suddenly tired, Colonel Boyd patiently begins. "You have seen the airplane, Yeager. And you've been through a preliminary briefing. Colonel Ascani and I want now to go a bit further into the question of whether or not you should be assigned to this project.

"Do you understand the hazards involved in flying this aircraft at the speeds proposed?"

"Yes, sir. I do." But you don't understand what's coming next and your mind runs on before each question, trying to stay one jump ahead of them.

"Do you realize why this airplane was designed to withstand tremendous stress? Why it has been designed to a load factor of 18?"

64

"I understand that, sir." If you knew what was coming next you could have the right answer ready. But you don't know. And all you can do is to listen and wait.

"You know, of course, that at the speed of sound air loads may go to infinite. Do you know what that means to the pilot?"

"Yes, sir. That would be the end. That would be it."

"That is correct. It has been anticipated—" Colonel Boyd brings his finger tips together now and fixes his eyes again on yours—"that this may happen, that the aircraft may be crushed or its wings torn off, that the pilot will not survive. That is why we have been so insistent on safety, Yeager. That is why safety must be the primary factor here."

"Yes, sir," you answer, wondering which of the things you've done but you shouldn't have done they've discovered now, whose property you might have buzzed, what God-awful mistake you might have made.

"Yeager!" the colonel's voice snaps suddenly. He asks the question as if it required an answer he didn't want to hear. "Are you *married?*"

"Yes, sir." You feel yourself beginning to smile. "I'm married, " you admit. For a moment you're tempted to ask, Aren't you? Because it's less than a month since the colonel himself set a new world's record for speed in the F-80R. But the colonels are trading serious glances now. You begin to worry again.

"And you have," Colonel Boyd asks quietly, "*children?*"

"Yes, sir."

"How many children do you have?"

"Two boys, sir. Donald is a year and a half. Mickey two months old."

"Where are they now?"

"In West Virginia with their mother, sir."

"And if you were assigned to this project," Colonel Boyd asks carefully, "have you considered what might happen to your family?"

"Yes, sir. I planned to take them out to Muroc with me on temporary duty."

For a moment the colonel stares at you. Then you can

see his face break into a sudden grin. But he swivels around in his chair, his face to the window now. The back of his neck is red.

Then Colonel Ascani clears his throat. "Well, Yeager, in view of the risks involved, don't you think we ought to choose some other pilot for this project?"

"That is right." Colonel Boyd swings suddenly around again, his face expressionless. "This *is not* a safe project. A great many reputable people think we won't come out of this project with either the pilot or the plane. Don't you agree that the selection of a pilot who has a wife and children would be simply adding to the risk?"

Feeling now that you're losing whatever ground you've gained, you say, "No, sir, I don't agree with that."

"Why not?"

"Well, sir—" But you don't really know what to say. You want this project. It's unique. The ship itself is a challenge. It's a rocket and it's fast. It's more than that. You have the feeling as you sit there wondering how to answer the colonel's question that flying this airplane is something to which the whole of your life has led, that here in this moment you've reached a point of departure from the past. Whatever you say, whatever decision the colonels make, nothing will be the way it was.

You want this project, not just to prove yourself or to measure yourself against the rest, and not for the fame it might bring. You've had a glance at the future, touched the unknown. You've got to go on and see what's there because you can only go on alone. This is the thing, this chance to accomplish something alone, something that's really important, and to do it without depending on any other man. The pilot who flies the X-1 into the sonic range will, in the last analysis, make the decision himself. And when he goes, he'll go alone. This much you know. But you don't know what to say.

"Why don't you agree—" The colonel repeats his question—"that your having a family, Yeager, would add to this project's already considerable risk? It seems to me you'd have just that much more to worry about."

"My being married and having responsibility," you

answer finally, trying to turn the colonel's argument, "should be in my favor, sir. Having a wife and children have made me more careful as a pilot and not less."

"There is an argument—" The colonel is almost grinning again—"I hadn't thought of, Fred."

"Have you discussed this with your wife?" Colonel Ascani wants to know.

"No, sir. I have not. As far as I know, I haven't been finally assigned. And I thought this project was more or less secret, sir. I haven't discussed the project with anyone except Hoover and Ridley and the men we met in Buffalo."

Colonel Boyd swings suddenly around in his chair again. "What do you think your wife would say," he asks, his back still turned, "if you told her you were the pilot assigned to fly an airplane at the speed of sound?" He swings his chair back to face you now.

"Just what she's always said. She might tell me to be careful. She usually does. But she knows that flying is my job. She knows it can be dangerous. I've never heard her complain. I was flying when she married me. I've been flying ever since. We have two children now. Glennis would like to have more."

There is a moment of silence in which the colonels trade glances again. You feel somehow that their decision has been made.

"As far as I'm concerned," you finish your argument, "I want this project. I'd very much like to be assigned. I've seen the airplane, sir. And I'd very much like to fly it."

"If that is all—" Colonel Ascani comes to his feet.

"Thank you, Fred," Colonel Boyd dismisses him.

"Good luck, Yeager," Colonel Ascani says. And the door clicks quietly shut behind his back.

"All right," the old man tells you. "Now we can begin. What do you know about this airplane, Yeager?"

Only then do you begin to relax. "We witnessed a ground run on it, sir. We were briefed on its history, on the plane and its power plant. Ridley and I have since gone over it all. The systems are new to me, but not as new as I thought they'd be."

"How do you mean?"

"You take pressures, sir. I knew what a dome regulator was when I was twelve years old. My dad, you see, is in the natural gas business back home in West Virginia. He used globe regulators then and uses them still. I know what a regulator or a valve is and how it works. I've had them apart. They're the same thing in the X-1. Just simple domes. And the pressure systems—we're just using higher pressures than my dad works with. Of course, I don't understand how it all works. But it doesn't disturb me too much. I think I can learn."

"That is, of course, an oversimplification. But it will do as a beginning. Now let me brief you," the colonel says, "on your part in this project." He leans across his desk. "We are sending you out there as pilot, Ridley as engineer. You're a team. You will work together and you will work with NACA and with Bell.

"I cannot emphasize too strongly, Yeager, this idea of the team. We've given a great deal of careful thought to the selection of everyone concerned, to your selection as pilot, to Ridley's as engineer. We think you can work together. I have more or less wagered my future on this, the future of the whole Fighter Test Section. So it is what you are going to have to do.

"You will also follow the schedule set for you. They will not let us take this in big bites. We are going to have to nibble away at the problem, moving in each of your flights to a higher speed, but moving only with the advice and approval of Ridley and of the engineers. Do you understand this fully?"

"Yes, sir, I do."

"Then, for yourself. You have a tremendous responsibility. You are the pilot. Once in the air, it's up to you. You alone will be responsible for the flight of this aircraft. And I meant what I said. Safety is the primary factor. Nothing else matters.

"The idea is, of course, to get this airplane up to the speed of sound. But don't stick your neck out. If at any time it seems to you that this can't be done, don't try to do it. If it scares you, say so. If you think we should drop the program, pick up the telephone and call me here. Don't be embarrassed. There won't be one word said about it and no one will think the less of you. If you think things are not going right, you say so. The program will be dropped. We'll cancel it. Is that clear?"

"Yes, sir. It's clear enough."

"My personal opinion—" The colonel gestures with one hand—"is that we are all being overcautious with this thing. But that is strictly for your information—" He raises the hand—"and not for your guidance. You understand?"

"I understand." You feel like grinning again.

"Now, what are your plans?" the colonel asks.

"They figure on getting us out of here Saturday morning. We'll pick up the B-29 in Buffalo and ferry the X-1 right on out."

"All right. But watch the weather. You're not to fly in any weather. And don't fly at night. You can plan to stop over in Denver. I'll make arrangements to clear you in. If anything should go wrong, fire in the B-29, for instance, you will land in the X-1. You drop out. But only if that can be safely done and without risk to yourself. Ridley and Hoover, of course, will go with you. And Major Cardenas will pilot the B-29.

"Are you all ready, then?" The tone of his voice becomes a shade more familiar now as the colonel leaves his desk and crosses the room.

"I'm ready, sir." But standing, you're suddenly tired. Your wet shirt sticks to your back.

"I'll see you again," the colonel says, "before you go. I want to see all of you together. But I want to wish you luck, Yeager. All you need." He grips your hand in his and for a moment it looks as if he's going to smile.

"Of course," the colonel says after a moment's thought, "I don't believe these wild predictions that this airplane will come apart or change ends on you or anything like that. If I did, you wouldn't be going to Muroc to fly the thing.

"I think you'll make it, Yeager, perhaps before we expect it. And when you begin to read about your exploit in the public press, I hope you won't believe a word of what you read. I hope you'll go right on being what you are, a military pilot and, in my estimation, a pretty good one."

"Yes, sir," you answer, not knowing what else to say.

"And, Yeager, about this schedule, if you think we can step it up— Well, never mind. And, Yeager, before I forget it. I want you to call your wife."

"Yes, sir. I will."

"It's not that much of a secret." The colonel grins and abruptly leaves the room.

10

You drop the quarters and dimes and nickels into the telephone box with clumsy haste and Glennis keeps saying, "Hello, hello? Is that you, Chuck?" Because it might not be. A call from the base might be a call from someone else to tell her you've augured in or you've been hurt.

"Glennis, it's me," you tell her, hearing relief in her voice as she says hello again. "How are you, honey? How are the boys? You don't know how I've missed you. Is everything going all right at home?"

"Everything's fine," she says in a rush of words. "I miss you, too. The boys are all right. The baby looks just like you. Donald is right here with me. He wants to talk to you, Chuck. Go on, Don," you can hear her saying. "It's Daddy. Tell Daddy hello."

You get really homesick then. "Donald?" you call him, wishing that you could see him now. "This is your dad. Can you hear me, son?"

In the silence that follows you hear him chuckle and you can hear him breathe. "Tell him hello, Don," Glennis whispers. "Here, talk into this. Say, 'Hello, Daddy.'" But then she says, "It's no use, honey, all he can do is grin."

"Daddy." Donald begins to cry. "I want my daddy!"

"Well, talk to him, sweetheart," Glennis says.

But there is only silence again. "Where's my daddy?" the boy's voice finally cries. It's the saddest sound in the world.

"I'm right here, Donald," you tell him. "Here I am." But you can't make him understand.

"Mom," you hear Glennis saying, "take Donald, will you? I've got to talk to Chuck."

"Come on, Grandma's big boy," your mother calls him. "Come with me." And his small voice gradually fades as he's led away.

You want to go home. You haven't been home for over two weeks. But you don't know when you'll get back to Hamlin now. "Don seems upset," you say. "I wish I could see you all."

"Donald's all right. It's just his bedtime, honey. He's tired. When are you coming home?"

But you can't go home. There isn't time. You tell her the good news first, that you've got a new job, that you're going back west to Muroc and that you'll be permanently stationed there. "I'll be coming back to get you just as soon as I can find a house." You tell her it won't be long.

"A house," she says. "We won't have to live with anyone else. Your mother's been wonderful, honey. But you know how it is. I guess I'm just tired. I'm tired of living out of a suitcase. Most of all, I'm tired of living without you."

"I know."

"Oh, honey, I can hardly wait."

"We'll make it, all right," you tell her then. "Now listen, this is a real good deal. The old man just picked me to fly the X-1." You tell her what little you can about the project. The plane is experimental. It's a rocket-propelled airplane. The program will last for several months, maybe a year or more. You're going with Hoover and Ridley. The plane is expected to fly at the speed of sound, to crack the sound barrier.

"And you're going to fly it?" Glennis asks quietly. "Isn't that what that English pilot was trying to do? The one who was killed a few weeks ago? Wasn't he trying to smash the sound barrier, Chuck?"

"Oh, that. No," you tell her, "it wasn't the same thing, honey. He was just flying an ordinary jet. This airplane is really different. This plane is built."

"You be careful, honey."

You don't know whether she understands or not just

what the program is. You don't really want her to. She knows it's important. There's no reason why she should know about the risk. You don't really admit the high risk factor yourself because until a man is really hurt, he doesn't believe he can be hurt. You'd rather believe what the colonel says, and Ridley, too. "There's nothing to worry about," you tell your wife. No airplane in the world will change ends on you or fly apart without giving you warning. You'll have plenty of time to get out.

"How soon are you coming back for us?" Glennis asks then.

You tell her you just don't know. There's nothing for her to do but wait, just as she's always done. But she doesn't want to wait. She's tired of waiting. Why can't she drive the car to Muroc and meet you there in a week or two? How many miles is it from here to there? That's not too far. There's not much packing to do, no furniture.

"Honey, you can't drive all that way by yourself," you tell her. "It *is* too far. Too many things can happen. I'd be worried to death."

"What do you think I do, Chuck? Twenty-four hours a day. Oh, well," she says, submitting suddenly, "do you want me to ship your clothes?"

You tell her no. You'll be back before you'll need them. Her voice brightens then. This will be good for all of us, you tell her. She'll be able to visit her mother and father in Oroville. You'll have your own home for a while. You'll all be together. The sun will be good for the boys. The winters in Muroc are wonderful.

"Honey?" Glennis interrupts you.

"What?"

"You don't have to give me a sales talk about life on the great American desert."

"I didn't mean—"

"I love you. Just be careful."

"Don't worry, Glennis."

"Are you leaving tonight?"

"In the morning." You're going to Buffalo first. You'll call her from there. And you'll send her a telegram from Muroc just as soon as you land. You'll call her again a week from tonight. You'll know more then about where you can rent a house, how soon you'll be back to get her, how long the project will last.

"All right, honey," she finally says. "Good-by."

You hang up the telephone, beginning to wonder whether it's worth it all or not, whether you'd rather fly or work in an office and live at home. The project seems less important now. You see it not just as an eager pilot but as a homesick guy with a wife you don't see often enough and with two little boys you don't really know very well. You can still hear Glennis saying good-by and hear Donald crying as he's led away.

It makes you feel guilty because your life is so much apart from theirs. Why do you keep on flying? Because it's all you know. But why did you want to fly in the first place? How did it happen? Where did it all begin? Back in the past, so many years ago that it's hard to remember now.

Part Two

11

Summers were the best of all, and walking stilts. There wasn't a thing they didn't do in the summertime, things boys will do; they hunted and fished, played tops and marbles and made slingshots, too. But they started walking stilts when they were really young, just six or seven years old, and walked plumb up until the end of high school, taking long trips back into the hills, seeing who'd go the farthest without getting off, going a mile or more back into the woods and over fences and streams and everything.

And then sometimes they'd climb young sapling trees and ride the top of one to the top of another, go all through the woods that way without ever touching the ground, like monkeys, really, the way boys are when they're out in the open all day long and it's spring or summertime. They fished a lot and hunted, too, beginning when they were very young. He'd got his first rifle, a .22, when he was only ten years old, but an old hand then at hunting. They fished the Mud River and caught mostly bass with grasshoppers and worms or little frogs for bait. Hunting, there were rabbits, squirrels, deer, quail and grouse, pheasant and bear, 'most anything a boy would want to hunt. His dad had gone with him at first. But later not so much any more. Later his father's business kept him away from home.

Mom raised the family, mostly. She raised them almost alone. She was always after his brother Roy and him about keeping clean, getting home early at night and doing whatever was right. She raised them the same way she'd been raised, kept the same customs she'd always known. He could remember her telling them how they'd had Christmas when she was a girl and that was the way she'd made their Christmas, too, the big family meal and everything. Things hadn't changed very much in Hamlin in her lifetime, or in his.

As far back as anyone could go on either side of the family, the Yeagers or the Sisemores, Mom's family, they'd always lived in Lincoln County and always been farming people there. Even his folks had been able to keep a big garden and a cow or two. And his own chores had always been just what his father had done when he was a boy.

Hamlin is right on the Mason-Dixon Line and there's always been two of everything. Mom belonged to the Republican Methodist Church. She sent her children to Sunday school every Sunday the whole year around. And in summer they went to Bible school. But when it was over there were a million and one things they found to do back in the woods and rocky hills.

Sometimes he went with the others but it was better to go alone, to walk by himself off through the brush and under the quiet trees, to climb in the hills and find someplace you'd never found before, some little draw you'd missed or ledge whose height you'd never reached. He'd walk sometimes all afternoon along the river bank or stand high on a cliff's edge looking down, watching the wind move in slow waves across the treetops, hearing it stir pine needles, oak and poplar leaves until the wild caw of a lonely crow would turn him away or nightfall send him home. On the way back he'd bring the cows into the barn, feed them, milk them and turn them out into the yard again. Mom would be calling everyone then. It would be dinnertime. He'd walk back up the hill, feeling the summer all around him, feeling it rich in the air and soft in the ground beneath his feet, not really wanting to go in the house but going in.

In wintertime the cows stayed in the barn. He'd feed and milk them and clean out the stall. Other than shoveling snow and going to school, those were his only winter chores. His folks weren't hard. It was just the idea of keeping him busy enough. He'd come home from school at four o'clock and his mother would say, "You change your clothes."

"Yes, ma'am," he'd answer.

"And don't forget your chores."

"No, ma'am." He'd clean out the barn, throw down some hay, milk both the cows and go back to the house again, the fresh milk steaming a little in the buckets, catching a few snowflakes until the door to the kitchen opened and Mom helped him inside, saying, "Mind your feet, son," and, "Now run along and wash your hands." When he'd done that she'd say, "Let's see those hands." Sometimes he'd pass inspection, sometimes not, and he'd have to scrub again at the kitchen sink while hot food scented the stove-heated air, waiting for him, waiting for grace to be said, for Mom to remember if it was Roy's turn or his or their sister Pearl's. "Amen." Their mother would end the prayer and rush right on. "Now, Roy, you eat your vegetables tonight," as if this too were part of the blessing asked.

"Yes'm," Roy would promise.

Right after supper he'd go to bed, sometimes while it was still daylight. That's when he read. Jack London's books were favorites for a long, long time, *White Fang* and *The Call of the Wild*. The Tom Swift stories, too, he read them as fast as they came out. And he liked Mark Twain. Hannibal always seemed like Hamlin to him and Tom Sawyer's home much like his own. Their lives were pretty much the same with the same seasons, marble time and top time, and he'd had the same ideas. He talked with Roy about it when it got too dark to read or Mom called up to say, "Put out that light," because he talked with Roy about everything there was, just everything under the sun, how things are born and what makes motors go, what happens when someone dies, how to skin rabbits, the best way to hunt a bear and how to take care of rifles, fishing reels and high-top shoes. There wasn't a thing they didn't talk about between themselves. Sometimes they talked all night, it seemed to him.

"Roy, what's a 'dominant, primordial beast'?"

"A bear, maybe."

"What if you had two bears? Would both of them be that? Or what if you had a bear and a dog that could fight better than him?"

"Why, I guess the dog would be."

"What's primordial mean?"

"I don't know, boy! That would be some fight."

"What would?"

"A bear and a dog, if the dog could take care of himself."

"You think a dog could lick a bear?"

"Some dogs could."

Then spring would come again. In April he worked in the garden, so he'd get up at six and plow for an hour before he'd eat. Right after breakfast he'd go to school, something he didn't really enjoy. School was just something he had to go through with and that's all it was. A typical school day was just a matter of going to school until it was out. He wasn't necessarily a good student. He could do most things just about average. Geometry and mathematics, anything with figures in it he liked, and he'd get pretty good marks in things like that. In history he was just average. He never did flunk but did just manage to pass sometimes, in English mainly. He thought it was pretty dull.

But he liked sports and playing in the high-school band. He played football and basketball and he played trombone in the band. They marched a lot and he liked that, too. About all they learned to play were hymns and marches. They'd stand out in the open air and it would be crisp and smelling of wood smoke in the fall or snow in winter or the thawing ground in spring. The sun would be bright and the brass trombone would glisten or shine and they'd play the *National Emblem March* or *Lights Out* and *When the Saints Go Marching In* or *When the Roll is Called Up Yonder*. It would really stir him, more than he'd ever admit. But other than that, school was just something he had to go to and that's all it was. He was always glad to see summer coming again.

He spent more time than most boys do talking to

older men. Like J. D. Smith, for instance, who was a
lawyer in town and a former state senator, too. He'd sit by
the hour listening to J. D. Smith recall the past and they'd
talk about everything together, gardening and growing
things, old wars and ancient history, what books to read
and how to live. But the men he was really close to were
men like the high-school football coach. He'd even hunt
sometimes with him. Louis Hoff, too, who led the band
and taught them to drill and march. He liked him, too.
But still, when it came to hunting, he'd often go alone.

He could remember even before that time, when he
was ten or eleven, not much more. He'd go off by himself,
go wandering through the hills alone, climb way up high,
as high as he could go to cut his name into the rocks. He
could remember lying stretched out on the ground and
watching some big old airplane up in the air, a C-47
probably, on airways between Huntington and Charleston,
though he didn't know that then. He'd look up there and
watch it, wondering what made it fly, how it stayed up
there, what it was like to be above the ground that way.
But as far as wanting to fly—he didn't know anything
about it then. He didn't make up his mind until he
finished school.

He finished in May that year and went right to work.
He worked in the pool hall there at home, worked there
for two or three months. There wasn't much else to do. He
could have gone out with his dad, drilling wells for natural
gas. But he was a little small for swinging big sledge
hammers, dressing bits and doing heavy work like that.
He would have grown enough to handle them. But he was
restless and dissatisfied.

In a small town like Hamlin there isn't much to do.
Twelve hundred people. It's just a residential country
town with a little farming and some natural gas. There's
not much future there. He'd worked for the town photographer, cleaned up the studio in the evening and after
school. He earned five dollars a month at that. Why, even
after he'd finished school, ten dollars a month was all he'd
been able to earn, and he'd worked in the local pool hall to

make that much money. There was nothing else for him to do. In a town like Hamlin there seldom is.

His father knew. "You can't stay here," his father said. "You've been a boy here, son. I guess that's all you can be in Hamlin. It's a good town to grow in but that's all it is. You're restless now. You want to do more than there is in the whole of Lincoln County to do. You can't stay here. But you don't know where to go or what you *can* do. It will be that way all the rest of your life unless you go now. Where? You can't just go to Huntington or Cincinnati, son. Just work in a factory and live in a rooming house to get the things you want. You want much more than that."

His father wanted him to go to school. There was Marshall College down in Huntington, his father said. But there was no money to send him there. He could have gone anyway. He could have worked his way. He didn't know that then. He wasn't aware. Having lived in a small town all his life, he just didn't know what things there were in the world to study and to learn. He didn't know all the things there were to be done in the spring and summer of 1941.

But then Jake Markham came back home. He'd been to flying school. He was an army pilot. "It's a good life," Jake Markham said. "You go to school. You're trained, and that in itself is an education. You've got a profession then. You're pretty well paid. They're liable to send you anywhere in the world. And flying is fun. It's the easiest thing in the world. But once you've flown, it's all you want to do. I'd do it again, if I was your age, Chuck. That's what I'd do."

. And there was J. D. Smith, an old man then and wise. "There's a big war going on in Europe," J. D. Smith had told him. "And it doesn't seem logical to me that we can go on forever ignoring that war. It might be a good idea now for a young man to learn how to fly."

He began to hear, then, more about the war. Recruiting sergeants came to town. The Army would take him, the recruiting sergeants said. He'd be a sergeant pilot in no time at all. He had all the requirements. He'd finished high school. He was eighteen years old. He'd have basic training first, of course, and maybe a few months on the ground. But if you enlisted for flying training, that's where they'd put you. You'd go to flying school.

He tried to imagine how it would be, how it would feel to fly. The rest of it didn't worry him. He knew how to march and drill. He'd been in a military band. And he'd spent two summer sessions with the CMTC at Fort Benjamin Harrison. He knew how to wear a uniform and how to salute. It seemed like a pretty good deal to him. His father agreed. "They'll draft you anyway," his father said. "You might as well get what you want. Learn how to fly."

"I suppose you're right," his mother said. "You won't get anywhere playing pool. But when you go away, son, don't forget for a minute who you are and what you are. Remember the things I've tried to teach you all your life."

So he went down to Huntington on the twelfth day of September in 1941 and he enlisted. His father went down there with him. "Don't gamble any," his father said. Of course, he'd been exposed to gambling all his life. They played poker in the poker hollow back in Hamlin. All towns have their poker hollows. He'd known gambling from the start. But that's the last thing his father had said to him, "Don't get to gambling or you won't have any money."

He never had any money anyway. Twenty-one dollars a month—you can't gamble much on that. And all he wanted to do was learn to fly.

12

He didn't know why he'd wanted to fly. He'd never been close to an airplane, not even to see one on the ground. But he'd enlisted to learn to fly and his impatience grew all through the first six months of service in the Army Air Corps. It was six long months before he was even given a ride in an airplane. And that, when it finally happened, was just an accident.

He'd been around by then, from Hamlin to Huntington and from there to Fort Thomas, Kentucky. Inoculated, uniformed and scared, he was transferred to Ellington Field in Texas for basic training in the school of the soldier, infantry drill and military courtesy. Two months later, older and wiser, he arrived at Moffet Field in San Mateo, California. Since he had been taught again to march and to drill, they made a mechanic of him now. Three months later he was a corporal, crew chief on an AT-11 twin-engine Beach at Victorville Army Air Base. He'd never been in the air but he still wanted to learn to fly.

"If you want to go up," the engineering officer said to him one day, "come on along." It was just a maintenance hop and, of course, he'd gone along. They took off and got way up in the air. He looked down then. But it was no thrill, really. It was like standing on one of the cliffs back home. That's all it was. Then he got deathly sick. He went on a second flight and got deathly sick again because there was nothing for him to do, just sit and watch. They were high in the air and it was cold. Sitting like that with nothing to do, uneasy, cold, you'd naturally get sick. You'd think you were going to die and then you'd wish you

would die. It was an awful feeling. But it didn't last. Back
on the ground again, he still wanted to learn to fly.

He was a good mechanic. Everything on the airplane
interested him. He learned to taxi the airplane and to run
the engines up. He'd sit in the cockpit touching each
control, one at a time, and in his mind he'd trace its action
within the plane and the effect of this action on its flight.
He studied its systems, taught himself, asked questions
when he didn't know. He began to understand the basic
principles of flight. By the end of July in 1942 he knew
that old twin-engine Beach from tail to nose. They sent
him then to flying school.

He was eager to fly and he was full of confidence in
himself when he reported to Santa Ana for preflight training in the beginning of August, not even fazed by the
prospect of having to learn all over again how to salute and
to drill and to march. But he avoided that this time.
Preflight, he learned with pleasure, was just for the cadets
who came directly from civilian life. He and the other
enlisted students were shipped on to Ryan Field at Hemet,
south and east of Riverside. There they were joined by
more cadets, but these had been taught, in a way, to
salute.

He'd never liked them, the cadets. His friends were
enlisted students, all of them, from the first day at Ryan
Field when he came dragging his gear into the barracks.
They were cabins, really, with six men assigned to each.
Three men had arrived before he did. They all turned to
face him as he opened the cabin door. There were two
enlisted men, a tall buck sergeant with a hatchet face and
a nervous-looking Pfc. And there was one cadet.

"Help the man in," the sergeant said. "He's one of
us." But the Pfc and the cadet began to unpack their
things. The sergeant was stretched out on his bunk. "You'll
have to excuse my friends," he said. "One of them is a
gentleman and the other guy is too busy looking after
himself. I guess I'll have to do it." The sergeant got up and
helped him drag his gear into the room.

"Notice the young lieutenant there, how neat he is,"
the sergeant continued as he began to unpack his own

things, too. "He's not a lieutenant, really, Corporal. But he's going to be, aren't you, sir?" The cadet kept putting his clothes away. He didn't answer. The sergeant grinned. "You and me, Corporal, and this sad-looking Pfc, we're in a business which in peacetime—well, most people think we're in it because we're too damn poor or not smart enough to live on the outside. We're just government issue. But you take Junior. Excuse me, I mean the lieutenant over there. He's smarter than we are. He was in college until his draft board began to nose around. Then he called up his congressman and got appointed as a cadet.

"You and me, Corporal, will live with Junior, see? We'll eat just the way he eats and we'll march, drill, study and learn to fly with Junior. Only he's going to be a second john, an officer. Whereas you and me—" The sergeant lay down on his bunk again—"we will be sergeants. Staff sergeants, yes. But still we will go on being dogs. Ain't it enough to make you want to bark?"

You could feel the strain in the air, but the cadet said nothing. He went on putting his clothes away with slow precision. And as it turned out, the sergeant was right. The cadets all treated the student pilots pretty sad and the students kept to themselves. There was only one good thing about it. They all learned to fly together.

First there was classroom instruction. They learned about planes, air frames and engines, how they were put together and what made them fly. He found that simple because he'd been working with airplanes for almost a year. Up in the air it was different. His instructor took him up in the air to give him the feel of the plane in flight. It was strange and new and it meant hard work. You had to concentrate. You had to watch air speed, keep the plane level and keep your head. It had taken him seven long hours of dual instruction in the back end of that little Ryan, seven hours to get the feel of the plane in flight.

"Wake up," his instructor would shout back through the Gosport tube. It was a conelike tube that ran from the instructor's helmet into his. The instructor sat in the forward cockpit. He smoked cigars. He'd blow smoke back through the Gosport tube and it burned your eyes and your ears. "Get out of that fog back there," he'd say, or, "Get out of that cloud."

He'd answer, "Sir, I'm right behind you."

"You're too cocky, Yeager," his instructor said one day. "You're too damn smart." And later he said, "Don't be so wise. You'd better get straightened up. And fix that hat. We're liable to wash you out of here."

It was an enlisted man's service hat. He wore it the way he'd always worn it, low down over one eye, peaked up in back. It was in a way an act of defiance each time he put it on. He was an enlisted man and, by God, he wasn't going to let the cadets forget it. But he tamed down then. He wanted to fly. Hat or no hat, he was going to be a pilot.

He could remember his first solo, remember the way it felt to be taking off alone. He got off the ground all right. But up in the air he leveled off and the sight of that empty front seat frightened him. "Do just as you'd do if I were sitting there," his instructor had told him on the ground. It was easier said than done. But he set up his pattern, picked out the field and nervously came down. He landed the plane and they waved him right off again. He flew all right but there was plenty to worry him. They covered the air-speed indicators in those training planes. You flew by the feel and the sound of the ship. He landed a second time and they waved him off again. When he knew he could do it, it suddenly got to be fun.

He'd fly all morning by himself, doing air work, all the things he had to do—stalls and rectangular patterns and S's that taught you to bank and to turn. One day he was really frightened. There was a cumulus cloud sitting up from the field, a towering Q. It went up to 12,000 feet. It took him half an hour to climb that high in the little Ryan and when he got up to the top, he wouldn't go near the cloud. He was too damn scared. He circled it once and came back down to the field.

In October they finished the primary course at Ryan Field. Still cocky and eager, he went on to intermediate training in BT-13's at Gardiner Field near Taft. The BT-13 was a much bigger airplane than the Ryan he had flown.

Instead of just seven cylinders, there were nine, and the engine ran much smoother. But there was more to do. There was a prop pitch control, a fuel pump, fuel selectors. Flying became more complex then. There was more hard work than ever. But to the sixty hours he'd had in the Ryan, he added seventy more in the basic training plane, the BT-13. Then, in January of 1943, he was transferred to Luke Field for advanced training. The hatchet-faced sergeant and the nervous-looking Pfc were still with him. So were the cadets.

At Luke Field they began to learn gunnery, aerial and ground. They flew in formation, too, in tighter and tighter groups as the weeks wore on. They learned to do acrobatics, cross-wind landings. The risk increased. The cocky and eager students were favored now. It was hard work, but more like flying than anything he had done before. He began to feel even more confidence in himself.

"Tomorrow you guys will get your wings," their instructor finally told them the night before graduation. There were five of them in his group, two student pilots and three cadets. "It's an old and honored custom of the service," their instructor said, "to celebrate this occasion. I'll have a few words to say to each of you."

Later that night they sat in a bar and talked. And they listened to their instructor talk. "You're all going to be good pilots, of course. That goes without saying. I wouldn't take anything now from any one of you. But flying is just like anything else. Some guys are good at it. Others are better. In one way it's a game." They all had another drink on that and then he went on.

"What I mean to say is this. Some kids are good at baseball. Others that never get up to bat are damn good boxers. Each of them has a special skill. And the same is true for each of you." Then he went on to tell them what he thought each of them would do. One of the students, he said, should be an instructor. They needed them then and he'd be good at that. There was one cadet who ought to go on to multiple engine planes, to bombers or transports. "That's where you'll shine," he said and they all had another drink on that. He went all around the table that way, telling each one of them what he'd do.

"What about Yeager?" somebody finally said. "What's he going to get?"

"Yeager's a fighter pilot. I think," he said, taking another drink, "he'll make the best fighter pilot of all the cadets or students I've ever trained."

That came as a surprise, of course. He didn't know what to say. His face had burned and he had grinned with pleasure. A fighter pilot, that was all he wanted to be. It was what all of them wanted, to be assigned to a fighter outfit. They were the best, he thought. They did the flying and they got the planes. But how in the world could one instructor know whether you'd be any good or not? It was something you didn't know yourself.

"You want to know why?" his instructor had asked him after they'd all had one more drink. "It isn't because you're so cocky and eager, Chuck, although that's part of it. It's the way you fly, the way you do acrobatics. And it's the way you are. The whole pattern of your performance here suggests the pattern of a potentially damn good fighter pilot. Of course," he said, "you're not there yet. There's a lot of hard work ahead of you. But you can make it, if you try."

He got his wings in March of 1943. A few days later the sergeant pilots were all promoted. He was a flight officer then, half-man and half-dog, the hatchet-faced sergeant had said, when he reported in to the 357th Fighter Squadron in Tonopah, Nevada. It was a brand new squadron and it was wonderful. There were only six pilots and ten new planes, all P-39's. They were all eager and all they did was fly. They raced and whipped one another in dogfights and each pilot did his best to fly faster and better than anyone else and lower than anything else in the air. There were gunnery ranges and bombing ranges. They shot gunnery, aerial and ground, dive bombing and skip bombing, too. They averaged over a hundred hours a month, each pilot, during the three months they were there in Tonopah. And that's the way to really learn to fly. It was wonderful, always.

Not just the flying alone. It was the idea that he was a fighter pilot assigned to a regular outfit. He had achieved the first real goal he'd set himself. More than that, he had a new goal now. He'd be going into combat soon. That's why he was there. That's what all the long months of training had been leading to. That's why they'd put him on aviation pay. And all of his eagerness centered now on this, to get into combat and to fight, to measure himself against something unknown.

But first there was Glennis. It was the summer of 1943. He was twenty years old. And the first time he saw her he didn't know what to say.

13

The group moved to a temporary fighter base near Oroville, California, in the summer of that year. But there was no change in the pilots' day to day routine. Up early in the morning, they'd eat a big breakfast. Then they'd be briefed on something new or lectured on something they had to know. And then take off. They'd fly for two or three hours, land, eat lunch, fly two or three hours more. And there were always classes. There was always something to learn, flying or on the ground.

And all the while the squadron was shaping up, growing into a tighter and tighter unit within the group itself, each pilot coming to know more about each of the others than he would ever know about anyone else, what each could do, where each was weak or strong, the habits, traits and idiosyncrasies of each man, whether in flight, wing tip almost to wing tip, or brushing his shoulders on the ground in barracks, classrooms, mess halls, hangars and briefing shacks. They were never alone.

Even at night the pilots would all go off together, their squadron almost intact, taking the whole day with them from the base into the town, flying it over again in taxis and in buses, flying in restaurants and in bars, their sun- and wind-burned hands always in flight, flight on their lips and in their eyes, creased still against the sun, reflecting, even when they saw only the walls and faces in a room, the bright blue sky.

So that a twenty-year-old pilot taken away, set suddenly apart from the others and facing a man who'd never flown, or facing a girl, became almost inarticulate, a stranger in a foreign room, groping for words or even silent. What could he say, whose whole life seemed to be airborne now, whose consciousness was fixed so firmly on flight and its experience, on men who shared this and the planes they flew? Nothing in all of his younger life compared with this. It was almost all he knew.

So there he stood in the USO in Oroville while Flight Officer Chuck McKee found all the words to say. ". . . having a dance," he heard McKee's voice saying, "the squadron is." There wasn't a word of truth in that. They were looking for girls.

She was pretty and dark and very small. "I said, my name is Glennis." She must have had to repeat it a couple of times. But he hadn't heard. Half in the air, but still aware of her, he saw her finally and he heard. But he didn't know what to say. And then McKee was gone. He was alone with her.

She had two jobs, she told him, not knowing what else to say to him. Glennis did all the talking. She was secretary to the principal of the high school and she kept books for the Oroville dairy. Four or five evenings a week she spent at the USO, not to meet soldiers, not even to meet the pilots there. She was very emphatic about that. "I feel sorry for all of you," she explained. "This town is so small and there are so many servicemen and nothing for them to do."

Her mother and father were farmers, she told him then. But she called the farm a ranch. She liked to ride, she said, swim and hunt. What did he do besides fly?

He must have found something at last to say to her because he saw her again the following night and the night after that, the night after that night, too. He talked about flight and planes at first, then slowly about his life at home. He told her of hunting alone in the hills, of fishing and playing ball. "My older brother and me," he said, or, "Me and my brother Roy." They talked about school and what they'd liked and how each of them really wanted to live. And then, as they talked about after the war, they found themselves saying "us" and "we." "It would be fun if we," they'd say or, "That couldn't happen to us."

The others began to accept her then, the pilots with whom he flew. She was "Yeager's date" for a while and then his girl. But they finally called her Glennis. "What are you and Glennis doing tonight?" they'd ask him during the day. But then as suddenly as it had begun, it came to an end.

"We're leaving," he told her one night. "The squadron is being transferred." He never said group, although the other squadrons were going, too. "We're going to Casper, Wyoming. I don't suppose we'll be seeing each other any more."

It seemed to them as if the war would go on forever the night they said good-by.

"Let's just not say it," Glennis said. "I mean, let's say so long or something. But let's not say good-by."

"All right," he agreed.

"Chuck?"

"What is it, honey?"

"Couldn't we meet somewhere?"

So they studied a map and a calendar and all the timetables, too. They could meet halfway. "In Reno, Nevada," he said, "on the last week end this month." It was October then. There was only one train from Oroville to Reno.

"That will be all right," Glennis said. But it was a freight train. She rode with the brakemen in the caboose.

"It was a long, cold, lonely ride," she'd written him later on. "I talked and talked but all I could think about was you. Then when I got to Reno you weren't there. I called the base. They didn't know where you were. I thought I'd been stood up. Can you imagine how I felt? I'd made a fool of myself for nothing, for nothing at all.

"I left a call for you at the base. 'You have him call me,' I said, 'just as soon as he gets himself found.' I was so mad at you that I couldn't talk. I guess my feelings were hurt, or my pride. I sat in a cafeteria and drank cup after cup of coffee. The more I drank the worse I felt inside. Then I came home again. But that was after I knew what had happened to you. I was ashamed of myself then and I was frightened sick."

It was one of those things that happen. The squadron had been assigned a new C.O. that morning. They were always hampered by being the favored squadron because the group commander always flew with them. That's why they were always attached to group headquarters, always around the brass, the adjutant or executive officer. "Non-pilots, lieutenant colonels usually," he explained to Glennis later, "and that's the most useless rank in the Army, as everybody knows."

He'd had to fly that morning she'd waited for him in Reno because the squadron commander who had agreed to let him off had been transferred out. He'd done something he wasn't supposed to do, according to all the headquarters brass, something that any one of the other pilots would have done. But they booted him out. The new squadron commander didn't particularly care about Flight Officer Yeager's personal plans. "You'll have to fly," he said.

And there he was, leashed off and leading the flight, wishing to God it was over because he wanted to be with her and there hadn't been time to call. He was up around 18,000 feet with eleven planes behind him in elements and flights when they spotted a B-24 below them at 5,000 feet. "Let's go," he told them. "Let's make them jump!" They echeloned over to the left and dove in past the bomber's nose, split S, just rolling it back and coming through, making a head-on pass at the B-24. Every other fighter went above or below the B-24, really making those truck drivers or bomber pilots get plumb down there under their seats. He went past the bomber himself, rolled over again as he went by, split S and came out on the deck. He was going straight down when the impeller section, the compressor or supercharger failed on his P-39. There was a bad explosion behind his back. Fire came out from under the seat and one of the doors blew off.

Fire, that's the one thing a pilot is afraid of most, flame or fire in an airplane because they blow up fast. He knew he had to get out, knew he was going fast and losing altitude. He tried to go out through the open door but the rush of air tore off his helmet and his mask. Then doubling up somehow, he rolled himself out.

Things happened fast. He saw his plane, smoke coming from its tail section, as he reached up to pull his rip cord. He was on his back then, going backward, tumbling. He could remember seeing his parachute stream out. When it opened it made a noisy plop and flipped him over. It was the flip that knocked him out.

When he woke up he found himself in the base hospital. The other pilots had seen him bail out. A sheepherder who'd found him unconscious had dragged him out to a nearby road. An ambulance had been sent out to bring him in. He'd cracked a vertebra, the nurse said, but he'd be all right. She gave him the message Glennis had left, just "Please get well. I'm going home." He could imagine how she must have felt.

They'd frightened her badly, told her finally where he was, that he'd bailed out of his burning plane and was still unconscious in the hospital.

"You'll never know," Glennis had written to him later, "how awful that long ride home to Oroville was that night. I felt just like a widow. I thought you were going to die. The brakemen tried to be nice and understanding but they only made everything seem much worse than it really was.

"Then when I came home I found your telegram. I cried all day. I wanted to rush right back to see you but I couldn't go. And now you're going overseas. When will I ever see you again? What's going to happen to us now?"

He hadn't known what to answer. He couldn't say anything but, "Wait." It was all she could do because the squadron was ready. They were going overseas. In less than a month they were on their way.

14

They landed at Greenock in Scotland on a cold, raw winter day in January, 1944. The sky was gray and thick with the smudge of soft coal smoke. You could smell it in the air. The men on the deck stood crowded along the rail, some of them laughing, some just staring at the land. There was a band that looked like a Salvation Army band huddled together on the dock, wrapped in their overcoats and gloves. They played very badly for a while and then they stopped. When he left the ship an hour later they were gone.

He walked through the cold, wet air to a waiting railroad train. It was very old, with a door to each compartment and no inside aisle, like the trains you saw in English films but never expected to see yourself. Out on the station platform two old women poured hot coffee into Dixie cups. But no one had time to drink any coffee. The train tooted and pulled away, leaving the two old women standing helplessly beside their table full of steaming cups.

It was a long and uncomfortable ride down through the center of England. Stiff and weary, he sat in the hard, old-fashioned seat remembering Glennis. He thought of her sadly riding from Reno back to Oroville in the caboose. He'd seen her once since then, just briefly to say good-by. Now it all seemed unreal and far away. Now there were strange, new scenes and the whole of life seemed to have changed. The waiting was almost over, the training and preparation for whatever might lie ahead. Now it was almost on him, and as the slow train jolted and jerked along, he found his impatience almost impossible to hold within himself. He wanted to act, to move, to do

96

something, to do anything at all. But he could only sit as the neatly landscaped English countryside slipped past the window, gray in the mist and heavy fog.

How would it be? he wondered, asking the question over and over again. How would he measure up to pilots with whom he'd fly in combat? And how compare with those enemy pilots with whom he'd fight? It was the question each of the others asked himself. And for the answer, each of them would have to wait. That was the worst of it, waiting, waiting to act and waiting to know. When the train finally stopped they were all worn out with waiting. They were at Radenwood, somebody said. They were near Ipswich. It was still gray and cold. They waited for trucks. When the trucks came they climbed inside and waited for them to move. When the trucks moved they waited for them to stop. And when the trucks finally stopped they walked through mud to their Nissen huts and waited for something else.

But nothing happened. They sat there with nothing to do, no planes to fly, no combat, nothing. Then they moved again, this time to a new air base at Saxmundham, to Leiston Air Base north of Ipswich. But there was no change, really. There was still nothing to do but eat and sleep. The food was bad and at night it grew so cold they had to sleep in their flying suits. Then, gradually, the squadron settled down.

He and Chuck McKee were still pretty close. They'd gone to flying school together. They were still flight officers, the only two in the squadron. The others were all commissioned, but he had friends among them, Bud Anderson, Don Bochkay and Browning and Teedy, too. They all bought English bicycles. They'd ride into Radenwood eight miles away. He and McKee bought dogs, two wire-haired fox terriers they christened Mustang 1 and Mustang 2 after the planes they hoped to fly. They really had nothing to do.

But they began to work again, to go to classes every day, to study tech orders on the new P-51's, to become as familiar as they could with the cockpits of airplanes they'd never flown. There were lectures too on the Mustangs and on how to evade the enemy if you had to bail out of your plane, or how to escape if the enemy captured you. Whenever they could, they'd pile in a truck and visit the 354th Fighter Group, a Mustang group in the 9th Air Force. Their pilots had been fighting for a month or more. They'd watch them take off to fly a combat mission and wait there, watching until they came back to their base again. Wide-eyed and open-mouthed they'd listen, hearing almost the howl of engines, the rattle and bang of armament, and almost seeing the 109's and the 190's, the flak bursts and smoking planes as they had fallen to the ground. "Hell," they'd say, "there won't be any left for us," as the pilots' hands flew on from incident to nervous incident, saying, "Then we were bounced," or, "So I gave him a quick burst," and, "I clobbered him." While they themselves had done nothing but stand and wait.

Impatient, wondering, they'd go home then, back to their quiet, idle base to unearned rest. And chafing against the long delay, they'd go into the town again to drink warm beer or lemonade or gin and tonic in the pubs. Sometimes not even this attracted them. They'd stay on the base, irritable in their idleness, profane in their complaint, like leashed dogs growling at restraint. It was, they thought, a hell of a way to fight a war.

But anger died as it was born. There was too much wild exuberance in all of them. Each box from home called for a feast and each small feast was celebrated with determined zeal. The coke stoves in the Nissen huts would burn red hot with foraged coal and hastily acquired wood. They'd grill cheese sandwiches and make washbasins full of soup. Sometimes they'd sing, play records, talk, drink rationed beer or gin. Once in a while they'd all get slightly drunk. Then they'd put on their flying clothes and go to bed. In the morning it would begin again, the waiting. No one wanted to get up. It was always cold and there was always fog. Then it began to snow.

At last, in the middle of January, the group drew planes, brand new P-51's, the first in the 8th Air Force. Then everything changed at once as the squadron returned to a pattern broken by weeks of idleness. Up at five in the morning, hurriedly fed, jammed into cold and smoke-filled Nissen huts, briefed, lectured on new facts, fresh data, late reports, they sat through hours of instruction when they were not rushing from their barracks to the mess hall or from the scattered clusters of Nissen huts down to the X-shaped landing strip to watch their fighters being prepared for flight. And finally they flew again. But it was late in February before the squadron took off on the first of its combat missions.

Called at five in the morning as they always were, none of them ever knew whether they'd fly or not. It was cold and dark outside. The snow fell in a lazy slant and no one talked. Still half-asleep, he left with the others for the briefing shack and the cold air woke him as he walked. All he could see was the black path through the snow, the back of the man ahead of him and the small cloud of his own breath in the frosty air. He could hear only the footsteps of the other men and, off in the distance, the muffled sound of engines warming and of working men. There were the smells of winter in the air, of fresh snow and of pine wood burning in pot-bellied stoves, reminding him of home and hunting and of early mornings in white-wintered hills.

He came then to the briefing shack, another half-round Nissen hut, its corrugated steel roof black and wet with melting snow. Stepping inside, he passed with the others through two sets of blackout curtains, blinking against the sudden glare of yellow light, and walked half-blinded through the room to find a chair. It was the way each day began. He saw then on the big wall map the bright red line that ran from England into Germany. The others had seen it, too.

Now there was tension in the room. Excitement grew as the briefing officer waited in silence for the last man to come in. From the first whispers voices rose to ask, "Did you see the map?" and the room filled with talk and laughter rising in pitch and volume that culminated finally in a few wild rebel yells. Then they grew suddenly quiet as the briefing officer, pointer in hand, began to speak.

"Good morning, gentlemen. I see you've guessed the news."

He was afraid. Who wouldn't be? he asked himself. And yet what he really wanted was to get right up in the air and rush right into it, right into combat. He didn't know what he'd do. He couldn't be sure. And although his mind was full of this, he was still somehow aware of everything. It was the unknown that frightened him. On this first mission there would be a lot of unknowns. He didn't know what combat would be like. He didn't know where they were going.

"To Hamburg," the briefing officer explained.

But Hamburg meant nothing to him. He'd never been there. And suppose he had? Would he know how many Krauts to expect? Or where they'd come from? In what planes? Or what he'd do?

"You'll escort this bomber box." The briefing officer was calm. "You'll find flak here—" His pointer touched the map—"and here." The pointer began to hop like a rabbit along that red line into Hamburg. "Here, here and here. There will be plenty of flak. You'll have some fighter opposition—" The pointer moved back to mark a long rectangle on the Dutch channel coast—"within this area."

He was sweating now. But then he'd flown so many hours with this squadron. There's safety in numbers, he thought, his mind seesawing back and forth from fear to confidence. His back still sometimes bothered him. It hurt him to pull *g*'s. But what the hell, he told himself, you've had a rest. His confidence returned. They'd rehearsed this scene a hundred times or more, flown more than a hundred practice missions. They'd studied aircraft recognition all through training. He knew what 109's looked like and 111's, 190's, Heinkels, Junkers, everything the Germans had in the air. He'd been briefed enough on what to expect. There was nothing to worry about. But the same old question popped back into his mind. What would he do? He didn't know.

The briefing was over then. They left the hut. The morning was grayer now, less black, as he climbed into a jeep with several others and rode out to his plane parked half a mile away. The X-shaped landing strip was set in a big, rough circle flanked by trees. Around to the right they saw the planes of the 362nd Squadron being readied for flight. Around to the left they could hear them working on the planes assigned to the 364th. Their own aircraft were parked beyond these on the far side of the field, standing in groups of threes or fours, half-ridden under the leafless trees that rimmed the landing strip. On every group he could see mechanics working; and beyond each single fighter plane with its mechanics checking stabilizer, flaps and landing gear, another mechanic and another plane came into view. So that no matter where he looked, from plane to plane he could see more airplanes and more working men. There were thirty planes in the squadron. The number alone was reassuring.

Then in the squadron area they were briefed again. He found he would lead a flight and he was told exactly what this flight would be expected to do, where they'd rendezvous, what bombers they'd support, how the weather would be and what the last intelligence reports had said. He got into his G suit then and into his yellow Mae West, picked up his dinghy and went out to make one last check of his plane, *Glamorous Glennis*. He smiled as he always did when he saw the name painted on her nose.

But now it was almost time and he looked once more at his watch. He'd had his time hack, that is, he knew exactly when to get into the cockpit, when to start the engine, when to start taxiing and the time the first two airplanes would take off. He'd done all this before and all of his training had been to help him do it just as well right now. He was there to fight, to shoot an impersonal enemy down. But for one more moment he wondered whether he would, or whether he'd run or even jump right out of his plane. Then they took off and there was no more time to think.

Plane after plane now left the ground, each motor roaring to lift each plane, then rising in pitch to climb until its single roar was lost in the growing drone of all their motors as separate fighters formed into elements, elements into flights, flights into squadrons circling above the field until at last the group was formed. And he could feel for a moment the sense of this power spiraling in the air, know in this moment that all over England men like himself formed into fighter squadrons like his own, the squadrons becoming other groups and the groups forming into two air forces, uniting together with still a third, with British wings comprised of Free French, Danish, Polish, Norwegian, Dutch and Czechoslovak pilots, all of them like himself formed into squadrons and the whole of them coming together, joining now the fleets of bombers that had left their bases half an hour before and the entire vast armada heading now for Hamburg, Bremen, Essen or Cologne. And his excitement was immense.

They were all excited. "Bogies!" somebody shouted into the headphones through which all could hear. "Don't let them in!" the group commander shouted, too. His head kept going around and around and his eyes swept the sky as his hands moved with intricate, unthought precision. But nothing happened. There was nothing there. Along the coast he saw small, scattered puffs of flak. Still nothing happened. He saw land below him now and it was German land. This too excited him. But nothing happened. Then there was Hamburg and the flak increased. The bombers began to go in in steady runs. He watched the bombs fall tumbling down to strike, saw the first pattern running in blasts across the open ground leaving a trail of fire and smoke that soon became one black cloud above the rubble, graying finally and shot through with flames. But he and his plane flew as he watched and his head kept spinning to search the sky so that later he hardly remembered what he had seen.

Then they came back to England and his disappointment grew as the excitement died. He had seen no German aircraft. Nothing happened, he told himself as he landed his plane. But everyone talked as if this had been it, the thing they had each of them waited for. Hands flying or pounding each other's backs, they flew the whole mission over again until it became as many different things as there were pilots to tell them. He thought it was something he'd always remember. But the next day the mission was repeated, and a few days later and again after that and they all merged in his mind into one continuing experience. After a while he could hardly tell one mission from another.

On the second big strike he'd seen some Germans, though, and it was strange and unreal and nothing at all like the fierce encounter for which he'd prepared himself. He was leading an element that day but the flight leader had some engine trouble. He himself took over the flight and off in the distance he saw these ME-109's. "Look at them, stooging around out there," he complained. The Germans wouldn't come in. He didn't know what to do. He was hesitant about leaving the bombers to go out and get the 109's. But there they were. And licking his dry, dry lips he watched the Germans turn and fly away.

Then on the fourth of March he finally made it, shot down his first German plane, shot up another. It was the first big daylight raid on Berlin. There was a heavy snow that morning as the planes took off. The pilots could hardly see and the whole group was split up.

"There were two of us together," he told the others later, "Rogers and me. We each had wing men but we'd lost them in the soup and snow. After we entered weather on the gauges we couldn't find them again. We broke out on top together and joined up. He saw me first and just latched onto my wing. Then we went tooling in and got with the bombers. There were Krauts all over the place!

"We were up around 30,000 feet and I looked down—it was just like the picture on the card, an ME-109 going along there by himself. I said, 'Let's go and get him!' and I peeled off." His left hand then became the 109, his right his own P-51 as he went through the whole episode again.

"This 109 was in a slight dive, see? And I had my 51 really whammed wide open. I dropped my drop tanks, came on in and went past him so fast I overran him. Looked like he was standing still. He turned to the right and went into a 50-degree dive. I closed up fast and opened fire at about 200 yards, got real good hits on him as I went by him. And I got under him, shot into his underside and got good strikes on his wing roots and his fuselage. Pieces flew off and there was smoke and flame. His engine was smoking and windmilling, too. I overran him again, got strikes along his fuselage and canopy. Then I pulled up and did a wing over on his tail. His canopy blew off. The pilot bailed out and went into the overcast at about 9,000 feet."

That was his first plane. A few minutes later he got his second, an HE-111-K. Rogers, his wing man, had picked him up again and they'd gone off together to find their squadron's planes, the red-and-yellow-checkered tails and noses of their 51's. "We saw you guys," he went on to tell the others. "And then I saw this Heinkel 111-K way down ahead, setting on top of a cloud layer at 10,000 or 11,000 feet. I'd just used up quite a bit of my ammunition on this 109 and I only had one gun firing, but I peeled off on this guy and pulled up right behind him. I'd learned my lesson. This time I cut the power back, way back, and turned coming into him and slowed down. His gunner was back there shooting at me, so I got right up close and clobbered him. There wasn't but one of my guns shooting, as I said, but I was getting strikes back there on the fuselage and killed the gunner, or anyway he quit shooting. Then I tried to set an engine on fire and I got one smoking. But about that time the guy went into the cloud deck and I couldn't. So I pulled on up and we got with some of the boys and came on home."

He'd claimed one aircraft damaged, one destroyed. These were confirmed and he'd felt wonderful that night. He'd been in combat and he'd been all right. Even the G.I. food seemed good to eat. He talked and talked and listened to everyone else. They were all still talking as he fell asleep.

They took off early the next morning on a strike south of Bordeaux. It was Sunday, the fifth of March. He flew as spare. Besides the sixteen pilots in a flight, two others always went along to fill in vacancies that might occur, to keep the flight of sixteen planes complete. One plane dropped out and he went into the tail end of the flight.

They got to Bordeaux all right and were coming back across the south of France. It was late in the morning, almost noon. Ten miles southeast of Angoulême they were bounced by three Focke-Wulf 190's.

"We'd made the rendezvous with the bombers and were protecting them at the target area," First Lieutenant William R. McGinley reported that night. "I was leading the second element in a flight of four. We had just gone down to investigate some planes near the bombers. I was bringing my element into formation with the leader when Yeager called for a break to the right. I broke and saw an ME-109 making a pass at us. Captain O'Brien, who was leading the formation, called for us to keep protecting while he went after the enemy aircraft. I circled and kept looking into the sun. From the time Yeager called the break I did not see him again. I joined formation with two ships from another squadron and came home with them."

"Two FW-190's bounced Blue Flight." First Lieutenant Ernest F. De Nigris also reported the attack. "Captain O'Brien leading engaged one in combat, claiming one damaged. . . . Yeager was last seen taking evasive action."

Whether it was one plane, two or three, FW-190 or ME-109, he called break and broke back into them, making a head-on pass at all of the planes. And it seemed as if all of them hit him at once.

His engine caught fire. He lost his elevator control. The oxygen system blew up and there was a big hole in the wing. At 20,000 feet he got rid of the canopy and jumped, crawled out somehow and went over the back of the plane. There were flak fragments in both of his feet. He cut his head open getting out. He didn't know this then. He was numb, just scared and going from move to move as fast as he could. He delayed his jump until the ground came rushing up to meet him at around 5,000 feet. Then he opened his chute.

". . . regrets to inform you," his mother carefully read the War Department telegram to Glennis over the telephone, "that your son, Flight Officer Charles E. Yeager, has been reported missing in action over the south of France."

15

"Look," he explained to the woman again, "I'm an American pilot." He spoke in the monotone of fatigue. "I've got an escape kit." The woman was neither young nor old. Thirty-five, he guessed. "I want to get into Spain. If you'll just tell me where—"

"Wie heissen Sie?" the old man asked him in German again. The woman said nothing. She listened and watched.

"I don't know what you're saying," he told the old man. Nor did he know what the old man felt. A black mustache hid the old man's mouth and the eyes above this were fixed and questioning. Who are you? they seemed to ask. What do you really want?

"I want to get into Spain," he insisted again. "If you'll only tell me—"

"Just a boy," the woman said then in English. "Why, you're just a boy! Have the Americans lost so many men that they're fighting the war with boys?"

"I'm not just a boy," he insisted, wearily reciting the facts. "Lady, I'm twenty years old, the youngest pilot in my group. I was shot down this morning. I want to get into Spain."

"But you're wounded!" she said, as if she had suddenly noticed this.

"Yes," he admitted, not knowing his face had been cut and that the blood had dried on his forehead into a ragged scar. He sat wearily in a stiff-backed wooden chair, his hand resting heavily on its bare arms, the weight of his legs resting painfully on his heels. "My feet," he explained, "they're full of flak. It'll be hard for me to walk. But if you'll only tell me—"

"*Il est blessé, Papa,*" she said to the old man then. "*Il n'est pas Boche,*" then hurriedly left the room. She was back in a moment with scissors, a basin of water and strips of cloth. "I am sorry," she told him, kneeling beside him on the floor. "You must know how it is with us." She began to cut the thick laces on his boots. "We in France can trust no one, no more than you can really trust us."

"Yes," he said, flinching against a sudden pain. "I guess you're right." He gripped the arms of the wooden chair. "I don't know any more about you and your father than you two know about me."

"*Il est Americain, Papa,*" she said to the old man then.

The old man answered, "*Bon.*" And as the woman cut carefully into one of his boots he heard the old man's voice go on. "*Cachés dans l'encadrements des portes,*" the old man said.

"Hidden," his daughter translated without looking up from her work, "in the casements of the doors—"

"*Sur la route derrière les arbres,*" the old man's voice continued, "*nous assistons aux violents combats aeriens au dessus de nos têtes—*"

"How do you say, not *assisted,*" the woman explained. "It was as if we ourselves took part in the fight. Do you understand?"

"*Lors que sur notre droite, en direction de Cours les Bains nous voyons votre chasseur prendre feu—*"

"We saw your fighter plane take fire." The woman began to cut off the second boot.

"*Une angoisse nous serre le coeur,*" the old man said.

"There was," his daughter repeated slowly, "anguish in our hearts." Then carefully lifting his injured feet, she placed them gently in water.

He closed his eyes, his weariness overcoming fear. But as the hot water soaked into his wounds he grew slightly sick with expected pain.

"My father's name is Bertrand," he heard her saying now. "I am Madame Latrielle. My husband is now a

prisoner of the Boche. The old woman you saw is my
mother. The girl, my daughter." Then she went on trans-
lating her father's words.

"*Encore une victime—*"

"Another victim, we thought. One more poor devil
gone. But then—"

The old man lifted his hands and smiled. "*A notre joie
nous voyons tout de suite un petit objet se detacher, un
parachute—*"

"All at once, to our joy, we saw a small object detach
itself, a parachute—"

"*Au bout des ficelles—*"

"At the bottom of the lines—"

"*Le corps du homme—*"

"The body of a man—"

"*Se balancer—*"

"Was balanced—" As in the slow response to a litany,
the woman's voice followed the old man's voice, repeating as well as she could his words.

"We smiled," the woman explained, "but our smiles
vanished when the German plane came after you. We
shook our fists at the sky and helplessly watched your slow
descent.

"You may think," she continued, "that we felt nothing
of your fear." The old man's voice wound on a phrase or
two ahead of hers. "This is not so. Among us one man's
fear is every man's. We were deeply pleased to see one of
your comrades attack the Boche."

The old man struck a match and held it before him,
nodding his head as he breathed in smoke. He had
finished his story now and he sat remembering it all again.
"Deeply pleased," he repeated himself.

"We ran into the forest then," the woman explained.
"We found you there." She was standing now, carefully
soaking the wound on his head. "You must understand,"
she insisted, "why we were forced to hide you in the barn,
why we could do nothing more, why we are still uncertain
of what to do."

"It is all right," he answered wearily. "I understand."
And the mere act of closing his eyes put him to sleep.

Then the nightmare of falling and of escape repeated itself, the fire, the explosion, the hole in his wing. Again he fought clear of his burning plane and waited again through minutes of slow descent. As he hung in air, his feet had begun to hurt him then and the blood ran from his head wound down into his eyes so that when he came down to the treetops it was hard for him to see.

But they were sapling trees. He saw that much and blindly clutched at branches, gripping one with his hands, feeling it slip between gloved fingers until he could bring it against his chest. Then he hung on, his body dragging the sapling down to the ground.

There for a moment he lay motionless, not knowing what to do, free of one danger, facing a hundred more. Somehow he took off his chute and its harness and rolled them into a clumsy ball. Somehow he got to his feet. He wanted to run, to run and to hide. But not knowing where he could run or how to conceal himself, he stood for a few seconds feeling exposed and alone and always about to be shot. His whole body was braced against the expected crack of a rifle or the command to halt.

He saw the women then and they saw him. Waving, they gestured for him to follow them. And the old man suddenly appeared. Down they both ducked to run crouching along a hedge and over a patch of open ground, the old man pushing him into a barn, pushing him up to a ladder, pushing him up into the loft and pushing him far back under the hay. "*Silence, silence,*" the old man whispered, leaving him suddenly alone. Dust in his eyes and in his nose, he lay there listening, holding his breath, buried in hay. He was afraid to move. The sudden sound of German voices held him still.

"*So? Ganz nichts?*" a man's voice asked, then shouted, "*Bertrand! was machen Sie dahin?*" And heavy footsteps ran into the barn, slowed to a cautious walk, climbed up the ladder into the loft. Hay rustled all around him, prodded and spread with bayonets. But they missed him somehow and they left. How long he lay there after they'd gone he didn't know, hours it seemed, until the woman came in at last and called to him in whispered English,

"Are you there?" And he came crawling, stiff-legged and bloodstained, out of the hay.

"What is your name?" the woman asked.

"Yeager," he answered, "Yeager, Yeager!" He woke himself repeating his name, stirred in the hard wooden chair and opened his eyes to see the old man carefully watching his face, and the woman, too.

"There are many such names in America," the woman said half to herself. "Now you must lie down and sleep. Come," she said, helping him out of the chair, helping him to cross the room and climb the narrow stairs.

But he was unable to sleep. Fear and the Benzedrine he had taken kept him awake. All night he sat on a straight chair facing the open window and for two days after that this chair served as his observation post, a post from which he listened to sounds in the rooms below and from which he watched the sun rise in the morning, move through the gray winter sky and set at night. It was from here too that he sometimes saw the German soldiers patrolling the roads, saw the big He-177, a four-motored bomber, fly over the house at less then 300 feet. Looking for me, he told himself, feeling exposed and alone, feeling the strangeness of being close enough to the German plane to distinguish its smallest markings, yet being unable to shoot it down, unable even to fire a single shot.

Then he was finally moved. They dressed him in French civilian clothes, in a blue beret, a nondescript jacket, black baggy trousers. "My husband's clothes," the woman explained. They gave him a cross-cut woodsman's saw. "You must look as if you had some purpose in being out." And finally mounted on a bicycle, with the saw balanced precariously on his shoulder, he was prepared to ride away, his feet still sore in the missing husband's shoes.

"*Au revoir*," they told him, the whole family lined up in the yard to say good-by, old Madame Bertrand, her husband *avec le gros mustache*, their daughter, Madame Latrielle, whose hands were cold and rough, her own small daughter, shy and unsmiling. "*Tu vas retourner aprés la guerre?*"

He answered quietly, *"Au revoir,"* and cycled off with the stranger who had come for him.

Two days and nights they rode, stopping only to breathe or to rest for a moment along the road, stopping only once to eat in a farmhouse hidden among trees—two days and nights over lonely back roads—two days and nights to the south and west. At last they stopped again at another farm. There he was left with the farmer, his wife and their young son Jean.

"You are," they warned him in labored English, "the cousin of the father. You are to help on the farm because there is nothing to eat in the town." He drove a team. He loaded hay. The days passed nervously, the work not even diverting him but only serving to underline his fear. He worked, still half-expecting the rifle shot or the sudden "Halt!" he had come to dream about. Then he was moved again, this time into a town.

"Welcome to Nérac." These people greeted him in even more labored English. They were very young, not much older than he was himself, Gabriel and his wife, Marie Rose. He had nothing to do. There was nothing for him to do but to sit. They became very angry with him one day for allowing *les Boches* to see him plainly at ease on the steps of their home.

It seemed so unreal to him, that he should be sitting, the sun warm on his face, while German troops marched heavily along the road, their rifles slung, their black boots beating in muffled cadence against the snow. He watched until they were out of sight, and the full reality of the men he had seen, the danger he'd faced and its threat to them all, had not yet sunk into his mind when Gabriel hissed him into the house, saying, "Fool, fool!" over and over again. Back in the kitchen Marie Rose buried her head in her arms and wept with relief.

"You must understand," Dr. Henri explained to him—he was a French physician who had studied in England between the wars. "It is not just to be sent to jail that they fear. If you are found, that is the end for them, for many of us. Of course, you don't look like an American—" He smiled—"but an idle young Frenchman is as much of a

criminal in France today as a hidden American pilot.
There is one penalty for all of us."

Later this same man led him away to meet the
Maquis. "Twice weekly," Dr. Henri said as they rode
together in the back of a truck, "our friends, the British,
make regular drops of the things we need. You'll eat rather
well for a day or two and be well supplied. In time you'll
be taken into Spain. So, *au revoir, Charles, et bonne
chance!*" The truck stopped and he disappeared. The
truck started again and stopped once more. The door was
opened and he was pulled out into the night.

"*Êtes-vous un pilote?*" a voice asked him. "*Voilà des
camarades.*" And he was led off into the woods.

There were three others, all lieutenants. "Francis
Whitt," the first man introduced himself. "Swindel," the
second said, shaking hands. "Omar Patterson," the third
man gave as his name and added, "They call me Pat." But
none of them were at ease. Each studied the others as if
he were wondering which of the three might be the
enemy. And they were all at the mercy of the French who
moved with a suspicious freedom and who went about
their work with a deceptive ease, receiving their bundles
from Britain at regular intervals and visiting town with
equal regularity.

The drops were made in an open field at night. There
were weapons and food, counterfeit Vichy francs and
rations cards, the clothing and equipment peculiar to their
activity as an underground group and as a guerilla force.
With food and counterfeit francs a Vichy gendarme who
belonged to the Maquis bought false identity cards and
papers for the American pilots. Someone else arranged for
another truck. Locked up in the back, nervous and ill at
ease, the four were driven one night to Lourdes in south-
western France.

Somewhere in Lourdes the truck stopped suddenly,
the door was unlocked and they were waved out. "These
are your guides," somebody said. The door was slammed
shut again and the truck sped away as a voice called back,
"*Bonne chance.*" And there they stood, cold and uncertain, facing strangers.

"It is necessary to leave at once," they were told. Still cold and uncertain they set out on what became an uninterrupted four-day-and-four-night forced march. Hungry, tired and always cold they alternately crawled or ran from night into day and back into night again, only fear and the promise of escape giving them strength. At last, at sunset on the twenty-seventh of March, they stood at the foot of the last snow-covered mountain slope.

"When it is dark," the guide who spoke English told them, "cross the road. It is about 3,000 meters to the top of this slope and that is the Spanish border. It is from this point," he apologized, "very dangerous for us. If you are captured, you must insist that you found your way here without help. If you are not captured—" He smiled suddenly—"you will all be in Spain in the morning. In either event, we wish you all good luck." Solemnly the men shook hands. *"Au revoir. Bonne chance."*

"Merci, thank you," the Americans answered and suddenly found themselves alone.

"Well," somebody said, "the last couple of miles are always the toughest." They lay in a ditch and waited for night to fall. Then they moved off toward the road, not walking fast, spread out one man behind another, each stepping gingerly on slippery snow. It was very dark and from the end of the file the fourth man could barely see the first man slip across the road. The second followed and his excitement grew. Even his hunger and the cold were forgotten now as the third man moved across. His turn was next. But then there was the sound he had expected all these weeks, the crack of a rifle against which all of his nerves and his muscles were braced. The third man dropped, rolled back down the embankment from which he had climbed to the road a moment before and lay perfectly still. It was Patterson. He had been shot in the knee.

"Get out of here," Patterson said. "Get over the road."

But he found a stick with which Patterson could partly support himself and he dragged him back up the embankment and painfully pulled him across the road.

The rifle cracked again, a burst of three shots this time. There was one more burst as the sniper fired the rest of his clip.

"Go on." Patterson swore at him. "No sense in both of us—"

"Save your breath, Pat," he said, dragging him down off the road and into a ditch on the other side. He thought their chances were pretty good. It wasn't the whole damn Germany Army that threatened them. A single sniper, he thought, or maybe a small patrol. Swindel and Whitt had gone on ahead. But he and Patterson were armed. In the meantime it was dark, not as dark as it had seemed at first, but dark enough. Pulling and pushing the other man, carrying Patterson when he could, he began to climb. They slipped in the snow. Sometimes he sat, his hands under Patterson's arms and locked on his chest, and he dug his wet heels into the snow and pushed. Sometimes he crawled, one hand ahead of him reaching for something to hold to, the other hand gripping the collar of Patterson's coat. They did not always move ahead. Sometimes they slipped and skidded back down again. And all the while, Patterson swore and clung to the stick that supported his injured leg. "Go on," he kept saying. "Why should we both be caught?"

He stopped finally because he had to. Breathless, sick almost with the effort he had made, he lay in the snow, his hands still gripping Patterson's coat. And they listened. Down on the slope they heard distant, angry calls, ahead of them nothing but night sounds, the sweep of wind across open ground.

"Where," he gasped when he could breathe again, "are you hit?"

"In the knee."

"Hurt?" They were both breathing heavily.

"Hell," Patterson panted, "yes."

"Don't worry." Heavy-handed, wearily, he fumbled in one of his pockets for a first-aid kit, pulled off the metal strip that bound the halves together, clumsily ripped open the packet of sulfa powder. "Let's see." In the dark he bent over Patterson's knee, sprinkling some of the powder into the wound, more in the snow. Then he tied on the bandage and put on his gloves. "Now listen," he told the injured man, "I grew up in hills like this." It was still hard for him to breathe. "I'll get you up this hill." He lay on his back and closed his eyes. "Just let me get my breath." In a few minutes he said, "Come on. Let's go." He took a fresh grip on Patterson's coat. "Let's get up this goddamn hill."

On up the mountainside they crawled again, their progress measured in inches and feet, sometimes in an easy yard or two. They could see the thin, sharp line of the crest above them where the gray line of snow was faintly traced against the darker sky. Measuring, guessing, hoping it wasn't too far, he pushed and pulled the other man along with him. Patterson said nothing now and neither did he. There was nothing to say and they had no breath to say it with. You could swear at the snow, or the cold or the pain. But all you could do was stumble and crawl along. It became in the last few thousand yards a contest between that snow-covered mountain slope and whatever strength he had left. The Germans, wherever they were, had ceased to exist. There was only the mountain and him and the man whose weight he dragged behind him or pushed on ahead.

They finally made it. Up on the crest at last, he lay for long minutes unable to move, unable to speak. Only the cold wind kept him awake, and the snow into which he had sprawled. Below them in the early morning light he could see the graying stretch of a natural ski slope and down at the bottom a wooden shack.

"Where are we?" Patterson asked dully.

"Spain," he answered, his own voice flat with weariness.

The other said simply, "Thanks."

Then after a while he said, "Pat, there's food down there and a fire. You can see the smoke. Let's go." And together they slipped and slid down into Spain.

"*Hola!*" The guards came out of their shack. "You're under arrest!"

He laughed. Patterson began to laugh. The guards laughed with them. It was a thing they could all understand and appreciate together. Later he would be given the Bronze Star and the citation would read, "For heroism displayed while in enemy-occupied Continental Europe from 25 March, 1944, to 28 March, 1944," the days of their march from Lourdes.

"With complete disregard for his personal safety and well being," the citation would state, "Captain Yeager—" He'd have been commissioned by then and twice promoted— "carried a wounded comrade through the Pyrenees Mountains into Spain, a neutral country. This exhibition of courage . . ." But to him, to Patterson, to the frontier guards who had arrested them, it had seemed only amusing then. They had all laughed together, understanding this. And then the guards had put them in jail.

16

Back in England on the third of June, he sat all day in the interrogation section at Supreme Headquarters, Allied Expeditionary Forces in London. He was asked, and he had to answer, one question after another. There were two things they wanted to know. First, what had happened to his airplane? How had he been shot down? Had the plane or its armament failed in any way? Any, second, what had happened to him in France? Who had helped him? What had he seen? How had he evaded capture? How escaped?

"What is your name?" the questioning began. "Your age? How tall are you? How much do you weigh?" There was some discussion about that. Only 120 pounds on the fourth of March, he weighed even less when he crossed the Spanish border twenty-four days later. But now, after six weeks of idleness in Spain, another two weeks in Gibraltar with nothing to do but eat and sleep, he was heavier than he'd ever been.

"What do you weigh now?" he was asked.

"A hundred and forty-five."

The interrogating officer made a note of that and the questioning went on. "What is your rank? Your group? Your squadron? Where were you based? On what day were you shot down? How was your aircraft damaged? In what way did it behave?" And having disposed of the plane, the captain who questioned him asked him about his route through France.

"What are the names of the people who first came to your aid? How many live in the house to which you were brought? What kind of a building is it?

"Here is a map of Angoulême." A map was spread on the table top. "Can you show me where the Bertrand house is located?"

He marked the spot.

"Can you show me now the route you took from Angoulême? Who went with you? How did you travel? Where did you stay in Nérac? What are the names of the people with whom you lived? What do they call each other? Describe them. Here is a map of the town." Another map took its place on the table top. "Can you show me exactly where they lived?"

He marked another spot and the questioning went on, covering each of the links in the underground chain by which he had slipped from France to the border of Spain, asking the names of everyone he had met, asking what each had done, how each had looked, where he had met each one and how each one had worked.

"It has been important for us in the past," the captain explained, "to be able to contact these chains at various points in France." And the questioning continued as the interrogating officer led him back again over the route of his escape. "This," he kept insisting, "is very important. What German troops did you see? From what units? In what strength? Where did you see them? What did they do?"

This, on the third day of June in 1944, was of more than routine importance. For the third of June was D minus three in the vocabulary of the war. Operation Overlord was about to begin and all along the south of England ships lay in ports and harbors and in roadsteads off the shore. On the land itself the men of the allied armies waited to move from the marshaling areas down to the sea. And on every road the convoys stood facing south, long lines of tanks and trucks and carriers of every kind jammed bumper to bumper along the way, the entire massive, complex and interwoven movement about to begin. And each new scrap of information bore the weight of the whole.

"How did you travel to Lourdes? Over what route? You could see nothing on the way? Where did you stay in

Lourdes? Did you see any German troops? When did you leave?" The questioning went on monotonously. "What were the names of the men who guided you?" Repetitiously, "What did you call them?"—one question following another until he was almost unable to think.

"And you crossed the border into Spain on the twenty-eighth of March?"

"Yes, sir."

"There were four of you?"

"Two of us, sir. The others had gone ahead."

"What happened when you got into Spain?"

"We were arrested, sir. Lieutenant Patterson was sent on to a hospital. After a couple of days they moved me down into the town and I was released. We were all contacted by the American military attaché, who got us out of jail and into the hotel, the Alhambra de Aragon, I think it was called. And we really fat-catted it for a while. Then it was finally arranged to get us into Gibraltar and we were flown up here."

"All right." The captain pushed back his chair. "That covers it all. Now as soon as you've been identified, you can go on leave. We've notified your squadron that you're here. They're sending someone down to identify you. Then you can go for a visit, perhaps. And after that, back to the States. You're out of it for a while."

"Back to the States?" He began to protest. "But, sir, I want to go back to duty with the squadron. I want to—"

"Sorry. We've got a rule. You're an evadee, Yeager. You've evaded the Germans and you've had help from the French to do it. The fact is, Jerry would very much like to discuss all this with you, the things we've been talking about all day. They'd get it all out of you. Then you'd be shot. And the others who've helped you would also be shot. So they've made it a hard and fast rule not to permit escaped POW's or evadees to return to combat in this theater."

"But isn't there something I can do? I don't want to go to the States. I want to go back to my outfit, back to the squadron. Can't I talk to someone?"

"Good Lord," the captain said, "another one. Do you

know a Captain Glover? Fred L. Glover? He's as crazy as you are. He wants more combat, too. Do you really want to go back?" The captain was serious again.

"Yes, sir. I definitely do."

"Well, you can talk to the deputy for Operations. But don't count on anything. I wouldn't hope for much. Policy is policy around here and no exceptions are made. You are," the captain warned him, "as good as on your way to New York right now."

But the brigadier general to whom he talked was sympathetic. "Why?" he asked patently. "Why do you want to go back? And why should the Army make an exception of you?"

"Sir," he began, "I don't think I've had a fair chance at combat, having had only eight missions so far and only about a couple of weeks of it. But it's not only that. I went to the squadron from flying school. I trained with the squadron. My friends are there. I'd feel like hell if I had to go home and start over again. It doesn't seem fair or right to me."

Captain Glover had much the same argument to make. And facing these younger men, the general must have remembered a number of things, how aggressive young men are, what it can mean to have the conviction that there's a single slot in which you belong and only one place for you to live, what courage is, however blind. He must have remembered, too, how scarce good fighter pilots were, that it was D minus three and in a week or so they'd be in even greater demand, that it might not matter in a few weeks from now what French civilians they had known.

"Come back in the morning," he told them quietly. "I'd like to help but I can't change the rule. There is only one man who can. Perhaps if he's not too busy, we can get you in to talk to him. It's the only chance."

Early the next morning they returned to SHAEF and at nine o'clock stood face to face with the Supreme Commander.

He put them at ease, shook hands with both of them, asked them to please sit down. He understood, he told them with somewhat fatherly concern, that they were both evadees, that they had asked to be returned to their squadrons and not to be sent back to the United States.

A great many men have come into this theater of operations, the Supreme Commander said. And, he admitted, almost all of them would be glad of a chance to go back to the States. This, he thought, was no reflection on their quality as fighting men. Now, if they'd been away from home for almost a year, if they'd been in combat, had been shot down, had evaded capture and suffered the hardships of escape, what reason could they have for refusing a well-earned holiday, a rest at home?

"Sir," he tried to explain, "ever since I began to fly I've looked forward to combat, to getting into combat. That was the objective. It was the goal, to get into combat and see what you could do, to measure yourself against the other guy. Then I got into combat and as soon as it started, it was over."

His disappointment was understandable, the general quietly observed.

"And another thing, sir," he tried to explain again, "I want to go back to my squadron. As I see it, sir, that's where I belong. It's where I can do what I've been trained to do. I'll be of far more value to the government there than I could be anywhere else. If I go back to the States, I'll end up somewhere in the training command. I don't need a rest. I had a good rest in Spain."

Smiling a little, the Supreme Commander was inclined to agree with him, with Captain Glover, too, who had much the same thing to say for himself. But he wanted them both to understand that the policy stood and that it was not a policy he had made. More than personal considerations were at stake, his wishes or their own. Like all regulations, this one had been made for a good reason, to safeguard life, their lives and the lives of those who had helped them to escape.

He would do, however, as much as he could. He would ask permission from Washington to make an exception in their case so that they might remain in the theater, fight with the squadrons to which they belonged. He'd be glad to have them there. He wished them good luck.

They saluted again and hurriedly left, both of them breaking out into the hall like small boys suddenly excused from school. Now everything was fine. They had only to be identified. Then they could leave, go back to their units, fly, and in a few days fight again.

It was Teedy who came to London to identify him, Teedy who came officially to SHAEF to identify an unknown man who said he was an American fighter pilot. It was Teedy who walked quietly into the room where he sat waiting and carefully studied his face.

"Is this the man?" Teedy asked finally, carefully hiding a grin. "Is this the man who claims to be Yeager?" Teedy shook his head. "I have never seen this man before in my life!"

It was D minus two.

"Boy, did they raise their eyebrows," he wrote to Glennis later on. "They figured they had a big fat spy. Teedy knew it was me, of course, in spite of the weight I'd put on. But he couldn't resist the chance to have some fun with those headquarters characters. I didn't say anything either, just sat there and watched those gravel-crushers run around in circles until Teedy finally had enough and admitted it was all a joke. They gave us both hell then and sent us home."

17

It was good to fly again, even if only above the base. He gunned the engine, raced down the strip alone, feeling the plane airborne and light, alive around him. On up he went, climbing in lazy sweeps to right and to left, then suddenly breaking to the right into a series of rolls and loops and spiraling turns that brought him down almost to the ground. He climbed again to 28,000 feet and dove back down, then climbed to altitude again. But it was no fun, really, flying alone. He wanted to be with the others. He wanted to fight.

"Out of the question," the squadron commander had said. "You will fly noncombat only and only over this base until we hear otherwise. Those are the orders we got from SHAEF. Now relax," he added. "You're lucky to be here at all."

All morning long he flew alone, then landed and refueled and took his plane back up to practice stalls and loops and figure 8's, dogfighting with clouds and with imaginary 109's. It was like boxing shadows but it tired him. At four o'clock he landed again, waited impatiently alone until the squadron's planes began to come in from the mission they'd flown. He counted the planes as they came in, then listened to the inevitable talk. And in the morning he watched them all take off on another mission. He was alone again. And there was nothing for him to do but to fly alone. It was better than nothing, really. But he wanted to fight.

Back up in the air that morning he climbed to 30,000 feet. He thought that just for the hell of it he'd buzz the tower, make a few passes at the field. Maybe they'd all get tired of keeping him around, tell him to go away, get lost somewhere. He knew that he shouldn't but he was just getting ready to come back down in a screaming power dive and to buzz the operations shack when they called to him over the air.

It was the operations officer calling him. "How do you read me, Chuck?"

"I read you fine."

"Where the hell are you?"

"Right smack over the field," he answered dryly. "Anything wrong with that?"

"No. Listen, Yeager, how would you like to do a little hunting?"

"Boar," he asked, "or just rabbits again? If it's rabbits, I think I'll keep on flying awhile."

"Neither one," the operations officer said. "Just got a call from Air-Sea Command. There's a B-17 ditched up north off the coast of Holland. I've got four planes here and you're in one of them. We've got some green, green pilots down here ready to go. Will you look after them?"

He would have gone alone and said as much.

"I'll send three of them up. Take care of them. Have you got fuel?"

"Hell, yes," he said. "I just got up here. Plenty of fuel."

"Ammo?"

"Always loaded, just in case."

"Well, do a quick fly-by and pick up these three kids."

"Roger," he said and dove back down to the strip. The three 51's were racing across the ground together, one of them chasing the other two, as he came down. He wanted to buzz the tower still, not just for the hell of it but because he felt so fine. It was wonderful, really, to have some place to go, something to do. But he merely called out, "Thanks," to the operations officer and flew on by.

"Don't mention it," the other answered him with unofficial courtesy. "I felt kind of sorry for you, buddy. Just don't use any of that ammo, don't get into anything, or we'll have all those damn reports to make and we'll both be in the soup."

"Roger," he promised, grinning into the air, a mile away from the base by then. "You guys just latch onto my wing and let's get out of here," he told the three pilots, who were airborne now. They all came beautifully together into a finger flight of four and he led them off to the north and up to altitude.

For over an hour they dutifully searched for the B-17 but there was nothing in the area to which they had been sent. There was only a big, gray JU-188, a Junkers patrol bomber, cruising ahead of them and along the coast.

"Let's go!" he shouted, not thinking of anything except the chase. "Let's get that guy!" He closed up fast, giving the Junker a sudden burst that rolled him up on the beach. It was easy and it was wonderful. Then they went home. And there was hell to pay.

"You didn't!" the operations officer swore at him. "How could you do it to me, Chuck? You promised!" he complained. "Said you'd stay out of trouble. And now—Oh, God!" He stopped short, facing the prospect of explaining to the squadron commander, to group, to wing and to SHAEF itself why a pilot who had been all but grounded, who had been forbidden to fly except over his British base, had crossed the channel under his orders, engaged in combat, shot down a JU-188 and rolled it all the way up into the Netherlands.

"What do you mean, Yeager shot down a plane?" the squadron commander asked him quietly. "Was the base attacked? Are there Krauts around here?" His voice rose slightly. "Or did he shoot down one of our British friends?"

"Sir," the operations officer said bluntly, "he shot down a JU-188 up off the coast of Holland."

"Holland!" the other roared. "What in the hell was he doing up there?"

"I sent him, sir, to look for a ditched B-17—"

"You sent him?" The commander's voice dropped suddenly. "Oh, what the hell," he finished. "Get him in here."

It was a squadron matter and they settled it there. He

gave the plane to Captain Eddie Simpson, he remembered—made him five, made him an ace. And he gave the combat time to a kid by the name of Pascoe who had gone on the flight to Holland. So there was no paperwork.

There remained only five more days of impatient idleness until on the nineteenth of June, on D plus thirteen, the order came through from SHAEF reassigning him to the squadron and permitting him to fight.

Now he returned to that elite fraternity from which he'd been cut off. He was a fighter pilot again and an old man in the squadron with which he had trained. It was wonderful. He'd say that all his life and he would remember the months that followed his return, and they would always seem to be the golden days. No matter where he would go or what he would do in the future, he would always look back with homesickness to the squadron, to England, to combat during the last six months of 1944.

Not to the fighting, the killing, the winning of one encounter after another. Their own losses were too high—half of the old group killed or missing in action, every other man. It was the first result of this to which they would all look back one day, to the closely interlocking comradeship that grew from common risk and from the tension with which each of them lived as long as he lived. The half who survived were drawn together with each fresh loss into a tighter and tighter group and into this no one else could enter without first having accepted himself the same high risk with which they lived and died. It was a group with its own ethics, living apart with its own rules.

Twenty pilots start out together, he would try to explain it later on. Half of them are killed and the rest of you in the group come closer and closer together.

You know from the start that some of you will get it. But as long as it isn't you, you never really understand why it has to be anybody else. It's nothing you can talk about. You might discuss the flying elements involved, the things that happened, talk about *how* someone got clobbered. Never anything else. The personal factor you just shut off. You have none and you can't afford to worry about it all, just watch your tail.

Nonflying officers, the ground-pounders or gravel-crushers—intelligence officers, adjutants, supply officers, armorers—the pilots never associated with any of them. You'd all be in a bar together talking about the mission that day, or combat or how one of the guys got clobbered and they'd try to filter into the group. You'd all clam up, move off. They were good fellows and you liked them well enough. They'd been with the squadron as long as the pilots had. But they didn't understand.

"Too bad about So-and-so," they'd say. "Hear he got clobbered." It made you angry, forced you away from them. Because it's against all your rules for them to come into it at all, to say what you yourself can't say. If a guy starts trying to talk about something he doesn't know, if a supply officer tries to sound like a fighter pilot, you freeze or you move him out. He's immediately on your list. You lose your faith in him. You feel like asking him where his wings are, how many missions he's flown, how many shots he's fired or even heard. But you don't say anything at all, just move away. You live apart from them, from everyone.

He shared a Nissen hut with Don Bochkay, Andy Anderson and Jim Browning. They were all flight leaders in the squadron. Between them they would finally account for sixty-three German planes shot down or destroyed in the air. And in that hut their lives were centered all through those fall and winter months of 1944. At night the coke stove glowed and they talked about women and airplanes, the blitzed streets of London, how the war seemed to be going, what they'd done that day or would do tomorrow, talking, endlessly talking, swilling hot soup and drinking beer.

Meanwhile they flew together, too, so many missions that they established a fixed routine and a point of rendezvous to which they'd all return before flying home. It was high in the air above a lake in western Germany, a small lake on the edge of the Ruhr, a district better known to them as Happy Valley because it was always full of flak. There the four of them would meet, go chasing each other's tails, dogfighting to see who'd lead the way back home. Then they'd race back to the base together, land together, talk out the mission again, get dressed and go into town or cook more soup on the coke stove in their Nissen hut.

On the thirteenth of September he shot down another plane. "I was leading Cement Blue Flight," he reported later. "I spotted an ME-109 diving straight down around 15,000 feet. I rolled over and caught the enemy aircraft on the deck, diving around 450 to 500 miles an hour. I closed up fast and opened fire at 300 yards, observing strikes on his engine and his fuselage. The engine began to smoke and windmill. I overshot. Lieutenant Gailer fired at him until the enemy aircraft attempted to belly in, exploding when it hit the ground. I claim one ME-109 destroyed, shared with Second Lieutenant Frank Gailer." This was confirmed.

One month later on the twelfth of October he accounted for five more. Leading the group with Cement Squadron he went roving out to the right of the first box of bombers they were escorting. Over Steinhuder Lake in Germany, twenty-two ME-109's crossed suddenly in front of the squadron from eleven to one o'clock. The German planes were a mile and a half away, flying, as his own squadron was, at 28,000 feet. Coming straight out of the sun, he fell in behind the enemy formation, followed them for about three minutes, climbing to 30,000 feet. He closed up to within a thousand yards, coming within firing range and positioning his squadron behind the entire enemy formation. Then he struck.

"Two of the ME-109's were lagging over to the right," he stated in his encounter report. "One slowed up and before I could open fire, the pilot rolled over and bailed out. The other ME-109 flying his wing bailed out immediately, just as I lined him in my sights. My plane was the closest of all our planes to the tail end of the enemy formation, the only plane within shooting range. And no one was firing.

"I dropped my tanks and closed up to the last Jerry, opening fire from 600 yards. I observed strikes all over the ship, particularly heavy in the cockpit area. He skidded of to the left and then, smoking and streaming coolant, went into a slow dive, turning to the left."

Closing up on another German plane, he did not follow the burning 109. Lieutenant Stern, flying in Blue Flight, reported this enemy aircraft on fire as it passed him and went into a spin. Yeager, he saw, had pulled up by then to within a hundred yards of the next ME-109. He saw him skid to the right and take a deflection shot of ten degrees. After a three-second burst of fire from Yeager's plane, the whole fuselage of the 109 split open and blew up.

"Another ME-109 had cut his throttle and was trying to get behind us," Yeager continued in his report. "I broke to the right and quickly rolled to the left on his tail. He started pulling it in and I myself was pulling about 6 g but I got a lead from around 300 yards and gave him a short burst. There were hits on wings and tail section. He snapped to the right three times and bailed out at 18,000 feet.

"These ME-109's," he concluded, "appeared to have a type of bubble canopy and had purple noses. They were a mousy-brown all over. I claim five ME-109's destroyed."

After the fight they rendezvoused over their lake on the edge of Happy Valley and came on home together. His claim was confirmed. He was given the Silver Star. "For gallantry in action," his citation read, "while leading a squadron of fighters in support of heavy bombers over Germany, 12 October, 1944. . . . The fact that Captain Yeager destroyed five (5) and his squadron two (2) enemy aircraft during this action attests to his courage, tenacity of purpose and determination to destroy the common enemy."

But it was not all violent action and wild victory. There were the dead to be buried quietly with a drink. There were the missions on which nothing happened and there was no release from the tension with which they began. They would return still taut with expectation and unable to relax. Then they'd go off to town, stand quietly in pubs until the inevitable "Time, gentlemen, time," sent them back home again.

There were good days, too. They'd all get horses, ride

out across the flat fen country of Suffolk, hunting, they said, and finding a few wild rabbits in the muddy ground. These they took back to their hut and fried. Soaking in rich, brown gravy, they were a welcome relief from their diet of pork chops, spam and powdered eggs.

They hunted one day with the British, and it was a rare occasion, one that was hard to forget. They'd met some RAF pilot officers in one of the pubs in town. "Look here, you chaps," the British pilots said, "you like to go hunting. Why not go for a spot of shooting with us?" They said they'd be glad to. Each one of them drew a batman who carried hot tea in a Thermos and a full flask of gin. The British gave them each a shooting stick, and there were Italian prisoners of war to flush the game.

"All right, you ruddy Wops," their squadron leader ordered, "into the bloody brush!" And a long, ragged line of miserable Italian soldiers moved off through the mist and mud while the RAF pilots and their guests perched on their shooting sticks, drank their hot tea and washed it down with gin.

"Sorry we've got no brandy," the British apologized. "Jerry's been getting it all these last few years."

And now and then a covey of grouse or pheasant would take the air, reminding them all that this was a hunt. Once in a while they'd manage to pepper a few with shot. But it was largely a convivial affair, an act of friendship gratefully received. Then they went back to the war again.

On the sixth of November he shot down his first German jet and damaged two more. "I was leading White Flight in Cement Squadron," he reported. His flight was at the extreme right of the squadron formation. They flew at 8,000 feet in haze. Suddenly, below and to their right (at two o'clock low) three German ME-262 jets zipped past them going 180 degrees or in the opposite direction to the squadron's flight. There was no opportunity to attack. The jets were gone as quickly as they were seen.

But Cement Leader sighted two more jets, low and traveling on the squadron's course, but off again to their right. "Cement Leader to White Flight Leader," the squadron commander called him then. "Bandits at four o'clock!" The whole squadron maneuvered to the right, putting White Flight into the lead. "They're jets!" somebody said. "Go get them, Chuck!"

He attacked from above, coming down to head off the latter of the two faster planes, getting a 90 degree deflection shot at the jet from 400 yards away. Keeping their loose V formation, the enemy planes took no evasive action. Depending on their superior speed, they simply pulled away, sped out of range in the hazy air.

Cement Squadron flew on then in a thin overcast, its edge being over to their right. They'd come down to 5,000 feet. Yeager, still in the lead, dropped down to get under the overcast and met three jets head on. They were now at 2,000 feet. He split S on the leader and the Germans broke formation as he fired a high deflection burst from above. Getting behind their leader now, he fired three more bursts to get hits on his wings and fuselage from 300 yards. The faster jets pulled away, and again he lost them in the haze.

He found then that he'd lost his own planes, too. Alone, he climbed to 8,000 feet and headed north. At 5258 N-0643 E he came to the jet air base, a large airfield with wide, black runways at least 6,000 feet in length. Skirting the field he drew a few bursts of inaccurate flak, then spotted a lone 262 approaching to land from the south at about 500 feet. He split S on him at that same low altitude and going 500 miles an hour. The flak became very thick and accurate. He fired a short burst at the jet from 400 yards, got hits on the enemy's wings. At 300 yards he had to break off—the flak was too close for comfort now. He broke straight up and, looking back down, saw the jet crash-land short of the strip in a wooded field. One of its wings flew off.

This time he won the Distinguished Flying Cross, "For extraordinary achievement while serving as a fighter pilot on an escort mission over Germany. . . ." His courage and flying ability were both commended.

That night they fried jack rabbits on the coke stove in their hut, sopped up the rich, brown gravy with G.I.

bread and washed it down with French champagne. "It's just like sody pop," he complained. They opened a bottle of bourbon for him and they all got slightly tight.

Two weeks later he shot down four more German planes. They were escorting Jonah this time, another fighter squadron with a strafing mission north of Berlin. Fifteen miles southeast of Madgeburg the strafing squadron reported enemy aircraft.

"Jonah to Cement leader, bandits at eleven o'clock!"

The squadron wheeled to the left to face two gangs of enemy aircraft, fifty plus in one gang, more than a hundred and fifty FW-190's in the other. The turn to the left had again put Yeager, leading Green Flight, at the head of his squadron's formation.

"You guys are there, go after them," the squadron leader said.

He led his flight in past the smaller group of fifty planes, climbed up to 32,000 feet, positioning his planes behind the larger gang. Then he attacked, jumping the nearest enemy aircraft. The FW-190 went into a rolling dive to the right and then pulled up into a tight turn to the right. But he fired a side-deflection burst from the right, getting hits, good strikes from 200 yards. The 190 snapped and its tail flew off. He saw no chute as he pulled up into the bottom of the gang.

A second 190 jumped him then. He broke back into him, getting deflection shots from 90 degrees at 100 yards. Smoking, the Focke-Wulf went into a sudden dive. He followed it down to 15,000 feet where it blew apart. He saw no chute again. He climbed back now to the tail end of the gang and jumped a third 190. This one started a circling turn with him but he turned inside, closed up to 100 yards and fired a burst that sprayed the plane from tail to nose. The German pilot bailed out at 25,000 feet.

On his way back up to attack the gang again he saw a lone 190 circling to his left. Attacking this, he got into a Lufberry with him, closed up to 100 yards at 29,000 feet and gave him a burst of fire. All of his hits were concentrated in the cockpit area. A sheet of flame shot out from the pilot's canopy and the 190 nosed down into a dive.

Watching it burn, he followed it down to 12,000 feet. Again he saw no chute. He circled once, then climbed back to the tail end of the larger gang, whittled down now to less than a hundred planes. He started to make another pass at a fifth 190 but he was jumped by a stray P-51.

"I broke into him," he said in his encounter report, "and he joined up. When I looked back the enemy aircraft were all splitting up, heading for the deck and going east. None of them dropped their belly tanks. They were rather aggressive when engaged. I claim four FW-190's destroyed. Ammunition expended: 889 rounds .50 cal. MG."

And he won a cluster to his Silver Star, "For gallantry in action while providing escort and cover for a fighter group on a strafing mission over Germany, 27 November, 1944. . . . Captain Yeager's dauntless courage, zeal and combat aggressiveness during this action set an inspiring example for other members of his unit. . . ."

Back at their rendezvous point on the edge of Happy Valley, he and Browning, Anderson and Bochkay fought each other doggedly for the privilege of leading the flight back home. Anderson won, leading them out of the overcast at 7,000 feet. They broke out over the coast of Holland and into heavy flak.

"Some flak," they reported tersely, "was encountered in the coastal area of Holland."

The missions continued, day after day, flight after flight as increasing numbers of allied planes ranged farther and farther into Germany. But the Luftwaffe was broken now. On their last mission Yeager and Anderson flew as spares at the tail end of the group. They'd see no Krauts, they told each other. They broke to the right and headed for Switzerland. There they dropped their tanks on the top of Mont Blanc and peppered the snow with a hail of slugs. High in the air they looped and rolled and climbed back up to come screaming down again, twisting and turning, dogfighting just to amuse themselves. Six hours late, they finally returned to their base to face a vast disappointment and a terrible chagrin.

"What happened to you guys?" they were asked.

They answered, "We got lost," and then listened sheepishly to wild talk of wholesale victory.

For while he and Anderson had toured Mont Blanc, Cement Squadron pilots had shot down sixty-three German planes. "Sixty-three!" they told them. "It was lousy with Krauts! We all got some. They were all over the place! You sure could have padded your scores."

His score wasn't bad. He'd flown sixty-four combat missions, 270 combat hours. He'd been shot down and he'd escaped from France. He had destroyed eleven aircraft, shared a twelfth with Gailer, damaged three more in the air. He had the Silver Star with an Oak Leaf Cluster, the Distinguished Flying Cross, the Bronze Star, the Air Medal with six Oak Leaf Clusters, the Purple Heart, four battle stars on his ETO ribbon and the Presidential Unit Citation with which the squadron had been decorated.

But he was sadly disappointed on that night of January 14, 1945. Anderson was, too. They'd missed the last act of the show and it had been the wildest act of all. Sixty-three Krauts! They solaced themselves with a fifth of rye. He filled his canteen cup to the top and drank it off. "Cheers," he said and they applauded him. He tried it again. Approximately eighteen minutes later, the Flight Surgeon conscientiously reported, he passed out. When they had brought him around again with coffee and wet towels, they all went out together to get those gravel-crushers in their damn headquarters shacks. But somehow they never got that far.

He woke up in the morning under a dripping tree, wet with the rain that had fallen all night long. The best of the war was over. He was ready to go home.

Part Three

18

Mated, hugging the bomber's belly and lashed securely to its underside, the X-1 appears as only a small protuberance beneath the bulk of the B-29. The bomber's tail section alone is longer than the whole of the little plane, its inboard engines longer and almost as large in girth. Seen together, the planes appear in vivid contrast to each other, the long, high-tailed and big-engined B-29; the short, bright orange X-1 tucked under her belly—a fat little parasite hugging a whale.

But it's not the smallness of the X-1 that impresses you, crossing the ramp to board the B-29. Nor is it the purpose for which the X-1 was designed, to fly at the speed of sound. That much speed means nothing now and its significance to flight is equally meaningless. The plane is a symbol of something more immediate, much more real, as you cross the ramp to board its mother ship. It is the project itself for which the X-1 stands, the setting out with a handful of other men, the working together toward a common end, the opening of a familiar pattern. It is the present, but it is the past and the future too that envelops you now. It is like going back to the squadron as you climb with the others up into the B-29 to begin something entirely new.

Up into the pilot's seat Cardenas moves with lazy ease and Ridley, following him, sinks with routine precision into the co-pilot's seat. With Hoover you settle yourself on the metal deck beside the navigator's compartment, propping a chute behind your back for comfort. Turning to look back through the narrow passageway into the belly of the plane,

137

you can see the bright skin of the X-1 framed in the bomber's open bay. You can also see portions of the ramp below.

Converted by Bell engineers for the specific job of air-launching the X-1, the whole midsection of the B-29 lies open above the ground. It's a long rectangle into which only the top of the small plane fits. The B-29's bomb bay doors have been removed and the ship strengthened with steel beams running from just behind the navigator's compartment and the forward cabin bulkhead for a distance of almost 40 feet. Beneath this open section hangs the X-1, suspended by a standard D-4 bomb shackle with which it it also hoisted up under the plane. It is snug and secure in its hold. But it doesn't seem to be. The shackle seems small, the cable thin that holds the little ship.

Beyond the belly of the plane, in the tail section of the B-29, three civilian crewmen ride. They will observe the X-1 from the tail. There's not much to worry about. You know the X-1 has been ferried many times before, from Buffalo to Miami and from coast to coast. But this is the first for you and it's a matter of concern.

Cardenas fires the B-29 then and your excitement suddenly grows. You've flown enough. You've made so many take-offs you'd think this would be just another one. The starter whines and there's the old, familiar *plop-plop* of the engines, settling finally into their familiar roar. And there's the same routine.

"Okay, sir," the flight engineer says, calling the pilot on the interphone. "She's all yours, Major."

"All set?" Cardenas asks him.

"Roger, sir," the engineer repeats. "It's all yours."

Cardenas answers, "Okay. Rolling."

And you feel the big bomber begin to move. Its speed increases and you can feel the beginning of the take-off roll. The deck lifts under you now and you slide back up against the bulkhead. The B-29 is in the air.

"Left gear moving up," the left scanner reports.

"Right gear moving up," the right scanner echoes him.

"Left flap moving up."

"Right flap moving up."

"Fifteen degrees on the left flap."

"Fifteen degrees on the right flap."

"Left gear full up, left flap full up," the left scanner calls out now. "One and two look good on the take-off."

And the right scanner repeats, "Right gear full up, right flap full up. Three and four look clean on take-off."

Once again you suddenly sense the purpose of this flight and you're completely aware for a moment of the whole history and intent of project MX-524 to which, with these others, you've been finally assigned. Then you come back to the present, hearing the engineer say, "Roger," and hearing Cardenas calling the tower now, making a final radio check.

"B-29," Cardenas is saying. "How do you read me?"

"Loud and clear," the tower answers. "Take it easy and good luck."

The B-29 is still climbing now, into the west and away from Buffalo. It is early morning, the fourth of July in 1947. The sky overhead is clear and blue. Above its brightness lies the high frontier this project will assault, the dustless, thin, contrasting air of altitude where the sun is always a bright round ball in a dark blue sky, where there are no shades but light and dark, where you will fly alone in the fastest airplane ever built at speeds no man has ever known.

"Well," Ridley says, "we're off the ground."

"Aren't we supposed to be?" you ask.

"The voice you have just heard," Cardenas answers you, "is the voice of Lincoln County's Huckleberry Finn—"

"The Will Rogers," Ridley interrupts him, "of the jet age."

"The darling of women all over the world," Hoover suggests.

And you say, "I'm tired. You guys are keeping me awake." You try to relax then and to settled down into one more cross-country flight.

But it isn't easy. Excitement moves in you as you move on through the air. From time to time you turn back to the X-1 in the midsection of the B-29. "I'm scared to death," you admit, "that that damn thing will fall right out of there." Yet nothing goes wrong. The B-29 flies steadily on. You're restless. You always are when you don't have anything to do in a plane, in any plane. You go through fits of drowsiness and sudden starts. You have to get up and move around. You all shift places from time to time. You sometimes talk.

"Looks like a pretty good deal to me," you say to Ridley after a while.

"Yes, it does," he agrees. Bob Hoover is flying co-pilot now, and Ridley is sprawled beside you on the deck. But there's not much conversation. The last few days have been full of tension and excitement. There have been meetings, briefings, last-minute plans and changes in last-minute plans. You're tired, all of you, and as you fly this tiredness grows.

"It's a funny way to make a living," Ridley says after a while. "Why, why would anybody that could go off fishing or hunting or something, strap himself into one of these buckets and go flying around?"

"He'd have to be nuts," you agree.

"The pay is lousy."

"Not only that, the hours are bad."

"How did you get into this business, Jack?" you ask him then. "How come you don't build these things instead of just jockeying them around all day? You could have made a lot more money—"

"Boy, that's right. That's very true. But who wants money? What can you buy?"

There is much loud laughter at this from everyone. But Ridley shrugs it away, grins wryly and goes on. "Hell, figure out what it costs to fly for an hour and multiply that by your time in the air. Then think of how much a guy would have to earn to buy all that flying. No, Chuck, I'll tell you, if I had to start all over, I wouldn't do anything else. Neither would any of these guys. When I got out of flying school, of course, I did want to go into combat and I wish I had. We all wanted to then, to see how good we were. But I had an engineering degree from Oklahoma and I didn't have any choice. I went right into Air Matériel Command."

"Where did they send you?" you ask him, suddenly remembering the war.

"Convair plant in Forth Worth. I was acceptance pilot and also engineering liaison officer on the B-32 and then on the B-36. Then they sent me to Cal Tech to get a master's degree in aeronautical engineering. I got out of there in 1945 and went on to Wright Field."

"I should have gone to school," you say then, "and I could have. My dad wanted me to go—"

"You're doing all right," Ridley says. "Hell, you're the one who's giving to fly that thing back there, not me."

"What's it going to be like?"

"Same old thing," Ridley answers. "It's just another airplane. You'll learn its systems, see how it handles, what it will do. As far as the rest of it goes, the engineers aren't much ahead of you. This business of supersonic aerodynamics—we've got the theory of it, maybe. But no practical experience except in the handling of an F-80 in a dive. You want to remember, the X-1 is still a pilot's plane. That's why you're here."

You doze some more, half-thinking about it all, and after a while you begin to feel restless again. "Say, Jack." You turn to Ridley again. "This is the Fourth of July."

"Sure is."

"Wonder what my kids are doing."

"The baby's probably asleep."

"Don, I mean. He's old enough to get a kick out of the parade. I wish there'd been time to go home."

You think about that for a while, about Glennis back home and waiting again. And you make all sorts of resolutions, wishing the time away, wishing the boys were old enough, wishing you had a settled home. "I'm going to get a house," you say.

"Chuck," Ridley asks after a while, "when you came back from Europe, when you put all those medals away in the dresser drawer, how come you didn't settle down on a nice, steady milk run with Pan American or TWA?"

"New York to Miami all year long?" You shake your

head. "I never thought of it. I went right on out to the coast to Newcastle, California, so I could pick up Glennis. She turned her green ring around and we rode the train back to Hamlin. Boy, it was nice. They had a parade and all, right through the town. Then," you remember sadly, "I wound up in the Training Command. What a sad situation that turned out to be.

"And Andy Anderson and me," you remember, "we'd been in the squadron together, came back together, married girls from the same home town and they both had boys within a month of each other. Then, well, there we were down there at Perrin Field instructing bombardiers, combat returnees, all first lieutenants and captains who'd applied for flying school."

"How did you stand it?" Ridley yawns.

"We didn't. Andy and me, all he and I would do—go up and meet each other and get in a big dogfight, just us two. Just every day we'd make our students sick and scare 'em half to death and everything."

"Just for the hell of it?"

"Well, yeah. We were—that's what we'd been doing all along."

"You must have been browned off."

"Boy, that's really too mild. We just couldn't stand it, couldn't stand to face it. You never heard two guys bitch and moan so much in your life. Every night. Even our wives got sick of it. You could see it. They took pictures of us when we reported in and you never did see two such sad characters."

"How did you ever get out of that?"

"Well, they sent me up to instrument school at Chanute Field. When I came back they assigned me as an instructor. But about that time they came out with Project R. Being an evadee, having escaped from France, I could pick any spot in the continental limits for my next assignment. So I picked Wright Field. It was right near Hamlin. Glennis was back there having a baby then. And I liked Wright Field. I'd been there a couple of times before. But I had no idea in the world that I'd ever be a test pilot. They just assigned me there because they were short of pilots in Fighter Test. I'd had all my time in fighters and I was still pretty young—"

"Some guys," Ridley says, yawning again, "are just born lucky."

You lapse back into weariness and doze some more. But the sounds and the motion of flight keep you awake. And the thought of the X-1 hanging out under the B-29 keeps taking you back for another look. From time to time you walk back through the door and along the catwalk into the belly of the ship. You stand for a moment looking down. It's cold out there and you can see the ground below you gliding past.

How in the world, you wonder, do you climb down there on a ladder with all your gear on and crawl into that little door. There's only a foot and a half or so between the end of the ladder and the door. You'll have your chute on and your flying clothes. The wind will be whipping past you at the air speed of the ship, 200 miles an hour or more. You'll have to get down, feet first somehow, and work your way into the cockpit of the X-1. Then what do you do? How do they lower the door?

Still looking down, you begin to feel faintly sick. You go back into the cabin then and lie down on the deck again. "Jack," you ask, "how soon will we get to fly that thing?"

"We'll find out soon," he says calmly. "How do you feel?"

"Okay."

"You look a little green."

"I'm hungry," you answer. "Who's got the sandwiches?"

The B-29 flies on, the sun coming up from behind you, passing high overhead and moving on ahead into the west. Flat on the deck, hands underneath your head, you settle yourself to wait the long hours out. Impatience dies and flight becomes pleasant again. "Hey, Jack," you say, "just think. They pay us for doing this." And at Denver, finally, the B-29 comes down. You open the hatch, fix the small ladder into place and one by one drop to the ground.

Now everything is suddenly different. Away from

Wright Field, halfway to Muroc, off on your own, you feel for the first time that the project really belongs to you. Nothing can happen now to take it away. There sits the X-1, lashed to the B-29. Tomorrow you'll land at Muroc. Your eagerness and your impatience grow with every step you take away from the B-29. You'd just as soon take off right now and get out there, get to work, get in the air and fly again.

But you can't. You begin to talk instead. "Ridley?" you ask. "What do you really think of this deal? What do you think of the plane and all?"

You talk as you walk; all through the mechanical business of signing in, you talk. Still talking, you check into a room together and walk on out to the club. There, over a bottle of beer, you talk still more. You listen, too. And as Ridley goes on, you begin to realize how green you are as far as aerodynamics is concerned; the terms are new, the concepts unfamiliar. Ridley tries to explain. Still talking, he leads the way into the restaurant. Still talking, you eat and, listening, learn something of what you'll have to know as you fly up through the range of critical speeds below Mach 1. Then when you've eaten, you go on up to your room, still talking about the plane. "Built to take 18 g's, remember," Ridley reminds you again. "If the plane is going to go, you'll be long gone yourself before it's crushed or comes apart on you.

"Remember, too," he tells you again—you're each in a bed now and ready to go to sleep—"no airplane will ever change ends on you without giving you some sort of warning, letting you know."

"But, Jack—" You sit up suddenly in bed—"if something does go wrong, how in the hell can you get out of the thing? It's not like a 51 where you just get rid of your canopy and jump. What in the world do you do?"

"At that speed? Nothing," Ridley admits. "You've got to slow down your speed and lose some altitude, then jettison the door and drop right out. Depends on how much of a warning you get, on how much time—But I wouldn't worry. I don't see how it can come to that, the way that airplane has been built."

Then you begin to wonder again what it will be like to fly the plane. "Ought to be nice and smooth," Ridley thinks. "Everyone says it is who's flown the thing."

And you make a rough flight plan, talking together of how you'll fly the pattern at Muroc, how you'll land, not on the strip but on the dry lake bed where you'll have more room. And long, long after you should have been asleep, you're both still talking about it all. Because you can't sleep. You're too excited, ready to start. "Could have been out there now," you complain, "if the old man hadn't insisted we didn't fly at night."

"You'll get there," Ridley says. "Relax. You'll fly the plane."

But a knock on the door interrupts him then. Out in the hall there's a man with a badge. They've picked up a crewman in one of the downtown bars, he says in a flat and official voice. The crewman talked. Somebody had called the police.

You stand in the door, your mind still up in the air. You're worried at first, then angry as you begin to understand that this means trouble, this means a delay.

"What did he talk about?" Ridley asks from behind your back.

"What could he have talked about? Nothing," you answer emphatically. "He doesn't know—"

"Isn't this project classified?" the man in the doorway wants to know.

"It's just another research project," Ridley answers calmly as he climbs out of bed. "We're all brand new on the thing. We don't know anything about it, not enough to give out any classified information."

"Why, hell," you interrupt, "as much as we know has all been in the newspapers."

"That is right," Ridley says, coming to stand beside you now. "We know this plane was built to fly at the speed of sound and we're taking it out to Muroc to test the thing. That's not classified information. What did the fellow say?"

"Not much," the man in the doorway admits cautiously. "Said he was a crew member assigned to the project." He reads from a small black notebook now. "Said it was the

X-1, hottest ship in the world. Going to fly supersonic—"
The voice goes on, importantly cataloguing the kind of
things a man will talk about between three or four bottles
of beer on a hot summer night, boasting a little, making
himself a little bit more than just a customer sitting in a
bar. Good Lord, you think, not wanting any trouble, not
wanting any more delay. Are they going to hold us here for
this? And in the back of your mind you can hear the old
man's comment, see the look on his face when he hears
the news.

"Look here," you ask the man in the doorway, "can't
we just get the guy and bring him back here to the base?"

"I'm not sure we can," he objects.

"We'll be responsible for him," you insist. "We leave
out of here in a couple of hours—"

"The man will be with us," Ridley interjects. "And
anytime you want him—"

The man in the door gives in a little. "Well, if you
gentlemen can certify—If there's nothing in his remarks—"

"What information did he give?" you ask. "The name
of the plane? It's in the newspapers. He said we're going
to fly it. That's what you do with planes."

"That," Ridley agrees without conscious humor, "is
why they build them."

"This supersonic business—that was in all the trade
magazines six months ago. And he couldn't have told
anyone how it works or anything. Hell, mister, I'm the
pilot and I don't even know how the damn thing flies.
Captain Ridley here is the engineering officer and he
doesn't know. What could a crewman possibly have said?"

The man in the doorway shrugs. "All right," he agrees,
not wanting to let you off the hook altogether. "You'll have
to come down and pick him up."

"Let's go," you say. You put on some clothes and rush
the man right down the hall and out of the building before
he can change his mind. And after a while the matter is
settled, the worried crewman safely bedded down for
what's left of the night. Back in your room again, there's
less than two hours of darkness as Ridley greets you
sleepily and you crawl back into your bed.

"Everything okay?" Ridley yawns.

"Yeah. But we should have gone right on out to Muroc," you complain impatiently. "Jack, what about fire in that plane? There must be considerable danger of fire or flame in there."

"Suppose there is," Ridley agrees and yawns again.

"If you have to get out, you'll have to get out pretty fast, I guess."

"Guess you would," Ridley mumbles. "Have to do everything fast."

"That's right. You don't get much time for anything, even for flight."

"Just a few minutes—" Ridley's voice trails off.

"How many minutes, Jack? How many minutes of flight with full power on?"

But there is no answer. Ridley is fast asleep. And you lie restless, waiting for time to pass.

19

But you don't just get in the X-1 and take off. You can't do that with any airplane that's new to you. You've got to study the airplane, learn its cockpit, learn all its systems so that you know where everything is and just what every switch, valve, gear or lever is supposed to do.

And you begin, finally, without any excitement at all, land at Muroc, sign in, check into a room and go to bed. The next morning you go back to school, sit in a classroom in a tar-paper-covered shack north of Hangar Two on the South Base. It's seven-thirty in the morning. The whole Air Force crew comes drifting in: Ridley, Cardenas, Hoover, Lieutenants Ed Swindel, flight engineer on the B-29, and Ed Smith, B-29 co-pilot, the enlisted technicians and civilians who will learn with you the complex systems of the airplane and the careful procedures developed for its flight.

Seated in the one-armed student chairs, supplied with sharpened pencils and with clean, fresh blocks of white note paper, you stare at the blackboard-covered walls and wait for this first class to begin. And waiting, you withdraw a little into yourself, each one of you reminded, perhaps, of an older time and earlier experience. You can almost smell the schoolrooms back in Hamlin, remember the waiting years ago. And you have the same feeling you always had on the first day of school, a feeling of being shut away from everything that's going on. Out on the base you hear the sounds of flight, you know what's going on in hangars, on the big apron, the long strip and in the air. Just as you knew back home that the woods were there and the wind and the bright blue sky as you faced the

148

blackboards in those older rooms, smelled new chalk, fresh paper, ink in its metal-covered wells and waited for the new teacher to come in.

His name is Frost, Dick Frost, he tells you, lounging at ease on a corner of his desk, a tall, young man with a flame- or heat-scarred hand. "I'd better tell you a little bit about myself before we get into the project," he begins. He's a graduate engineer. He's been with the Bell Aircraft Company for several years, worked first as a production test pilot, then as an experimental test pilot. He had a rather serious accident in bailing out of a P-63. It put him in the hospital for a while. When he got out he worked partly as a test pilot, partly as engineer on various radio-controlled airplane projects.

Then he begins and you listen and hear again the legend of the ship, how it began with a question and a vague idea, how this idea was sharpened by risk and by the loss of life into a theory that none could test—theory grown now into the belief that man will fly in level flight at the speed of sound. For the plane itself is more now than a dream in the minds of a few questioning pilots and engineers and aerodynamicists scattered halfway around the world. They've built it now and it's been flown. Listening, you hear again the names of the men who brought the X-1 bit by bit from the backs of their minds to the reality of flight.

These were the pilots who in ships now obsolete and slow came screaming down from altitude to chase an elusive answer through the dangerous air, like Major Pete Barsodi, dead now, who was the first to see and to photograph shock waves rising like heat waves from his power-diving P-51. And after the pilots, men like John Stack of the Langley Laboratory at Hampton Roads, Tom Tyra of the Navy Bureau of Aeronautics' Fighter Desk, and E. W. Conlon, lent to the Navy by the University of Michigan, who pushed their own belief up through Army and Navy brass to men like General Hap Arnold and General F. O. Carroll, Kotcher's chief.

Then Kotcher himself, Bob Woods, Bob Wolf and Larry Bell, the men you met in Buffalo—Emmons and Stanley, Hamlin, Sandstrom, Smith—deriving themselves from older men, extending primitive ideas into concise devices that would work, inferring, guessing and extrapolating, learning by trial and error, inventing, developing and discovering, putting together somehow all the scattered pieces begged and borrowed around the world from scientists and from mechanics, from aerodynamicists and engineers and from machinists, plumbers, pilots, electricians, glider pilots, rocketeers, from chemists, welders, physicists and riveters. There isn't a mechanical trade or science in the world whose most commonplace practitioner would not know and understand something of some part of this complex and intricate aircraft. And you've got to learn it all. In two or three weeks.

The list of names goes on and there is reassurance as the number grows. Jack Woolams, dead now, who flew the ship; Tex Johnston and Slick Goodlin, who have flown it, too. The team from Reaction Motors—Davis, Iwanoski and Sartore. Williams and Beeler of NACA. Pappy Dow, who flew the B-29 for Bell; Mark Heaney, his co-pilot, and Bill Miller, their crew chief. The Bell crewmen who maintained the X-1 and who'll help to train the Air Force crew: Sam Gray, electrical engineer; Wendell Moore, power plant engineer; Bob Brooks, foreman; and Jack Russell, crew chief; the technicians—Garth Dill, Mac Hamilton, Jim George, Al Heusinger, Bill Means.

The list goes on. Your feelings are divided now. They've done it, all these men. What each of them has done, you'll do yourself. But you've got to know everything all of them have known together, or enough of everything to satisfy yourself, not simply enough to fly the plane. You measure yourself this time against no single one but against them all. And your impatience flares up at the thought of all you have to do and everything you have to learn.

"When I was assigned to the project," Frost is saying, "the air frames had been built. The power plant was being developed at RMI. My job was to get this power plant development completed, to get into the airplane, to test it and get it up in the air for powered flight. Believe me, I was green as grass, greatly astounded at having been picked to do this. I felt too small for the job. There were, however, several fine engineers to help me, most of them older than I was, more experienced. We worked together, licked the problems as they came along—and there were many of them. The rocket power plant, for example, had a distressing habit of blowing up."

Frost tells you then how Bill Smith, chief of rocket engine development for Bell, was sent to Reaction Motors, in Pompton Lakes, New Jersey, as a resident engineer, how Smith contributed, not to the basic design of the engine, but to making it reliable enough to trust in an airplane carrying a man.

"We, however, had been working on a parallel program at Bell just as insurance," he continues. "We began developing a rocket power plant of our own. On the second day I'd been assigned to the project, Stuart K. Etelson, who was in charge of Bell's rocket engine program, invited me out to the test cell to see one cylinder of the Bell engine run."

Frost's voice goes calmly on and you move back with him into remembered time, step with him into danger beyond the wire fence rimming the area around the cell, a warning line stacked with extinguishers and fire picks. Within the fence, three weathered fire shacks and a thick revetment built around the cell. The cell itself, a pillbox half-buried in the ground, its rounded dome and textured walls glaring in sunlight, topped with a siren howling in the air.

Inside the cell were three compartments, one housing the propellant tanks, another the engine on its stand. The third, separated from the engine compartment by a foot-thick concrete wall, held instruments. In this third cell five men were crowded, Frost, Etelson, three other engineers. They gave him, Frost says, a gauge to read and went on with their mysterious business—much opening of valves, adjusting of regulators, and the strange noise of gas rushing through its lines. Above all this the siren howled its warning in the air.

The engine began then with a tremendous shrieking roar. Even Frost knew something had gone wrong and everything urged him to run. But he stayed as the others nervously worked to avoid catastrophe. At the last hurried moment the propellant valves were suddenly turned off.

The resulting water hammer ruptured a two-inch line and alcohol shot under pressre into the crowded cell. The fumes were sickening, the fear of fire and explosion even worse.

"As the new project engineer," Frost says. "I could not be the first one to run out of there. I tried to stay out of the way while they worked frantically to shut off lines, get rid of gas pressure, operate the fire-extinguisher system which would not work. They knew what to do. I simply stood there waiting. And let me assure you, gentlemen, I waited most anxiously for some sort of a signal to get the hell out of that cell."

It was Etelson who finally said, "We'd better go." And the five engineers came tumbling together through the narrow door. There was a wild race for safety then, the gasping for air while fear died down. Then furious activity as someone called out, "Fire!" In wild confusion the men ran after fire extinguishers stacked along the fence. Untended hoses snaked on the ground, tangled and snarled. One hose burst suddenly, exploding fear.

And in the midst of this a tall young engineer, the scientist type dressed in a blue serge suit, a high shirt collar, vest and rimless glasses, his Phi Beta Kappa and Tau Beta Pi keys swinging on his watch chain, came leading a volunteer crew dragging a six-inch firehose through a foot of mud to put out the flame in the burning cell.

"This scholarly character and his crew," Frost now recalls, "brought their hose up to one end of the cell as another crew reached the door on the opposite side. The scholar opened his nozzle. The other crew opened their door just in time to receive the full force of that six-inch hose.

"But there were," he says, "no cowards in the crowd. In spite of the wild confusion and the real danger of explosion, the fire was put out, the Bell engine saved." And Frost goes on, remembering more, bringing it briefly back to life, talking at random and without design, without any purpose except to awaken interest and to impart the mood of the men who have built the ship.

But the effect of this, as he continues, is to make everyone aware that something tremendous has been done against tremendous odds, that the story of this project, the history of the plane, is a story of danger and a history of risk. He tells you now, for example, how the plane was brought to Muroc in October of the year before, how on the very next day the first test flight began with a minor error, finished almost with a final, tremendous bang. The pilot was Goodlin. Stanley flew chase in a slow P-51. Frost paced the tower, a microphone gripped in one sweating hand, unable to ask what delayed the drop, unable to hear the pilots talk. He could only guess which of innumerable parts and pieces might have failed.

"I could not," Frost says, "communicate directly with the X-1 and the chase plane simultaneously on the channel that had been assigned to us. We've since corrected this but at that time, although the P-51 and the B-29 could talk to each other and to the X-1 during flight, we in the tower could not listen in. Goodlin, Dow and the pilot flying chase had to switch channels to talk to anyone down on the field. Had we been able to listen to them, we might have avoided a bad ten minutes for Slick, for all of us."

For by the time the B-29 had reached launch altitude of 20,000 feet, there was below-sea-level pressure in the cabin of the X-1. Not knowing what had happened or what else could be done to lower the pressure in his plane, Goodlin decided to jettison the cabin door.

Chains used to lower the door from the bomb bay of the B-29 were carefully attached. Goodlin moved the release handle. And locked until now on 3,000 pounds of cabin pressure, the door shot out, smacked the welded aircraft-steel boarding ladder with a tremendous sock that bent it back beyond the pilot's reach. Goodlin looked out, saw only that wind-swept gap and the ground below, decided to stay in the cockpit while Dow landed the B-29 with the X-1 still attached.

Casually, Frost goes on, from this remembered danger skipping to another, telling you now how the crash landing of both planes was barely averted on the Bell crew's first powered flight. "It was to be," he says, "a great event. Directors of the company came out from Buffalo with Larry Bell. But the X-1 was never even dropped. The valve admitting nitrogen gas into the lox tank froze."

With no gas entering to force lox back to the rocket engine, the cylinders could not be fired. Goodlin could not even jettison lox to avoid the danger of explosion as the B-29, still carrying the X-1, came down to land. This had been done before but never with heavy and highly explosive propellants and fuel aboard. To add to the difficulty, the nose wheel of the X-1 dropped down.

Frost, flying chase, told Goodlin to pull up the gear. He pulled it up. The nose wheel dropped again. Even with this nose wheel retracted there is less than eight inches of clearance under the X-1 when it's mated to the B-29. If the wheel stayed down, it might rip the X-1 out of the B-29. Both planes would crash.

"You'll never get down that way," Bell warned from the tower.

Frost thought he knew what could be done. The up-lock holding the nose wheel would not engage. But if Goodlin retracted the gear just as the B-29 came in to land, the wheel would be almost up as the B-29 touched down.

"Can we try that?" he asked Larry Bell.

Bell said, "Try anything that will work."

The gear stayed up. Bell waited long enough to learn what had happened. "Keep trying," he said and hurried his worried directors home to Buffalo. Two days later, the flight was repeated.

"It was," Frost says, "a routine operation." The plane caught fire in midair.

It is routine, you understand, as he concludes at last, for something to go wrong on a normal flight in the X-1. The ship is dangerous. One rubber disk torn or a faulty part, a drop of fuel sucked from a dripping cylinder back into the fuselage, a lock improperly installed can kill, destroy with a blast or scatter the lives of half a dozen men with scraps of steel, smashed engines, burning rubber, fabric, human flesh and boiling hot magnesium across the desert or the red surface of the dry lake bed.

But Frost says now, "This afternoon we will begin with the ship, see how it is built, what makes it fly."

And danger is forgotten. You can hardly wait.

20

For the first time now you begin to see what's under the skin of the fastest airplane in the world, how each component functions in air frame and power plant, how the whole works together with precise complexity, how the 6,000 pounds of thrust exploded from its stubby tail will force the foil of its slender nose through the sound barrier and beyond.

Back from a hurried lunch in the service club, you find a chalk sketch of the X-1 on the blackboard, cross sections of the wing and tail. In these ground classes—Frost is waiting as you come in—you will learn all he knows about the plane, take each component in its turn, study and see each part itself, not just a schematic diagram or sketch. As often as possible you will go out to the ship itself. And the first lecture begins on the basic air frame—wings, stabilizer, fuselage and vertical fin.

For the first time now the project comes to life. This schoolroom lecture is as much the beginning of something you've waited for as the first student flight or combat briefing was. This, you can tell yourself, is it. Time falls away as Frost goes on, and walls recede. Your mind slips for a moment from the present, leaves ground with the B-29—the X-1 drops, its engine blasts and the plane shoots up into the dustless, deepening blue of altitude, then glides to earth again and stands with fuel still dripping from its tail, its nose still pointing to the beckoning curve of space.

"It is of conventional, mid-wing design," Frost's voice

155

is saying now. "The difference between this air frame and that of any other plane is only a difference of strength."

Nothing in this first lecture is new to you, none of it difficult to understand. But there is continually rising interest as Frost patiently disposes of those obvious facts that wrap the secret of the X-1's speed. The tension mounts and expectation holds off weariness, dragged like a weight all through the last few days. With the plane still in your mind, you leave the classroom late that afternoon, talk with the others though sunset, dusk and the first hours of darkness until at last speech lags and with unfinished thought you fall asleep.

In the morning you go back to school. The lecture is on flight controls—flaps, rudder, elevators, ailerons. At noon you rush to the service club again, talk through big bites of sandwiches and gulps of milk, through sips of coffee and half-finished cigarettes. Then you rush back to class, listen again, learn something more about the ship. That night there is more talk and argument, all of you wondering at what you've heard, guessing at what you've yet to learn in the next session of the class. This is the pattern, the routine that will go on for days. It never varies except with brief excursions out to the ship to see, into the hangar or out on the concrete apron to do the things you've discussed in class. And listening always, you impatiently learn each aspect of the X-1's flight.

On the third morning Frost starts with the power plant. Up on the blackboard there is a sketch now of the airplane in side view, a cross section showing the pressure vessels, their position in the ship, the piping that connects them. You will spend some time on this, Frost warns. It is an important part of the power system in the plane. It is the system developed, as you know, in place of the turbine pump that had been specified to force fuel under pressure into the rocket chambers of the ship. You remember how the decision was made to pressurize the tanks, how the nitrogen evaporator was developed, the principle on which it works. You know that pressure vessels were placed throughout the airplane, wherever there was room. You know, too, that gas is stored in these at 4,500 psi.

This high pressure storage system, you learn next, is connected by welded, stainless steel tubing. There are no joints, no removable connections until the first stage regulator is reached. The function of this regulator is to reduce gas pressure from 4,500 down to the 1,500 psi at which it is first used to feed auxiliary systems in the ship and to retract the landing gear and flaps.

"Here is a regulator," Frost says, showing you how it looks. It is a commercial product, a simple item but extremely important in the plane.

"This," Frost continues—and you thank Heaven you know what a regulator is as your mind slips back for a moment to all the hours you worked with your dad—"is simply a valve that opens and shuts in demand for a given output pressure."

You take it apart in class, study each piece—the forged body and its dome, the valve, stem, springs, back-up plate and diaphragm. Then you go on to learn what can go wrong with it, that if dirt settles between the valve and its seat, it won't shut off. Pressure builds up. If this continues, the lox tank, for example, might blow up. If the lox tank explodes, you, the plane and the project too will all blow with it into kingdom come.

"We hope, of course—" Frost grins—"that the relief valve will pop and the frangible disk will rupture, relieving pressure before the tank blows up. But these safety devices might not work."

If this does happen, if the lox tank pressure increases, creeps up to 340 or 350 psi, where the relief valve is supposed to pop, and if dome pressure is where it ought to be, you spill the dome. If that doesn't work—and it won't if dirt holds the valve open—you start the engine. Lox is used at such a rate that it will more than make up for any gas leakage through the regulator. If you can't start the engine, jettison lox.

"You can wait," Frost says, "for the relief valve and frangible disk to blow. But that is dangerous procedure."

There is a second weakness in the regulator. Its rubber diaphragm might rupture, tear where it's clamped down or where it bends up over the back-up plate. If this happens, pressure will equalize. The regulator will close. This is a fail-safe condition. It will not cause pressure to increase. But the ship won't fly. The pilot will have to jettison his fuels. If the rupture is severe enough, you may not be able to jettison all the fuel. You should, however, be able to get down to a reasonable landing weight, to get back on the ground and replace the diaphragm.

Through with the regulator now, Frost takes you back to the first stage of the pressure system and you trace its course throughout the ship, follow the diagram down to the second stage regulators. There are two of these—their function, to reduce gas pressure from 1,500 to 330 psi used in the lox and fuel tanks and to extend the gear and flaps. Since these are retracted with 1,500 psi, this smaller amount of pressure is just to insure that the free-falling gear goes down, to make certain it will stay. But even at that, Frost carefully admits, the system doesn't always work.

Then you go on back through the ship, tracing the gas to still another regulator that brings pressure down to go psi to operate the stabilizer actuator, an air-motor and screwjack affair. Frost shows you how this works. And you go on to the auxiliary functions, to operation, for example, of the jettison valves for lox and water-alcohol.

There is one other important gas function, Frost finally explains. In the cockpit there is a regulator reducing the first stage pressure from 1,500 to 400 or 420 psi to supply bleed pressure to the rocket engine. This is a constant source of gas flow through the engine prior to its operation. This bleed pressure must be higher than the 330 or 335 psi of the lox and fuel tanks, in order to keep the lines purged, prevent the danger of liquid oxygen seeping into the fuel line or vice versa. And that is the basic system. That is the system designed to replace the turbine pump for the development of which there's been no time to wait. Without this relatively crude idea of evaporating nitrogen into gas, condensing it under tremendous pressure, and reducing pressure through this complex set of regulating valves, the lox and fuel could not be fed back to the engine and the ship would not be flying now. But for this system, the whole project would have been delayed.

And having gone through it once, you go back through it again, from the screen-mesh filter downstream of the filling point where gas enters the ship, through the first needle valve on the cockpit panel into the first stage regulator, on to the second stage regulators, into the fuel and lox tanks and from that stage off to the auxiliary systems it supplies. Then you go through it again, retracing over and over its course throughout the ship until you know by heart exactly what happens from the moment nitrogen gas first centers the filling point until it has finally left the plane.

Now you go through the whole system again, this time considering each of the safety devices for each of the pressure stages—the pop relief valves and frangible or blowout disks that protect the ship. You study the couplings and the valves, methodically inspecting each so that by the time you've finished, you're certain you know where everything is, what each part does, how each can fail, what you must do if it ever does.

Then you go out to the ship itself, sit in the cabin, crack the first needle valve. And you know precisely what happens as you follow imagined nitrogen gas, thinking ahead, tracing aloud its flow all through the line, touching each separate part with your hand as you check it off. Back in the classroom, then, you draw on the board thin-lined and at first uncertain diagrams—the fuel system from start to finish, the lox system, each auxiliary line—until you have finally learned all this so well that you can give immediate answers to the questions Frost throws at the class.

If you can't answer, he'll ask again. He never lets go, won't let you rest until he's certain you know all you will ever have to know. There is no final examination in this course, just the continual, ultimate test that actual flight will finally impose. You'll either be clobbered or you won't. Frost, facing this, can only question you, hoping to fix in your mind each part of the plane on which your life will depend, each item that might fail.

"Chuck, what do you do if the lox tank pressure increases? Gets up to where the relief valve is supposed to pop?"

"You spill the dome."

"And if that doesn't work? What does that mean?"

"There's dirt in the valve."

"And what do you do if there is?"

"You start the engine or you jettison lox."

Through with the power plant gas-pressure system, you go on to something else, to the electrical system in the plane, to its hydraulic system and to the rocket engine, finally, studying each of its parts, seeing how each of them works and how they work together, exploding lox and fuel into 6,000 pounds of thrust. Back and forth you go over the ship day after day, tracing the plane from tail to nose and back again, adding each time to the simplicity with which the first outline began. Each day's knowledge overlays the things you learned the day before; so that into the simple air frame with which Frost began the X-1's whole complexity is finally charted, diagrammed, etched into your mind until this airplane in which you've never flown becomes, at last, as familiar to you as all the ships you've piloted, from the first Ryan in which you learned to fly to the Mustang in which you fought and from the Mustang to all the rest you're qualified to fly—conventional fighters, F-47, F-61, F-63 and XF8B-1; transports, C-47 and C-54; bombers, B-17, B-24 and B-25, B-29, B-45, B-52; jet fighters, the P-59, P-80, and P-83 and 84, P-86, P-92, F-91 and 94; jet bombers, the B-43 and the B-45.

But you've not ready yet, Frost says, to pilot the X-1. There is one more gap in your education, a gap filled now with constant practice of the things you'll do, not just in flight but from the moment a flight is scheduled until it's been completed and you're on the ground.

"A typical flight begins," Frost says, "the moment the last flight ends. The ship is examined immediately, gone over with great care as crewmen search for leaks, for ruptured diaphragms, for anything that might not work on the next flight. It is tested again on the ground, its engine fired before the next air drop. Then it is mated, attached to the B-29, its nitrogen system pressurized again and its lox and fuel tanks filled. All of this takes time. And for all these hours in sometimes days of preparation, there is at last a mere twelve or fifteen minutes in the air, less than three minutes of actual powered flight in the X-1."

There is, therefore, a careful plan for each of the steps that leads to the brief objective of a two-minute high-speed run at altitude. Procedures for loading and servicing both the X-1 and the B-29 have been fully developed, sharpened in weeks of practice by the crew of ten men who service the ship for Bell. Procedures for the flight routine have been developed, too. Each step in each procedure has been written down and there's a mimeographed script or write-up for every member of the Air Force crew, telling each man just what he'll do in every operation down on the ground or in the air. There is a write-up for the pilot of the X-1, for the pilot and co-pilot of the B-29, for the pilots flying chase, high chase above and ahead of the B-29 and low chase at its tail. There's a write-up for the B-29 flight engineer, for its crew chief and for the scanners in its tail, for the X-1 crew chief, who will ride in the bomber on every drop, for each mechanic and technician in the ground crews of the plane. There is a script for everyone.

And there is laughter when the write-ups are handed out, some awkwardness and much self-consciousness in the first classroom rehearsal you all go through together. But the group settles down at last, runs through the whole procedure several times, each man in his turn taking cue from another man, reading aloud each step of the job he'll do, moving in clumsy pantomime through every move he'll have to make. Then you go out to the apron and to the planes themselves, to the X-1 and to the B-29, go through the whole procedure again and again until each one of you knows just what his part in a typical flight will be.

It isn't easy. None of it is. From the first lecture to the last, it's one of the toughest things you have ever had to do, this learning of something entirely new under the pressure of time and of your own determination not to fail. You're not satisfied—and neither is Frost—until you know the plane from tail to nose, inside and out, and the whole flight takes form and shape within your mind, the whole carefully rehearsed, remembered movement from that moment you leave the quiet ship at rest on the landing strip until its small wheels touch again the hard-packed, red and welcome surface of the dry lake bed. And even then you can't relax.

For now, you fly.

21

You've practiced it over and over again. But it isn't easy to climb down into the X-1 while it's mated to the B-29. Even when both planes are at rest and sitting firmly on the ground, it's difficult. In actual flight it's worse. There is wind to contend with and there's fear.

At the last moment, just before take-off time, you jam your oxygen mask and helmet behind the pilot's seat in the X-1 so they won't work loose and roll through the open door while the plane is being carried up. You can reach them easily once inside the cabin.

That done, you climb into the B-29 and put on your chute. Then you sit down wherever you can and wait. Just sitting with nothing to do, you begin to tighten up. You're honestly frightened of the drop. And on this first glide flight you're just as worried about the business of getting down into the plane. Sitting alone you think uneasily of wind blast under the bomb bay, of sliding down on that ladder and of climbing into the ship.

There's some diversion as Cardenas fires the engines and the big bomber turns. He taxis off. The take-off roll begins. But once in the air, you tighten up again. And your anxiety keeps mounting as the B-29 climbs up to altitude. Fear is an old companion in the air. All men who fly know what it is. The feeling is always there, just under the surface of your mind, ready to flare up at the first sight or sound of danger. You'd be a fool to say you've never been afraid. And yet you never admit it when you are, none of you do. It's one of your rules, if there are any, not to come out and say, "I'm scared." You don't even like to admit it to yourself.

Because fear feeds on fear, it fattens on itself. Fear can destroy you and the plane. And it's contagious, one man can give it to another. Sometimes when everyone around you is frightened of something, smoke or fire, a belly landing or gear that won't go down, you can almost smell it, feel it in the air. If one man breaks, it's that much worse for everyone to keep a grip on his own fear.

So you build barriers within yourself, the conviction that no one else is frightened. Why should you be? And you pretend that you're really not. Sometimes you admit that all the rest are worried and the grip of your own fear weakens somehow and let's go. Most of the time you don't even know it's there.

You've flown so many hours through so many years with fear that it comes to seem perfectly normal, like an old pair of shoes. You've got them on but you don't really feel them on your feet until you have to run. That's the way fear is in the air. It's always there but it never bothers you until it bothers you. Then it makes every minute worse.

You're never badly frightened as long as there is something you can do, some action you can take against whatever it is that's dangerous, going on with the business of piloting the plane. But when you just sit waiting with nothing to think about except the danger that faces you, then fear slips up into your mind. It begins with tension and uneasiness. Your stomach tightens and you begin to sweat. Your mouth is dry. But you don't think of fear itself. You've simply got to move. You have to do something— walk, talk, tie your shoe or pare your fingernails. If you can't do anything else, you watch the man who has something to do.

On the take-off roll you sit there. The B-29 begins to roll. You're getting accelerations now that add to your uneasiness. Your muscles tighten. You hang onto the box, the bench on which you sit. You haven't fastened your safety belt. You should. There's a regulation that requires it. But you never do. You slide along on the box until the bomber picks up speed. Then you just watch the pilot up in the cockpit of the B-29, watch him take off and, once in a while, you look back through that door into the bomb bay where the X-1 hangs, always expecting it's going to fall right out of there. That may be just because sometimes you wish it would.

Airborne, finally, you stand, walk nervously around, easing the tension, hurrying things along. At 5,000 feet you can say gratefully, "Well, let's get going, Jack," and step back into the bomb bay where the first danger really lies. Gingerly walking along the catwalk now, you make a point of not looking down through the gap between the plans. It's cold back there. The small steel ladder, on which you drop down to the level of the cabin door, slides in a frame, a set of tracks. Designed to drop down under your weight, it's cold and stiff. The ladder sticks.

"Hell, jump on it!" Ridley shouts.

You bounce on the platform and with a sickening lurch slip down to the open cabin door. All other sounds are lost now in the engines' roar and in the wind. You swear and cannot hear yourself. Even with all your clothing and equipment on—G suit and pressure suit, coveralls and parachute—it's cold on the platform. The wind whips past, pulls at your clothing as you bend to enter the narrow door, through which you crawl.

There is a certain way you have to get into the X-1. You put your right hand up inside the door, hold on tight to the top of its frame. You slide in feet first, your left hand still holding the ladder behind your back. There is a bad moment as you release your right-hand grip, shift your weight from the ladder into the plane. You don't look down. Once in the plane, you scoot around, bending your body double to turn and slide across the floor and into the pilot's seat. That much is over, you think, until you have to do it again.

You straighten your parachute now, get into its shoulder harness, pull it down, fasten the safety belt, then wriggle around until you're comfortable. Just like a dog before it settles down. You fasten the oxygen-mask clip and the dehydrator-hose clip, reach for your helmet, shake out the mask and put them on. Each move more tiring now, you plug in the mask and hook it up to the oxygen, all this is difficult. Your hands seem weighted and your arms.

But Ridley comes down the ladder then to fix the door. Looking down through the canopy above your head, Ridley can see that you're finally set. He lowers the door on its cable, follows it down the ladder to manhandle it into place. You reach out to help him, catching the door as it hangs in air. Heavy and solid as it is, it bumps and bounces in the wind.

Outside there is not much room in which to work. The B-29 climbs steadily at 200 miles an hour or more. It's cold and windy and the air is thin. Jack works without oxygen. Pushing with feet and hands against the ladder, his back shoving against the door, he makes a lever of himself until at last the door slams into its frame. You lock it shut and peck at the canopy overhead. Ridley, still standing on his precarious perch, catches your signal, unhooks the chain with which he lowered the door, then through the thinning air climbs wearily back into the bomb bay of the B-29.

You've turned on the radio meanwhile, plugged in your headset and its microphone. "Okay, Cardenas," you call the B-29. "How do you read me?" There will be no more first names until you're on the ground. Chuck, Jack and Dick all sound too much alike in the metallic voices that come through the air, and there are just too many Bobs.

"I read you loud and clear," Cardenas answers. "How did it go?"

"Rough. Really rough. Is Ridley all right?"

"Ridley says he's tired out."

"You can say that again." Ridley comes on the air. "Wasn't too bad, though, Yeager. We'll get used to it."

"Ridley," you answer, "I will never get used to that!"

You call Frost now, and Hoover, check with the tower on the ground, make sure you're in radio contact with everyone. "Its dark in here," you complain to Frost. "I can hardly see."

"I know you'll be tempted," he advises, "but don't

look out into the sky. You'll be blinded a moment when you drop. But you know the cockpit thoroughly now. It won't be bad."

"Roger. Making my check now." There is no power on this flight. You will merely drop out and glide back to the ground. All you have to do on this check of the plane and its control, therefore, is to see that the landing gear handle is in the *up* position, that you have plenty of oxygen breathing pressure, that the voltage is up. You then place the cabin pressure valve at the door in the *pressurized* position. You vent the cabin and check your bail-out bottle, a reserve supply of oxygen strapped to your leg. It is tied to your parachute too and plugged into your mask, ten minutes' emergency supply of oxygen in case you have to bail out—if you can get through that narrow door.

"Completed my check list," you report to Frost. "Everything is okay." At 15,000 feet there is nothing to do now but sit and wait.

"B-29 to Muroc Tower," Cardenas calls, giving the bomber's position to the field, to NACA and to Hoover and Frost. "We are at 16,000 feet," he tells the two chase planes. "Fire up and come on."

It is dark in the cockpit of the X-1. You begin to realize that it's cold. Forgetting Frost's advice, you look out curiously and see a slot of bright and blinding light on either side, and the propellers spinning on your right and left. If one of those props comes off, you tell yourself, it will slice right through this cockpit, chop the plane to bits. It never has happened, you think, and it probably never will. But it would make a big mess of everything in here if it did. Including you.

You can't sit waiting for that. Better get busy, you tell yourself, practice the drop.

And you practice neutralizing the X-1's controls, sit firmly in your seat, arms and body in position, feeling the quick response of flight controls to every move you make. Right about there, you think, feeling the stick in neutral. That's the position for the drop. You set the stick again and again.

Then you go around the cockpit once more, go through

the check list a second time as Hoover, down on the ground, calls the tower. He's ready to take off.

"Muroc Tower. Air Force two-zero-one. Taxi instructions."

Frost calls in with him. But Frost stays in the background as much as he can, leaving this first flight up to the Air Force crew, letting you get the feel of the flight, build confidence in the planes you will fly and in yourselves.

"Two-zero-one, cleared runway six," the tower calls. "Winds are out of the east at seven miles an hour."

"Am I cleared to line up and roll?" Hoover asks.

"Roger," the tower answers.

A few minutes later, airborne and climbing to altitude with Frost in his F-80 on his wing, Hoover calls to the B-29, "Where are you? What is your position?"

Looking out again, you blink at the light, examine the ground below. "Looks to me, Hoover," you answer, "as though we're sitting over Rosamund Lake at 18,000 feet."

"Roger. See you now. I'll be right there."

"Yeager?" It is Ridley again. "How are you doing?"

"Why just fine," you answer, blinded again by the bright sunlight. "I haven't a worry in the world."

Hoover takes care of that, shoots out of nowhere to make a quick pass at the B-29 as he goes past. Just shining his fanny, you think. But the B-29 climbs with a sudden, frightening jolt into the jet wash of Hoover's plane.

"Hoover, you bastard!" you shout at him, angry with fear. "If I weren't stuck here like a setting duck, I'd shoot you down! I'd really clobber you!"

"Well, drop out, buddy!" Hoover calls back. "Come and get me."

Off in the distance you see him flipping his wings at you. He waves and yaws and rolls his F-80 around in the sky.

"Just look at that," you say with envious disgust.

"Yeager—" Ridley comes on to reassure you—"take this thing easy, now. You want to make one more check?" Talking, talking, his steady voice goes on. "Got anything on your mind?"

"I'm going to get that Hoover one of these days," you

promise him. "I got that on my mind." But you're not really angry any more.

And Frost comes in from time to time to remind you or to suggest. "Don't look out. I'll tell you where we are. I'm right back on your tail." You want very much to know where you are. The B-29 is grinding, climbing to altitude. You want to make sure Cardenas stays within gliding distance of the lake. If something happens, if you are inadvertently dropped, you want to be able to glide back down and land again. But there is nothing to worry about. The B-29 climbs in a steady spiral centered above the lake. NACA radar tracks the bomber as it climbs, calling in every few minutes to make another radio check. "NACA radar to B-29, eight-zero-zero. How do you read?"

"Loud and clear," Cardenas answers, or, "I read you fine."

"You okay, Yeager?" Ridley asks again.

"Just doing fine. They ought to ground that Hoover, though. They really should. He ain't got sense enough to fly."

"I'll ground you," Hoover says.

"Boy, that will be the day!"

"Stick around."

"You guys just listen to that. He's asking for it."

"Five minutes to drop," Cardenas says.

You're frankly scared. You lick dry lips and wait, setting yourself in position again, checking controls, squirming uncomfortably in your seat. Just about there, you tell yourself, resetting the stick again.

"Three minutes," Cardenas warns.

You sit and wait.

"Two minutes."

"All right down there, Yeager?" Ridley asks.

"Yeah, sure," you answer as casually as you can. "All set."

"Starting the count-down." Cardenas begins to count. Your body stiffens into position for the drop. "Ten," he begins. Your hands freeze on the controls. "Nine—eight—" You're anxious and still scared. "Seven—six—five—" But you're excited now, eager to get it over with. "Four—"

Cardenas counts. It seems as if there's a minute between each of the numbers in his count.

"Three," Cardenas says.

Come on, come on, you think. Let's get it over with. Let's drop this thing!

"Two." Cardenas finally finishes. "One."

From the time he says, "Drop!" until something happens it seems as if whole slow minutes have gone by. Then there's a great big crack, more of a thump, really, or a snap like when you pull a strand of wire apart that suddenly breaks. The X-1 drops. You leave the seat, hunch down, expecting to crack the canopy with your head. You don't, of course. You just float up to the canopy, just barely touch it as you drop out into a roller-coaster ride. The plane drops. You can't see a thing and the bright sunlight burns your eyes. You have this weird sensation of floating or hanging in the air. Your heart's in your mouth, your stomach right behind it, choking your throat. And your hands grip the stick so hard your fingers hurt.

Then you begin to see again. Your body sinks back down into the seat. You're all right now, heart and stomach are back where they belong. You're flying. It's suddenly wonderful. To Frost's surprise you do three slow rolls in a row. Then Hoover comes up from nowhere and you break right into him and laugh.

"The best damn airplane I ever flew," Jack Woolams said. And you agree with him as you go through the flight plan typed on the card strapped to your knee.

But you tense up for the landing again. It's suppose to be tough to land. The visibility is bad, marginal, they said. You have no trouble. The X-1 almost lands itself. Fear forgotten and anxiety gone, you leave the ship regretfully. You've flown the plane and it's been wonderful. "Like nothing I've ever flown," you tell Frost later that night.

But on the next glide flight you go back through the whole routine again, back through anxiety and fear. There is the unpleasant anticipation of the drop, the careful preparation, jamming your helmet and mask behind the seat in the cockpit of the plane, the unwilling climb into the B-29, the nervous waiting to take off, the slow and irritating climb to altitude, the pacing up to 5,000 feet until there is finally something to do.

Then there's the walk back into the bomb bay, the cold, the sudden roar. You bounce on the ladder again, slide down again into the wind. Again, the contortion of your body, the twisting and squirming into the plane, the fear again as the B-29 climbs for the second drop. This time it's just as bad. You know what to wait for now as you go through the motions, practice the set of your body, the feeling of the controls. Once more Bob Hoover makes a wild pass at the B-29 and you ride through his jet wash swearing and scared. Once more you carefully check the list as Ridley and Frost talk reassurance into your head. And all this while you're tensed up, waiting to hear, "Three—two—one. Drop!" Waiting to hear that separating snap. And you're all hunched down against expected shock, certain this time your head will smack that canopy. So your whole body flinches this time when Cardenas finally calls out, "Drop!"

But once again from the moment of drop it's wonderful. The X-1 is a beautiful plane to fly. On the long glide back down to the dry lake bed, a feeling of sudden exuberance takes hold of you. Hoover, flying on your wing, looks down into your cockpit, asking, "How does it feel?"

Grinning, you put both feet high on the instrument panel of the plane and wave both hands in the air. "Hoover!" you call back. "Look, no hands."

On the third glide flight you wait for Hoover to come up on your wing, then without warning make an abrupt and unexpected pass at him. And you come dogfighting all the way down to the ground.

"Absolutely," you tell Frost that night, "the best damn airplane I ever flew. How about turning the power on? How about making a powered flight in the thing tomorrow morning, Dick?"

But Frost says no. "We'll do this by the book. Besides," he adds, "your orders are in. You can go back home this week and get your family."

22

You've dreamed about going home for weeks, felt somehow guilty ever since that lonely night you called your wife to say good-by. You've called as often as you could since then, written whenever there was time. But now, as you leave the base to go back home, you feel more lonesome than you've ever been, and more divided and confused.

Beneath the sound of its engines as the plane takes off from Muroc, you can hear again your son's voice crying loneliness and wish again that you were home. But even so, the fat little X-1 sits explicitly within your mind, you hear Cardenas counting, "Three—two—one. Drop!" as Donald cries and the slow ship in which you ride turns into the east and grinds its way along.

Held now to the slower pace of normal speed and everyday routine, you wait with restlessness for the dull hours to move slowly past, for the tempo set at Muroc to die down and for the taut spring of your impatience to unwind. And all the while you see alternate glimpses in your mind of Glennis, Donald, home, spliced between scenes of wild activity, the preparation of the X-1 for its flight, the climb to altitude, the drop. Neither in Hamlin nor in Muroc now, you're caught once more between the two halves of your life, pulled one way, then another, from air to ground and back again, not even knowing what it is that knots your stomach as the plane flies steadily along.

For what is there on the secure and quiet ground that can compare with flight? So much of your life has been lived with speed and at altitude that in the whole cata-

172

logue of things men do for a living down on the ground there is nothing to measure now with flight, nothing to match it's last bright promise, to outdistance sound, to do this alone, to do this first. Given your first half-hour in the air and the years between, you'd want to make this flight even if it might be your last. You don't believe it will. You're sure of the plane and certain of yourself.

But if you leave down on the ground the calm and quiet of your home, your wife and sons and all their happiness, you fly with fear and with the second fear of its reacting consequence in your own mind and on their lives. So that now you sweat through idle minutes of uncertainty, not knowing whether to ground yourself or not, whether to live with the risk or quit this business, which is all you know, whether the simple questioning of yourself alone will—as you think it will—make you a better pilot than you've ever been, or whether it won't.

It's a rat race that goes on and on, this questioning to which you sink in moments of fatigue. You add again the small account that stands between your family and the years ahead—a few hundred dollars in the bank; a National Service Life Insurance policy paid at the rate of seventy dollars a month; a pension—only a fraction of your pay— and another ten dollars apiece for each of the boys each month. It isn't much. But that's all there is. That is, that's all of it. Glennis would have one hell of a time with nothing but grief and three hundred dollars a month. You add the figures again, come up with even less. There is at the end of this deary calculation only your own conviction that Glennis understands, accepts with you the risk with which you live together. One question remains, Do you have any right to ask her to? And the whole thing begins again until at last your mind slips back to Muroc and you see again the X-1 hugging the belly of the B-29, feel once again its cockpit small and compact around you, sense the small plane's pulse and pressure as it comes to life in air.

"My God!" you say aloud, facing again the sense of guilt, appalled at the ease with which you slip even in thought away to fly the plane.

"How's that?" the pilot asks you.

"Nothing," you answer. "Just thinking about the problems I've got."

"You've got problems?" the pilot answers. "Here, fly this thing awhile."

You take the controls. Kansas slips past, a piece of Missouri. It would be, you think, one hell of a note to auger in in this old crate, funny. But damn few would appreciate the joke. It happens too often that casual disrespect for slow and simple planes creeps without notice into the mind of a pilot accustomed to fly at speed and altitude.

"Remember this about airplanes," the old man told you once. "They're all potentially dangerous as soon as they leave the ground. All you've got to be to prang an aircraft is up in the air. Speed doesn't mean a thing; the closer you fly to the ground, the higher the risk." You can almost see the colonel as he talks, realize with a sudden start that you're guilty as hell of the very thing he meant.

"Take it for awhile," you tell the pilot, and sink back into yourself, plagued once again with the same old doubt as the same conflict rides haphazard through your mind. Once more you shoot like a shuttlecock from air to ground and back again, your mind divided, your emotions all confused. It is a feeling that lasts until you open the door at home. And then it's gone.

"Hey, Donald!" Glennis shouts with arms outstretched, "your daddy's home!" And he comes scooting around the corner, barely able to run on his eighteen-month-old legs.

Then you begin to talk and the whole past and all hope for the future tumbles out in a rush of words. "What an airplane! It flies itself. Nothing to worry about," you say, "built to take 18 *g*'s, more than the pilot can take. You couldn't prang it if you tried. And listen, honey, there's a house in Rosamund, twenty miles from the base. You can get up in the morning and shoot quail from the kitchen door! Jack rabbits—" You spread your hands—"as big as dogs! Cool in the morning and at night. And the desert all around. It grows on you, honey. It will be wonderful for the kids."

Long after dark you sit, still talking together of all the

things you've seen and done, your mother and father
proud to have you home, content to listen as you and
Glennis trade moments from the past, the lore of the
project for stories about the boys.

"Bright orange," you say. "Built like a brick house,
solid, strong."

"Mickey eats like a young horse," Glennis answers.

"Son," your dad says, "when are you coming home
again?"

And your mother keeps saying, "You be careful, son."

"There's nothing to worry about," you say, and go on
talking as if talk alone would bring to your family all the
time you've lost. Glennis knows what you mean. A long
time after you've gone to bed you lie in the darkness,
talking away each other's loneliness and fears.

Then at last there's the business of getting away, the
shipping of boxes, the packing of heavy crates, the cradle
for Mickey slung in the car, the bed on the seat for Don.
And there are all the good-bys to be said.

"Be careful, son." Your mother is anxious still.

"It's a shame you have to go." Your father is still as
proud.

There's the last-minute rush, the feeling of homesickness
with which you finally leave. And the long, long drive
together back to the coast, a drive through cities and
towns you've seen only briefly from the air, on roads that
have been only thin strips on the ground or red lines on a
printed map. It's a holiday, the only one you've ever really
had. You tell her about the house again, the sunsets and
the quail, the big jack rabbits and the way the sun paints
red and blue on the desert rock and sand. And your
impatience suddenly expands again, runs riot as you race
through the last hundred miles, rush into Rosamund and
finally stop.

"Well, there it it," you say. "Let's go in and make
ourselves at home."

But Glennis walks carefully from room to room and
you can feel with her the rented emptiness, the barren
ground and the dried shoulder of the world that rolls with
infinite harshness into the distant hills. Even at five

o'clock on an August night you can feel the heat of the sun at midday, the coldness of the night.

"Well," Glennis says, composing disappointment on her face into a smile, "it's lovely." And you can see her measuring curtains in her mind, weighing the dust and sand that will have to be scrubbed from the floor, rubbed out of woodwork, swept from closets and from halls. And all around there is the desert to come drifting in again through cracks and crevices, whenever you open a window, open a door. "Anyway—" She smiles again—"it's ours."

But when you've left she'll be alone, cut off from the world that might as well not be there if she can't move into it. You'll have the car. What will she do then, you wonder briefly, stranded alone in this isolated house? Worry and shrug it off, worry again and shrug it off again, filling the emptiness of daytime with smaller worries, lesser things to do. There are the boys to be fed and dressed, sand to be scrubbed out and the dust, dishes to wash and clothes to be ironed and pressed.

And there will always be fear of the telephone—the fear that this day-long loneliness might run on into the night and into days and years ahead. So that finally even the dull and routine trips into the store will become, in contrast to her loneliness, a kind of spree, a domestic orgy of sound and color, of voices and of things to choose—cereal, bread, salt in a red box or salt in a blue. And even these journeys will be finally dulled until at last there will be only five o'clock when you come safely home again.

You realize now you should have found a house in town or even quarters on the base. A tar-paper shack with company would have been better, you tell yourself, than all this room in the desert's emptiness. Glennis won't complain, you know. You know, too, that she won't be able to fool herself forever into facing days that will marshal themselves against her, each one an obstacle to be faced one hour at a time, ten more days taking the place of the one she's passed. She'll have to fight back.

And without waging open war on the surrounding loneliness, Glennis begins with a deceptive feint. "I'll drive you to the base today," she says on the third morning in the house. "I'll need the car."

So she escapes for a time from her imprisonment, drives you to work and then drives home again, alone with the boys. Now during each day she rides with aimless liberty from one pointless destination to another, avoiding loneliness and fear, not overcoming them. For why pretend? Her fear will end when the project does. And after that fear will be born again when a new project comes along. The loneliness will go on, pushed into the background only at five o'clock, rationalized in time, accepted finally, but broken only when you're just too old to fly.

At three o'clock she drives back to the base to pick you up, glad of the dusk that shrinks the world to wherever you are together.

"Well, how did it go today?" she asks.

"Oh, same old thing," you tell her. "Nothing to worry about."

This ritual over, the cycle begins again. You will never be able to close that gap between the two worlds in which you have to live. It will always be tough for her, much worse in a way than it is for you. For it is always easier to face danger yourself than to sit helplessly and wait for the man who does.

"How have the boys been?" you ask, lifting Mickey to set him on your lap.

"Just fine," she says, and begins to recount the day. But you really don't hear what Glennis says. The project has caught you up again in its race with sound. Tomorrow you'll check out the X-1 for your first powered flight. And the day after that, you'll fly.

23

Low on the ground, her weight flattening her tires, painted bright orange and with a nose like a humming-bird, the X-1 seems to be fast and powerful even at rest.

But the plane is short and fat, only 31 feet long with a span of 28 feet, and the sense of its power is of power compressed in a fat little belly no longer than two canoes.

Her smallness is heightened by the contrasting bigness of everything surrounding her, high walls forming the corner in which she sits, a yellow bulldozer backed up to her nose, big jets on either side of her, the men who stoop and crouch to work along her fuselage.

Stripped here and there of flaps of her metal skin, she shows the interwoven network of electric wires, tubing, tanks and valves that feed and ignite fuel blasted from her stubby tail. There are strips of silver, crimson, green and black, bright blue and and yellow framed in her apple-green belly and vivid against her orange skin. These are her complicated guts, bared now for one last check before today's ground run.

Then one by one her access doors are replaced. Resting his clipboard on her fuselage, the crew chief signs his maintenance report. Mechanics roll away their tools and equipment. And winding a long extension cord around his cocked left thumb and elbow, the last man walks away from the ship. The plan is clear. Rehearsals are over now. This ground run is for keeps.

Seen from a distance as it stands waiting to be towed away, the squat little plane becomes for a moment big with its significance. Your mind forgets mechanical details of thickness, weight and size and you are impressed at once with the smallness of its mass and the tremendous purpose of its flight, to assault the universe. It seems so small and slight to carry its pilot, 13,000 pounds of fuel and 500 pounds of recording instruments at a speed faster than the speed of sound. But tomorrow morning she will make the first powered flight in the last series of air tests for which she was designed and built. Tomorrow morning pilot and plane will begin to nibble away at the limits of transonic speed.

For this is the purpose, not simply to outrun sound, but to explore by slow and carefully controlled degrees those critical speeds in the transonic range and to record the strange and dangerous phenomena of flight within this range of speeds. And as the airplane has this double mission, it has two bands of partisans, two separate and sometimes opposing groups. There are the scientists, cautious, watchful, curious about detail. These advocate restraint and care, the strict adherence to a graded schedule of flights that move in imperceptible degrees toward the speed of sound.

And there is that handful of impatient men tagged by one of the project's engineers as the Stanley-Boyd-Yeager Group. Theirs is what used to be called the "Stanley approach" to the problem of supersonic flight—the conviction that it can be done, the willingness to take and to accept responsibility for calculated risk, to do what you can with what you have, and to keep a tight hold and a bright eye on the ultimate objection. You want to know whether or not you can fly supersonic? Well, get the hell up in the air and see.

And this is the ship these men have built and learned to fly, half-laboratory and half-rocket, into space, a missile aimed into the universe, and a workshop in which to examine carefully each minute detail of every inch of flight. Hooked to the yellow bulldozer, watched by her crew, the X-1, lately christened *Glamorous Glennis,* glides slowly across the hangar floor and through one open door. Her pilot rides in the cockpit, a technician on each wing. The others ride on the bulldozer or walk casually behind

the plane. It is almost nine o'clock on the morning of
August 28, 1947. The air is clear and bright. Sunlight
glistens on the X-1's orange skin.

The plane is towed carefully down the concrete apron
to the working area now. There she is filled with fuel
and with propellent gas. Here she will later be loaded
into her mother ship for tomorrow's drop. There is the pit.
And beyond this stands the liquid nitrogen evaporator, a
big sphere with three-inch-thick walls of stainless steel.
Mounted on skids, the sphere is framed in an open square
of supporting beams. A small shack stands against its face.
This houses valves controlling the liquid nitrogen it will
compress into gas and feed under pressure into the ship.
The whole structure juts up into the air and is crowned
with a red-and-white *No Smoking* sign.

Next to the sphere there is a cylindrical tank containing
liquid oxygen. Laid on its side, this too is mounted on
concrete pillars that raise it high above the men who have
begun to service the waiting plane. Crouched under wings
and fuselage, kneeling on heels and reaching overhead, or
straddling the X-1's back, they fix all their attention once
more on the plane. The oxygen filler valve is open, the
tanks vented. Long, black flexible steel hoses, thick as a
man's wrist, run from fuel storage tanks and nitrogen
evaporator into her belly and her sides. Through these
propellent gas and fuels begin to run, 293 gallons of a
carefully screened mixture of alcohol and water, 300 gallons of liquid oxygen. One of the black accordion tubes
turns quickly white with frost and the ship sits now in a
gentle fog of liquid oxygen that escapes from the vent and
rises like marshy mist into the desert air. Within this mist
the crewmen move like wraiths. Half-disembodied in the
fog, they seem almost to float from wing to nose, from tail
to landing gear. There is action everywhere at once.

While gas and fuels are pumped into the ship, the
nitrogen system is examined for leaks, and technicians
inspect the stabilizer flaps and landing gear. The crew
chief kneels, his head and shoulders above the fogging lox,
its vapor clinging to arms he brings out of the mist up to
the shrouded plane. Pilots and engineers have come mean-

while into the circle of action around the ship. Beyond them a second ring of working men has gathered, too, firemen hosing down the ramp, the air police who stand on guard. And all of them watch the waiting plane, her fat little belly frosted white and smoking now, her tires almost completely flattened under the heavy load of fuel and lox.

Then there is talk. Calm, curious, the pilot stands with the project engineer. Both watch the ship possessively, each seeing at first a different thing—the pilot, the plane he'll fly; the engineer, its power plant. Then their two images combine into the same composite thing and they discuss the ship.

"It seems to me," the pilot says, "that horizontal stabilizer has a tendency to stick. What do you think about it, Dick?" He will admit that Frost has taught him all he knows about the plane, and that is everything, or almost everything, there is to know.

"You're right," Frost answers. It's been his business to see a great many pilots prepare for flights of doubtful outcome. Yeager, he thinks, is the coolest pilot he's ever seen, certainly one of the best—"A natural-born engineer," Frost will say later on. "He took to all this like the proverbial duck to water. By the time he made his first powered flight he knew the airplane almost as well as I did, practically never needed any advice from me as to what to do when things started to happen in the airplane, whereas the other pilots who'd flown the X-1 used to just relay their instrument readings to me. They didn't know the plane well enough to trouble-shoot it themselves. But Yeager did.

"Chuck is also the best pilot I've ever known. I've known a lot of good ones. I considered myself fairly competent as a test pilot, but when I saw him fly, I felt like a beginner. All through the project he was extremely self-possessed, a lone wolf, maybe, with some of the qualities of an extreme introvert, some of an extrovert. And as I got to know him better, I found a great deal about him to admire. The guy has absolutely no nerves. In any situation that ever developed, and some of them got to be a little hair-raising, he never betrayed the slightest qualm;

there was never any change in the level or volume of his voice. He handled each situation with complete aplomb. And he handled it well. That's the kind of a guy he is."

But the plane is ready. There is no more time to talk. Action moves in a casual convoy down to the eastern end of the apron on which the hangars front. Fire trucks reel in hoses and grind away. The X-1 is towed down the ramp, her crew chief in the cabin, a technician sitting on one wing. She is towed even more slowly now and with greater care, and her tires are flatter than ever under her weight as she moved heavily along.

The rest of the crew, guards, pilots, project officers and engineers, ride in their cars and trucks around behind the hangars and back out onto the apron to meet the plane. When the last of them reaches this tie-down area the X-1 has been nosed in toward the buildings and lashed securely down. It is almost time to start.

The pilot walks up the plane. Four firemen, their hoses unleashed and running, come at the ship from either side. Crewmen and engineers disperse themselves, crouch, waiting to observe the run. The pilot enters the cockpit. Frost stands at its open door. The first needle valve is cracked. Item by item the men go through their written lists of things to be checked, some standing beside the ship with Frost, others at nose, wing tips and tail, each placed in such a way that no part of the plane is out of someone's sight. Each man can see and can signal to all the others.

Then it begins. The chambers are fired in series first, four separate blasts, one following another in a rising and falling scale of noise.

And finally it comes, the first dull roar as the pilot fires the number-one chamber again. The 15,000 pounds of the first cylinder's thrust blast off the concrete ramp in a visible stream of fire, vapor, dust and air that boils on the ground beneath the cold forced water from the firemen's hoses. The noise is terrible.

The second cylinder is fired, and the fiery thrust blasts with a doubled brightness almost twice as far. The noise is shattering. Hands cover ears. Three thousand pounds of thrust beat on the ramp and the X-1 bumps and strains at its leashing cables, fighting to rise.

The blast trebles and is suddenly almost unbearable as number-three chamber cuts in with equal share of roar. A long bright streak of transparent flame shoots off across the concrete into the sand that is blasted with three rockets' force along the dry shore of the dusty lake—forty-five hundred pounds of thrust. The sound beats into skull and heels and into the sockets of each tooth.

With still another blast the final cylinder is fired now. The full 6,000 pounds of thrust skids off the ramp, roars over desert sand and stone. It does not seem possible to stand the one or two minutes of this the pilot needs to check out his power plant and its controls.

Then, unexpectedly, one rocket quits, two, three and four. Silence fills mind and body with sudden rest. Some-one laughs. A man swears forcefully. All sound is flat in the static air. The run is over. The ship will be readied now to fly.

24

In the briefing that precedes this first powered flight you're told exactly what to do. It will be a flight with full propellant tanks, its purpose to acquaint you, Frost explains, with the handling characteristics of the airplane under power. There might be some trouble with the stabilizer actuator. You will, therefore, fly at a relatively moderate speed with only one cylinder on at a time, follow the same procedure established for ground runs of the power plant. It is the procedure made familiar now by constant practice—turn on one cylinder, turn on another; cut off the first, turn on the third, cut off the second, turn on the fourth. You will not exceed a speed of .8 Mach number.

You are told also that there will be official spectators watching this flight, some brass from Air Matériel Command. They will observe from the tower on the field. You'll do a fly-by for them, drop down to a few thousand feet and pass above the tower so they can see the plane in actual flight. Then you will land. And that is all.

It's difficult to say just what you feel before this first real flight. You're eager to fly—excited. It's a good feeling to walk into the hangar, climb into the cockpit of the plane, sit there alone, knowing you're going to fly it now. And sitting alone in there as the ground crew works to complete their preflight check, you suddenly feel the whole of the project around you again, sense all at once the power and purpose of this ship as its past comes suddenly alive in your mind.

But you move with a jolt back into the present as the

plane is towed from its hangar out to the pit. Still in the cockpit, you study the instruments again in a final test of your memory of each detail.

Out at the pit, you stand on the apron and watch them load the X-1 into the B-29, follow the bomber as it is nosed into its place, watch crewmen pressurize the X-1's nitrogen system, fill her tanks with lox and fuel, service the waiting B-29. It is all just as you've seen it over and over again in practice, except for the fact that woven through this fixed routine there is a tightening thread of tension now. This one is for the money, the first, official powered flight in the Air Force program.

And it is, step by step, almost exactly the way Frost said that it would be.

The pit is cross-shaped, sunk in the west end of the apron on which the planes are serviced. It is a trench crossed by a wider trench down one sloping end of which there's barely room to roll the plane. Nose hooked to a yellow bulldozer, wings just clearing the edge of the pit, the X-1 is carefully backed down this ramp and there it rests, a small bright-orange bird in a concrete nest.

The B-29, preflight inspection completed, its engines warm and ready to start, is then towed cautiously over the pit. It is a delicate job to bring the big bomber into position. Wide, bright-colored guide lines mark the path the wheels of the bomber must follow across the apron and into place. Once it is over the pit, crewmen lower winches built into the B-29. Broad slings are placed around the fore and aft fuselage of the X-1, hooked to their cables; and the four winches, one for each end of each sling, turn slowly, bringing the X-1 up into the belly of the B-29. When the bomb shackle has engaged the hook set in the top of the X-1's fuselage, the winches are slacked off, the slings removed. Four sway braces, screw jacks bearing in pairs against the top fore and aft fuselage, are jacked down into position to hold the X-1 rigidly in place. The planes are mated now and ready for flight. If the crewmen can tow the B-29 out over the pit without having to back it up and come in again, if they can load the X-1 up into the B-29 without having to lower the ship and try it a second time, they're really pleased, proud of their skill in getting it squared away.

You stand there under the bomber's wing and watch first, then help to jiggle the X-1 into its place beneath the shackel that grips its hook. The shackle is closed, the safety pin slipped in. On every flight the crewmen help you to learn one step in the process until you can do them all—lock the bomb shackle, slip in the pin, run one of the hoists that raise the X-1 up into the B-29, or tighten a sway brace down.

Then, once the X-1 is secured, you climb up into the bomber. Cardenas is having coffee now. You operate the bomber's brakes, in case a tub bar breaks or its landing gear rolls up to the edge of the pit. Then you go back to the X-1, climb into its cockpit again, go over its systems, check once more to see what changes may have been made since the last flight.

That airplane always gives you a friendly feeling, no matter how cold it is in there from the lox and the expanding nitrogen. It's neat and compact, well put together, each part well machined. The ship is solid and strong. Sitting alone in the pilot's seat, you can feel the beautiful precision of the whole airplane, sense its power and strength, notice small things you miss in the minutes preceding the drop and during flight.

But the B-29 has been nosed in to the lox tank and evaporator now. Still in the X-1 cockpit, you wait for pressure to come up, crack the first needle valve and set the first stage regulator at its 1,500 psi. Then you check out the landing gear, lower it once and raise it again. You spill the dome and leave the ship. The loading of fuel and lox goes on.

Ridley works on meanwhile, half-lost in the white lox vapor that fogs the area around the planes. Checking the lines, zeroing instruments, seeing that cameras are properly filled, he seems to be everywhere at once, but slips through the mist at last to where you stand. There, watching the crewmen work, you talk things over briefly, go over the flight plan, decide just what you'll do. Then you go off together. While the lox tank is being filled you leave the ship. There is the last-minute briefing with NACA engineers. Take it easy, Beeler says. The idea, he reminds you, is just to nibble away at speed, follow the flight plan, step by step. You listen, nod your agreement, leave. Then there's a final word with Hoover and Frost, who will fly chase. You go back to the airplanes then and there is the last, short wait until the lox tank has been filled and capped.

Now there's the rush to clamber aboard the B-29, the take-off, the climb to altitude. And from the moment this first powered flight gets off the ground, the long rehearsals, the hours of study, training, practice, thought and argument begin to pay off. You wait with the same nervousness, pace as before the narrow cabin of the B-29, move with the same anxiety back through the bomb bay, down with the ladder into the wind, and crawl with the same cold fear into the little ship. But the whole thing moves like clockwork now. You put on your helmet and your mask, hook up the oxygen, help Mac Hamilton fix the door, plug in your radio headset, turn it on. You check in with the chase planes down on the field, with the tower, with NACA and with Cardenas up in the B-29.

"How do you read me?"

"Fine," they answer, or, "Loud and clear."

Your eyes accustomed now to the darkness in the plane, you check your instruments again, this time against the check list strapped to your thigh. Beginning with the landing gear handle on your left, you work around to your right, first checking to see that the landing gear handle is in the *up* position. Then you make sure that the jettison valves are closed, that the first stage dome is spilled, that you're getting bleed pressure from the auxiliary tank up in the B-29. You make certain then that all your domes are spilled, that the tanks aren't under pressure now. And you keep on going right around, checking to see that the battery switch is on, the rocket chamber switches off, that the master switch on the throttle is off, the emergency cut-out button on. You make sure, too, that you have enough oxygen breathing pressure, that the voltage is up, that the cabin pressure valve at the door is set in the *pressurized* position. You vent the cockpit finally, check your bail-out bottle, resettle yourself at last in the seat.

Now you call Frost and Ridley. "I have completed my check list," you report. "Everything is okay."

"Roger," they answer. Ridley adds, "Take it easy, son."

And now the tempo is suddenly stepped up, and your tension mounts. Fear grows again and your anxiety. There are a thousand and one things that might go suddenly wrong, and the whole neat and orderly design Dick Frost has pounded into your head becomes for a moment disorganized and confused. Have you done everything you should have done? You're not sure and for a moment you can't remember anything. You know you've forgotten something but you can't say what it is. You stare at the instrument panel, your mind a jumble of domes and switches, valves and instruments. And all the carefully memorized details of patterns, charts and diagrams and of the ship itself slip for the moment out of place. You don't know whether you've checked any one of them or not or whether the way you remembered to set a switch is right or wrong. You read through the check list again, sweating; your lips are dry. Time speeds away. But it's cold in the cockpit, colder than you can remember it having been before. It's the lox tank up behind your back, you remember suddenly, and everything slips back into its place.

At ease again, you study the predrop check list, the things you will do in the last few minutes before the drop. First you say to yourself, you'll load that first-stage fuel up to 1,500 pounds. Then load the second-stage fuel up to 230 pounds, the second-stage lox to 240 pounds. Then see that you've got about 70 pounds' differential between the dome pressure and the tank pressure. That's it.

You check the card again. For today's flight the data switch that starts the recording and telemetering instruments has to come on just immediately before the drop. You'll turn this instrument power switch on, turn on the rocket motor master switch up on the wheel—it's a master throttle. You turn that up. Then there is nothing to do again but sit and wait. When the count-down ends you will reach up, flip the switch and be on your way.

Hoover and Frost, meanwhile, have cleared with the tower and taken off. They're airborne, climbing to altitude. The B-29 is grinding away. There's a radio check from time to time but not much chatter. Everyone practices his part. Tension is everywhere. Dick Frost alone is cool and calm, proud as a parent watching his kids. The rest of you sweat as the flight routine goes on. Hoover comes up and passes the B-29. Frost lets you know he's on your tail. Cardenas calls, "Five minutes to drop."

It is all in order. Everything's set. "All right," you answer Cardenas, "loading up first stage." You load the first-stage regulator up to its 1,500 pounds. "B-29," you tell them, "clear to disconnect the nitrogen hose from the X-1. Clear to disconnect pilot's breathing oxygen."

"I'll get it," Ridley answers. You can imagine him now up over your head, trailing his oxygen tube as he crawls into the bomb bay to disconnect the nitrogen bleed pressure hose and the oxygen hose through which you've been breathing to conserve your own limited supply.

"Nitrogen hose and oxygen hose disconnected," Ridley reports.

"Roger," you answer. "I am pressurizing the fuel tank." And you set the second-stage regulators, bringing the fuel tank pressure up to 230 psi. "I am pressurizing the lox tank," you tell them now. You get it up to about 215 pounds per square inch, then, as the domes cool off, reset them to make certain they're at the proper point.

"All pressurized," you finally report. "I am all set," you tell Frost, who flies behind you, watching your tail. "Are you in position to check jettison?"

"Roger," Frost answers. "We'll check jettison now."

You flip on the fuel jettison switch and flip it off as Frost reports, "Fuel jettison okay. Shutoff okay."

In the same way you check the lox jettisoning system next. You flip the switch. Frost tells you, "Lox jettison okay." You flip it off. He says, "Shutoff okay."

And from the B-29 Cardenas warns, "One minute to drop."

"Instrument power coming on now," you answer calmly. "I am ready to drop."

Then your anxiety returns. You've been busy until now. But now there's nothing to do but wait again. There's the tightening up in your stomach, the sweating as you go carefully through the final check. For the last time you make certain that all the switches are properly set, that all four chamber switches are off, that the master switch is on. And you're ready to go. When the count-down ends, you have only to turn on the data-recording switch. You touch it now.

You've dropped before and you know what it's like—a roller-coaster ride. There'll be that great big snap, your body will rise, float crazily in air, your head just touching the canopy as you drop clear of the B-29. Then you will settle into your seat, turn on one cylinder and fly. But fear expands again as you wait for the drop. How will it be this time? you wonder, and hunch down in your seat, your body braced for the jolt.

"Starting the count-down," Cardenas says. "Ten— nine—" He usually misses one count. "Eight—" he says, then goes on to, "Six—"

You lower your head, get your controls in a neutral position, set your rudder again and tighten up.

"Five—four—" Cardenas counts.

You've got everything real tight, your finger up on the data switch. "Come on," you say, "let's drop this crate!"

"Three—two—one. Drop!"

It seems like five whole minutes again until you drop away and into the bright sunlight. Blinded at first, you glide 500 feet or more. The air is silent. There is no sound now except the tick of instruments and the soft whir of cameras set up behind your head. On the ground below, in the B-29, in the chase planes too there is the tension of waiting.

You close the switch that ignites the first cylinder. The ship shoots suddenly ahead. Five seconds later you fire the second, shut off the first. Still carefully following the preset plan, you fire the third and cut off number two. You put the ship into a slow, exploratory roll.

"My God!" Frost calls with emphasis. "That's not in the flight plan, Yeager, not with the heavy load of fuel!"

You don't even hear him. "Zero g," you will later tersely admit in the pilot's report, "is reached in the roll." It is a sensation closer, perhaps, to delirium than to anything else—a feeling almost impossible to describe. The drop is nothing compared to this.

Your whole life slips in an instant into a soundless, pointless, directionless skid. It is like speeding along in a car that suddenly spins on ice. Whatever you do has no effect. There is no connection between the movements you make and the things that happen; no response to all the reactions you've ever learned. It is worse than that. You find yourself, for a moment that seems an hour, with no point of reference to any physical thing. You are weightless, helpless and directionless as the plane you sit in enters an arc in which centrifugal force erases the pull of gravity. It is like losing consciousness, like dying almost, but hovering an instant within the sense of life. Like losing consciousness of everything except the fact that you're still conscious and it frightens you.

With the last shred of reason you know only that you've got to do something to get out of there. It's as if your mind has left your body; you have to get back inside yourself or lose forever all contact with whatever is real, is solid, is fixed and can be understood.

And with the last light ounce of strength you push on the stick. But there is a sudden drop in the lox tank pressure. Number-three chamber abruptly quits and the plane is powerless. Nose down, the X-1 drops back into the world again. The dead chamber fires. You turn on number four and cut off three. Life flows back into you and it is wonderfully good to know again that *up* is up and *down* is down, that there is a canopy over your head and that the floor is at your feet.

"Frost," you call, still diving and gaining speed, "there's snaking or rolling in this thing. Feels like the fuel is sloshing in its tanks."

"Probably is," Frost says. "Hey! where are you going now?"

"To show that brass down there a real airplane," you answer him, still going down. At 6,000 feet you begin to

level off, then fly above the tower at 5,000 feet. You pass it
without a sound, then close the cabin-pressure regulator
and ignite the first cylinder to begin a shallow climb. But
something suddenly happens. Not to the ship. It happens
to you—something you'll never be able to explain to
Frost, who watches with his heart up in his mouth, or to
the old man, Colonel Albert Boyd, who'll hear of it later
with mixed emotions—official anger, professional pride
and personal glee. You won't be able to explain this even
to yourself.

What is it like to fly the fastest airplane in the world?
Even before you reach Mach 1 you're flying faster then
anyone else has ever flown. From .8 Mach you leave the
limits of the known, enter a region of speed, sensation and
experience where no other living man has ever been. No
matter how small the variance is from something that's
happened before, you know it has never happened to
anyone else. And you're tempted to go on from there, to
go a step further—a hundredth, a twenty-fifth, a tenth.

The figure is meaningless, the change sometimes
unnoticeable. It is not the risk you're after, the mere
sensation of greater speed, the pull of your guts or the
strange new feeling of being suspended in time and in
space, of floating in motion on top of the ball that moves in
every direction at once and never rests. It is the simple,
direct and pointed challenge that lies in doing what no one
else has ever done, in the fact that you're pitted alone
against some ultimate force.

You'd have the same sense of satisfaction, the same
feeling of profound achievement, in walking alone where
no other man has ever stepped, in going farther than
anyone else down into the earth or under the sea, in
lighting the first dim light or watching the first rough
wheel go around on its first working turn.

That is why, with the first chamber running, you fire
two, then three and four in rapid sequence. From 9,000
feet the small plane streaks like a suddenly shot orange
rivet straight up through the bright blue sky to 35,000
feet. The sensation is terrific, as if you've been violently
hurled against some force that shoves you back.

"Holy Moses!" you shout into the otherwise silent air. And there is no answer now from anyone.

"I don't know what happened," Frost will try to explain to Larry Bell in a half-hour telephone call to Buffalo that night. "I told him to do a fly-by and come in and land. His idea of a fly-by, Larry, was to dive down, power off but with the airplane going like a bat because it was still full of propellants. He dove down to 5,000 feet—that's only 3,000 feet above the field here which is at 2,300 itself. I was chasing in the F-80 and he outdistanced me by far, even though I went into compressibility doing a little *over* eight-tenths chasing him. I started to pull out at 12,000 feet but he went on down to five or six. And then the son of a gun turned on all four cylinders and shot up like a skyrocket!"

"Wasn't this," Bell asks patiently, "his first powered flight?"

"Sure, it was his first powered flight! And I specifically told him to stay under .8 Mach number. But I was going at the minimum safe speed in the 80, Larry, and he went by me literally like a skyrocket with that blast of flame coming out of his tail. And he kept pointing up and up, trying to keep the speed under eight-tenths, as I'd instructed him to do. Well, he couldn't, of course. He went straight up until he lost all orientation, couldn't see the ground any more. The sky was clear air and he was starting to flop over. So he finally cut the engine. But, my God! In the time it took me to get to 15,000 feet, he'd gone over five miles straight in the air!"

"Well, good," Bell answers placidly, proud of his ship and of the pilot, too. Safely in Buffalo, he chuckles. "Wait until Al Boyd hears about this," he says. "He'll either pin a medal on that boy or give him hell."

That's true enough. The old man is really going to burn when he gets the flight report. But you yourself, from the moment you cut those chambers on until the peak of that climb, don't think of this. There's you and the airplane there—that's all. And it's a wonderful ship to fly.

25

Seated alone in his office back in the Flight Test Division at Wright Field, Colonel Albert Boyd, his square face set in a stubborn frown, straightens the papers on his desk and reads them carefully again.

The colonel sits squarely in his chair, his body at right angles to the rectangle of his walnut desk. The papers from which he reads to himself lie squarely on his desk, framed on its surface now by his long, straight arms. The whole impression the colonel gives is one of precise and ordered action brought for the moment to attentive rest.

"Pilot's Report." The colonel's eyes scan the title of this typewritten page. "No. 1 Powered Flight, 29 August, 1947. Captain Charles E. Yeager, Pilot." It is now the third day of September. The colonel is not surprised at what he reads. He's read it before in the project engineer's report. He's heard it from Larry Bell, who laughed, and from NACA, whose engineers found nothing to laugh at in their report. But dammit—The colonel reads painfully on, his angular body almost motionless.

"The purpose of this flight—" The colonel skips that. He ordered the flight himself and defined its purpose. He reads on to paragraph two. "At a pressure altitude of 7,000 feet the undersigned entered the cockpit of the X-1 and the climb continued." Methodically and despite his impatience, the colonel reads carefully on into paragraph three.

"The release of the X-1 from the B-29 was made at 21,000 feet and indicated air speed of 255 mph." The colonel nods. In paragraph four he reads with interest, "With No. 3 burning, a slow roll was executed. When zero

194

g was reached in the roll, No. 3 chamber stopped, due to a drop in the lox tank pressure." And the colonel smiles his appreciation of this feat, a slow roll performed with the heavily loaded ship, the dizzy sensation of zero g.

But he frowns once more and his fingers begin to drum on the desk top as he reads carefully through paragraph five.

"During descent a slight 'snaking' and rolling motion of low amplitude and frequence were noted. It is believed this was due to fuel sloshing." The colonel's fingers continue to drum.

It is in paragraph six that his attention comes into sharper focus. His body stiffens as he reads. "Nos. 2, 3 and 4 chambers were ignited in sequence. After starting No. 2 chamber, the stabilizer was set in the two-degrees nose-down position. The climb was steepened as each chamber was ignited, in order to stay below the .8 Mach number. After No. 4 chamber was ignited, the climb was approaching 90 degrees."

The drum beat of the colonel's hand increases now. "In order to keep a one g fuel—" He sets one page neatly aside and reads hurriedly on—"the nose was pulled through to a 45-degree angle as in executing a loop. In this attitude .83 Mach number was reached and No. 4 chamber was turned off. While dropping the nose and rolling out into a normal attitude .85 Mach number was reached at approximately 30,000 ft. Nos. 1, 2 and 3 chambers were turned off during the recovery and the remaining fuel was jettisoned. During the above maneuvers no abnormal control characteristics were noted except a slight ineffectiveness of the ailerons. Due to the excited condition of the undersigned, there is a possibility that some other slight control abnormality was taking place but was not detected."

The hands which have risen come suddenly down to slap the desk top as the colonel's anger explodes. But even as one of the angry hands jabs at the summoning button on his desk, his anger begins to fade. He hears the buzzer sound in the office next to his and his hands fall loosely onto his desk again. A grudging respect for the pilot is in his mind now as he thinks of Yeager alone in his ship dropping to 5,000 feet, then shooting straight up again in a five-mile climb to thinning air. From his respect, good humor grows, creeping along the colonel's jaw. He finds himself grinning now, one pilot smiling at another's probably deliberate risk. The sharp angles of his body are broken suddenly as the colonel leans back reflectively in his chair and ponders his knowledge of the younger man. And a long-suppressed, forgotten-until-this-moment memory pops suddenly into his mind—*Pretty good for an old man*, he remembers, laughing suddenly aloud at Yeager and at himself.

For the old man is a pilot, too, and another country boy come from the hills. Born in Rankin, Tennessee, he went to high school in Asheville, North Carolina, and to junior college for a couple of years. He entered the service as an aviation cadet in 1927, completed flying school in 1929, went on active duty that year as a second lieutenant. A command pilot now and a combat and aircraft observer, the colonel has logged more than eleven thousand hours in the air, flown everything the Air Force has or has had in the air since 1929. He's a top-ranking test pilot himself, and, not three months ago, he set a new world's record flying the F-80R 623.85 miles an hour over a measured course at Muroc, bringing the world's speed record back to the United States for the first time in twenty-four years.

And all of this is in his past as he considers the problem of the pilot now. All this is in the colonel's mind as he decides what he will do. You can't blame anyone, he tells himself as the door opens and his secretary comes quietly in. But still—he leans forward in his chair—you can't let him get away with his. And in this divided mood the colonel composes a letter, dictated with no expression on his face to the unsmiling girl who writes it down.

"Just learned of your successful flight of Friday last week in the X-1," the colonel dryly begins. "We are very happy over the results, with one exception—" His voice snaps suddenly to attention—"and that is your exceeding the speed of .82 which was authorized." These words are underlined with the colonel's anger and with his concern. "I would personally like to have an explanation from you," he continues, his voice dry again, "as to your reasons for exceeding the authorized Mach number on this particular flight."

And in Muroc three days later you read the letter, worried at first because you know the old man can get really tough. You read it first on the base, then read it again at home. And you begin to sense the old man's understanding and his real interest and concern.

"Please remember," the colonel's letter continues, as you read it carefully again, "the instructions that I passed on to you personally here at Wright Field with respect to the value of the pilot and the plane to the Air Force and the cost per square inch of written data that we hope to obtain from future tests of this aircraft. The Air Force does not consider either you or the plane expendable so please approach higher speeds progressively and safely to the limit of your best judgment."

And it is signed, "Sincerely, Albert Boyd."

"Glennis," you admit finally that night, "I got a personal letter from the old man." You're flat on your back on the living room floor, Don jumping up and down on your stomach, Mickey just making noises in his crib.

"What did he say?" Glennis comes in from the kitchen to ask.

"Read it. It's on the table there." You lift Don up in the air, pumping him up and down as he laughs and shouts. "Way up you go!" you tell him. "Up in the air!"

"Daddy!" Don shouts. "You put me down!"

Your arms drop and the boy rolls tumbling across the floor. "The old man really hit the roof," you say reflectively. Hands under your head, indifferent to your scrambling son, you think for a moment of all the things the colonel might have said to you.

"Oh boy!" Glennis laughs as she reads aloud. "'I would personally like to have an explanation—'" And she grins down at you. "What are you going to say?"

"Why, I don't know."

"Don't you know why you did whatever it is you did?"

You grin back up at her. "Now don't get nosy!" You

reach up suddenly and catch one of her hands in yours. "Come on. Sit down here and let's talk this over."

"Here on the floor? Boy, you don't want to talk."

"This is pretty serious."

"Well, stop trying to kiss me then and—"

"I mean it."

"Oh, Judas Priest!" she says. "There goes the roast!"

Later that night she asks you again just why you broke the limit set for your first flight. But you still can't tell her. None of the reasons you can think of make any sense to you and they'd mean less to her.

"I'll talk it over with Ridley tomorrow," you tell her frankly. "Ridley knows."

But Ridley can only grin at you and shake his head. "Well, why in the hell did you do it?" he wants to know.

"Jack," you say, "I just don't know. No reason, really, except that plane is such a wonderful thing to fly. I wanted to really fly it—see what it would do."

"I see." But Ridley shakes his head again. "The old man isn't likely to buy that explanation. Hell, Chuck, that's why we're all out here—Bell, NACA and the Air Force crew—to see what that plane will do. And the first time they gas it up for you, you run off and try to do the damn job all by yourself. Colonel Boyd will really burn if you can't give him a better answer than that."

"Well, what in the hell am I going to say?"

"Sit down," he says, "we'll figure something out. First off, you better soften him up a little, apologize."

"I guess I better had."

"Here, shove that typewritter over here," Ridley says. He rolls in a sheet of paper and begins to type slowly. "Make it a personal letter. 'Dear Sir,'" he reads as he types, "'I am sorry that the first powered flight of the X-1 was not entirely satisfactory.'" He lights a cigarette then and carefully scratches his head. After a while he begins to type another line. "'We are taking every precaution and making ever effort to conduct these flights in such a manner that will lend credit to the Flight Test Division and the AFF.'"

"That sounds all right," you say. "It doesn't say anything much but it sounds real good."

"Well," Ridley defends himself, "it won't get you into any trouble. Let's get the meat out now and grind it up. Let's see." He begins to type again. "'The plan for the first flight called for a Mach number of .82 or .83 if no control difficulty or buffeting was encountered.'

"You can admit that much," Ridley says, lighting another cigarette. "Now how can we squeeze you out of this? Let's see."

"Hell, Jack, why not just tell him the truth? During the preflight conference we had with NACA and with Frost the consensus of opinion was that no trouble would be encountered up to .85 Mach."

"All right," Ridley agrees. "Let's put that down." He types again.

"Since everything was normal up to .83," you dictate to him now, "I do not feel that it was against my better judgment in increasing the speed up to .85."

"Well," Ridley says, "we ought to take a little of the pepper out of this. How about adding something like this?

"I can assure you, sir," he types, "that safety is a primary factor in these flights." He strips the paper from the machine. "That's true enough," he says and grins at you.

"That's fine," you say. "Let's get it in the mail."

"Okay," Jack says.

26

Now the whole project settles down to its work. A new pattern emerges and a new routine that varies only as tension mounts from day to day, anxiety from flight to flight. You don't fly every day. Flights in the series are set a few days, sometimes as much as a week apart. But by the fifth of October you've made six powered flights, each one at a faster speed than the flight before, each one for a different purpose—to obtain stability data in the .80 to .85 Mach number range at 30,000 feet, for example, or in the range from .85 to .88, or to investigate stabilizer effectiveness at 35,000.

Each time you go up for some new data, do something you've never done with the ship before, or something you've tried but at slower speeds and lower altitudes. And on every flight you manage to jump the limit, to fly the plane faster than NACA observers want you to, push the speed from .87 Mach number, for example, to .88.

You feel no hesitance in doing this. Your confidence in the X-1 and in your ability to handle it at any conceivable speed or altitude is complete. You know the ship. But you're impatient too, curious, anxious to pass Mach 1 and to get into sonic flight. You don't know why. It's as if something inside keeps pushing you, fear and the idea that something might happen to halt the program before you're through.

There are objections to this, of course, raised in advance at preflight briefings and brought up again at each postflight critique. Frost is always in these conferences, representing Bell. Ridley and you are there for the Air Force, Williams and Beeler for the NACA. It is Williams and Beeler who make the strongest objection to your slipping past the speed set for a given flight, who want to approach the problem cautiously, creeping up gradually in speed. "Nibble away," they both insist. Frost tends to side with you, however; Ridley, too.

And as time goes on the alignment within the group begins to shift. It is Frost, at first, who has the final say on what will be done and how, the old Bell crewmen who service the ship and set its pace. But Ridley takes over as Frost steps gradually down and the Air Force crew absorbs the work of servicing the plane. So that now, by the first of October, the project is all your own, an Air Force project with Frost advising, the Bell crew standing by. There is no friction in the change. It is natural, pleasant, hardly noticeable. The fact is, you're all eager, every one of you. Even the NACA men give grudging respect to the progress you make, submitting as much as they can to the drive and the push of the Bell and the Air Force crews.

"What else can they do?" Frost asks one afternoon. "I'm not going to say you guys are right or wrong, or whether I fully agree with your brute force technique or not. But—" Frost grins and shakes his head—"if a thing is done, it's done. All they can do is record the fact, give up the scholarly luxury of taking it step by step from day to day."

Meanwhile, there is fear. You never admit it in the air. You keep a tight grip on emotion of any kind. Even pleasure is controlled in flight. But there is that cold sweat when you land. You know you've been frightened. The details are deliberately obscured.

All through this project you've been under tension. It isn't something you can leave at the base, this fear of the airplane that grows in your mind. It isn't something you always dread. But no matter where you are, you know you will have to get back into the X-1 and that you will face anxiety again.

If you can slow the airplane down, you might get out—if there's time enough and you can control the plane, there won't be any necessity to jump. It is the specter of trouble at speed and altitude that frightens you.

There will be no problem with the door. The cockpit is pressurized. If you can set the handle properly, the door will pop right off. Then what? If you're going over 250 miles an hour, you can't get out. Wind alone builds so much pressure that you can't slide out. And if you can? The wind will tumble you back against the plane. You'll go back into that sharp little wing and be cut in two.

You will probably never have to jump, you tell yourself. But that's no consolation. You can be clobbered long before the plane gives out, even when there is no apparent necessity to leave the ship. Or you might have a fire. The damn thing might explode. So you begin to dream.

It is a peculiar dream, never technically correct and you are always somehow aware of this. You're flying in the X-1 or in a Mustang or some other ship, but mainly in the X-1. The plane is on fire and you're flying in weather on the gauges. That's where the dream is wrong. You never fly the X-1 on the gauges. And if it catches fire, you won't know it except for that fire-warning light. But in these dreams you visualize the flames, see the plane burning as if you were flying on its wing. Yet all the time you're locked in the cockpit, trying to get out. That is the primary thing, to get out. If you stay, you'll auger in. That is the tip, get out, get out of it! And in the process of getting out of that burning ship, you're so badly scared that it wakes you up.

"Chuck!" Glennis screams at you. "Where do you think you are? What are you trying to do?" She pulls at you, interfering with escape.

"Hell!" you shout. "Let me alone! I've got to get out of this airplane!"

"Chuck!" she shouts, and with half your mind you can hear the fear in her voice. "It's a dream, only a dream!"

You find yourself at the bedroom window then, not in any trouble, you tell yourself. You're in the sack at home, supposed to be sleeping. But you're trembling, nervous, excited still.

"Come on, honey," Glennis says. She's calmer now. "Get back to bed."

You're still half-asleep, and the fire still seems to be burning. It's as if you've really managed to jump. You feel that way, although you know you're at home and everything's all right.

"Are you all right, Chuck?"

"Foolish damn dream," you mutter. But back in your bed again you begin to trouble-shoot the airplane, running its systems through in your mind as if there had been a fire. You want to know where it started, how, what happened, why. Then finally you fall asleep again.

You don't dream every night. Maybe you make two or three flights between each nightmare. It depends on how rough it's been, how tired you are. Trouble-free flight in the X-1 is fatiguing enough. You depend on too many mechanical gadgets to keep you alive and the laws of failure are always there. You wait for trouble, you're always alert for something that might not work. When something does go wrong, fear drains the last of your strength away. You land in a haze and wearily leave the ship, fight off fatigue until you can go home at last, get into bed and sleep. But then you dream again.

You wake up swearing, your fingers fumbling with the window lock, or your hands red from the beating you've given the bedroom wall.

"Chuck," Glennis says, still half-asleep herself, "you're having another nightmare. Come on, Chuck. Let's go to bed." And she leads you away from the window murmuring half to herself. "Everything all right. Only a dream."

You're not in any trouble, you think again. You're in the sack at home. And after a while you finally sleep again.

"Chuck," Glennis finally says, after the third nightmare, "I want to ask you something."

It's six in the morning. The boys are asleep. Glennis is in the kitchen scrambling eggs. But even when you come into the room to ask her sleepily what she wants, she doesn't look up from the bowl held in her hands.

"How dangerous is this plane you're flying?"

"Hell, honey, it's built—"

"Please," she says sternly, still not looking up. "Never mind the specifications. I've never asked you before about anything you've had to do. But these nightmares—I'm scared, Chuck." She looks up now and the tears are running down her face.

Then Glennis, who has never questioned your right to fly, buries her head in your shoulder and sobs out the whole of her complaint. "All day long," she begins, "I sit here waiting. I don't even like to think what I sit waiting for."

"Easy, honey. Take it easy."

"It's bad enough when you're on an ordinary flight—"

"Don't cry that way, Glennis."

"But this—this *thing!* I hate that damn airplane!"

"Glennis, honey."

"And if it makes you dream like that—"

"It's all right, Glennis. It's all right."

"No, it's not all right!"

"Just another airplane," you tell her, hoping to calm her down, and she is almost quiet.

"If it's just another airplane—" She begins to cry again. "But it's not!"

"Look, honey." You walk her into the other room. "That plane is probably the safest thing I've ever flown." You sit her down, hold both of her hands in one of yours. "Listen." You raise her chin so she has to look at you. "It's just that I get too tired. I'm not really worried because I'm scared. Hell, I'm always scared in the air. Everyone is. It's natural. What makes me dream that way is the fact that there's so much at stake in this project."

"There sure is," Glennis says. But she's not crying any more. "There's you, and me, and Mickey and Don. In the beginning, before the children were born, I was perfectly willing to accept whatever risk there was. You were flying then and I knew you were going to fly. But it's different now, Chuck. It isn't just you and me. There are the children and they sense these things. I don't think we have any right to take any more chances than we have to take with the rest of their lives. I feel so terribly guilty when I see them alone, asleep at night, or when Don wanders through the house at three o'clock because he knows it's time to go after you and he senses, without knowing it, maybe, that you might not come home. I don't know." Glennis dries her eyes and stares at the floor. "I hate to talk this way. I feel as if I were letting you down somehow. But aren't we letting them down in a way?" She looks at you.

And you don't know how to answer her. "Well, honey," you begin. "The last thing the old man told me was—he said, if it gets too much for you, just get on the horn, pick up the telephone and let me know. Won't be a thing said about it, he told me. Nobody will think a thing about it."

"No," Glennis says after a moment. "You can't do that."

"Well, what do you want me to do?"

"Nothing." She tries to grin. "I guess I'm just tired. You and your damn nightmares—"

"Honey, I really mean it. That airplane is safe. Another thing, this project isn't going to go on forever. They say a year back in Dayton. Ridley thinks we'll be through by Christmas. I think it will be sooner than that."

"Then what?"

"Well, let's cross that bridge when we get to it. In the meantime, I'll be just as careful as I can. All right?" You're still worried, not certain she's as much at ease as she wants you to think she is.

"All right." She sounds resigned. "I'll scramble your eggs." And with a shy, self-conscious, ashamed and embarrassed smile, she walks back into the kitchen to pick up the bowl of half-beaten eggs. "Chuck?" she asks, after a minute or two.

"Huh?"

"Did you ever make out a will?"

"Sure did."

"How about your insurance?"

"It's all taken care of. You know that, Glennis."

"I know, but I mean, how much would it all amount to?"

"Not much," you admit. "Probably not enough."

"Can't you get more?"

"I want to. But, honey, the rates are too high. We can't afford any more right now."

"Can't we do without something else?"

"Sure, we can quit eating for a while."

"Judas Priest, how can you stand me?" Angry with herself now, Glennis begins to cry again. "I sound like a shrew!"

"Now, honey." Back in the kitchen you wrap her in your arms. "You sound like a worried mother of a couple of growing kids, with a damn fool for a husband. Don't worry. I'll talk to Ridley about it. Maybe we can work something out."

You can't blame Glennis. You can't blame anyone else. Maybe you have no right to take the risk. But you can't even blame yourself. Somebody builds an airplane. Somebody has to fly the thing. It doesn't have to be you. But it is. There's not much you can do about it. You can quit. But that isn't what any of you want, to avoid the issue, turn your back on the danger and on the challenge of the ship. You want—you both want to overcome it and to survive together. You honestly think you can.

And nothing happens as time goes on to change your mind, nor is there any indication that Glennis is still as frightened as she was except in the fact that she begins to visit the base. Whenever she knows you're going to fly, she stays to watch, sees the big bomber leave the ground, watches it spiral up over the field, watches until it becomes a speck in the sky and then is lost for a while from sight, watches the orange X-1 drop suddenly out, streak through the air and glide back down to the strip again, relaxing only when its small wheels touch the ground and you come wearily out.

"Well, how did it go?" she greets you when at last you're through.

"All right," you say. Then you go home and the cycle begins for her again, the waiting, the worry and the fear. But Glennis has a good attitude about this, you tell yourself. You keep her up to date on everything, carry as much insurance as you can afford, keep her briefed on all your personal affairs, tell her what she should do if you're ever clobbered. It will make it easier on her, you tell yourself. And Glennis is practical about it all. Hell, if you get clobbered, you get clobbered and there's nothing you can do about it then.

"Be careful," she always says, whenever she says good-by to you.

And you always are. But there is always fear.

27

Back in Dayton early in October, Ridley and you report your progress with the ship. You're getting close to Mach 1, you tell the old man, close to flight at the speed of sound.

"How close?" the colonel asks bluntly. "I mean," he explains, "I've followed your progress. Let us admit that on the last flight you made a level run to .925 Mach. Can you tell me what will happen in the last eight-tenths?"

"Looks to me, Colonel Boyd," Ridley says laconically, "like the airplane will just go eight-tenths faster."

"Yes, sir," you say in support of Ridley's argument. "I don't really anticipate a great deal of difficulty, Colonel. It's been easy, so far, easier than we all expected. Buffeting has been mild, and I've always had control of the airplane. Well," you correct yourself with a sudden grin, "most of the time."

"Let us look at the record," the colonel answers dryly. "You began with .85 Mach number on the first powered flight. On the second flight this was increased to what you thought was .865. NACA data reduction of their films showed this to be .9015, however. There is nothing to indicate that you weren't just lucky. You didn't get back above .85 until the sixth flight. And then you reported a heavy tail trim. At .86 the airplane began to feel right-wing heavy. You ran into tight buffeting at .87 and at .88 into a slight Dutch roll—all of which might mean nothing at all. But can you say this is the case?

"Well, I will say nothing at this time about variations from schedule, the pilot's excitement, or failure to note—

was the word 'detect'?—control abnormalities." The colonel glances a moment at his hand, then fixes his eyes on yours as he continues.

"As I told you originally, we are now in a region of a great many unknowns. Because you've been able to go from .82 to .92 Mach number is no guarantee at all that you can go on from there on to Mach 1 without disastrous results. You have proved only what you have proved, and nothing more. I must ask you, therefore, not to conclude that simply because this airplane flies under certain conditions at certain speeds within the transonic range, it will therefore fly at the speed of sound under any conditions that might exist.

"I must ask you—" The colonel pauses—"to accept the judgment—" He studies his hands again—"of scientists and engineers who are still of the opinion that at the speed of sound—" His eyes come up to yours again—"all things may go to infinite."

Like two kids getting a lecture back in school, you listen as the old man goes on. "I want to be perfectly fair with you," he says. "You may—just may be right. I may be wrong. But let us examine the record again. Let's see what we know.

"We know a little of where the buffet boundaries lie and we have some stall information. What else?"

"Well, Colonel," Ridley answers, "from .8 Mach to .87 there has been very little trim change—light stick forces. At .87 you do run into a little light buffeting."

"Yes—" The colonel's voice turns dry again—"and at .87 the airplane is right-wing heavy. You need three per cent aileron displacement to maintain level flight. Meanwhile—" He slaps the desk top—"elevator and rudder have lost effectiveness. And that's not all!" He raises one hand to keep Ridley silent. "As you go up from .87 the buffeting gets more severe and you note a nose-down trim change. At .90 Mach this trim change is reversed. The nose comes up now and the buffeting is—let me see, you said 'quite severe,' I think."

"Yes, sir," Ridley agrees. "But the airplane is still controllable."

"I know the plane is still controllable." The colonel silences Ridley. "But the elevators and rudder have become increasingly ineffective. All you have now is the stabilizer. And this airplane has never yet been flown with more than three-fourths of its power. For some reason one chamber or another is always out. Now what will happen with full power on and at faster speeds? Can you tell me? What if you lose complete control and the buffeting gets worse then it's been?"

"Well, Colonel," Ridley says quietly, "the buffeting may decrease."

"How do you know what will happen, Captain, at .98?"

"Sir," Ridley admits, "I don't know what will happen." He grins suddenly. "Let's just go back and see."

"Very good." Colonel Boyd agrees with him. "But you will go slowly. This is no time to rush. The good Lord alone knows what will happen at Mach 1. I don't. And neither do you."

"Yes, sir," Ridley agrees.

"Yes, sir," you echo him.

"We've got that settled? Good," the old man says. "Let's get some lunch. General Chidlaw—" He looks at his watch—"may want to talk to you. Let's join him on the hill."

But the lunch is pretty grim. All the enthusiasm with which you came from Muroc has been washed away in the old man's sober judgment of the facts. You feel this. Ridley feels it, too. So does the old man, who is enjoying it.

"Couple of hot pilots here," he quips to the generals with whom you eat. "Want to go back tonight and crash the sound barrier."

There is polite and appreciative laughter.

"No rudder, no elevator, buffeting getting severe at one speed, mild the next. Nose up at .87, nose down at .90. That airplane is liable to go in any direction, or all of them at once. But Captain Ridley and Captain Yeager here—" He smiles at both of you and grins at General Chidlaw—"anticipate no difficulty in, ah—" The colonel coughs—"attaining Mach 1 over the week end."

"Lucky to make it at all," the general comments between brief smiles at everyone.

"That's it." The old man reflectively rubs his chin and shakes his head. "They're just that lucky, General. They might just make it. So I've told them to slow down."

You don't know what to think of the old man's attitude as you leave for Muroc later that afternoon. "Can't tell what he's really saying," you complain.

"That's right," Ridley agrees. "I noticed that. Says take it easy, and all the time he's champing at the bit himself. Says don't do it, and you know, by God, if it were up to him, he'd have done it a week ago."

"What do you think we ought to do?"

"Why, hell, we'll do just what he wants us to."

"Okay," you tell him, "you're the project officer, Jack. I don't know what he means. I don't know what you mean. You guys run the show. I'll fly the plane."

"Well," Ridley says, "after another flight or two, we'll know a little bit more about what to expect. We can change the stabilizer setting, jump up the speed a little. And maybe give the old man a better argument in a week or so."

On the next flight you set the stablizer to almost two degrees to counteract tail heaviness caused by the high angle of your climb. With the Mach needle hovering between .85 and .86, you climb from launch altitude to 30,000 feet, turn off the cylinders then, one at a time. Still climbing, you go to 38,000 feet. Speed drops to .80 Mach. You do a stalled turn in level flight. Almost full up elevator is needed to produce the accelerated stall at 1.9 g's.

Dropping 2,000 feet, you fire a second cylinder, make a stabilized run up to .915 Mach. Firing three, you climb to 40,000 feet and your speed increases to .94. Everything's fine, you think—why not go on and get it over with? But the engine suddenly howls as it runs out of fuel.

"I'm shutting off," you say and cut off the motor. Still climbing, the plane goes up to 45,000 feet. Buffeting has been light. There is some instability from .88 to .90 Mach, but as speed increases this phenomenon disappears. At .90 Mach, however, you have to admit the old man may be right. Elevator effectiveness decreases appreciably. At .94, you can move the control column throughout its range with little force and very slow response. But ailerons are completely effective, the aircraft very stable. There is no Dutch roll.

Your mind is divided as you swing back and begin the long glide down to the landing strip. You don't know whether the airplane will slip through the barrier or whether it won't. You've had a few bad bumps, one of them today, something like a sharp turbulence bump. But the plane has always been controllable. You'd like to try. If you had a full tank of fuel and lox—

It is then that you suddenly notice how cold it is, colder than it's ever been before in the cockpit of the plane. The instrument panel is so cold that vapor begins to fill the cockpit, frosting the cabin, the windshield, too. You can't see anything as you glide back to earth.

It's like trying to drive your car with a frosted windshield. You keep reaching up to rub off the frost, and the vapor condenses again, frosting in streaks wherever you've tried to rub it away.

"Can't see a thing," you report to the tower, to Hoover and Dick Frost flying on your wing and tail. You're worried, certainly. But then you've landed blind before. It's just that your constant awareness of the value of this plane makes everything seem that much worse, more difficult to do.

"Go on in," Frost tells you calmly. "I will talk you down."

"Roger," you answer. "Thanks."

And from that point on, Frost in his F-80 flies the X-1 as well as his own plane. "Right on your tail," he tells you. "Hold her as she is."

The glide continues. You tighten up again. It's cold and your fingers are stiff around the stick.

"Hold her," Frost tells you, "hold her. Going nicely. Get ready to make your turn. Okay, now make your turn . . . little more rudder . . . little bit more . . . hold it! That's good. You are approaching now. You look okay . . . about ten feet up . . . hold it. Just hold it and let her settle. All right . . . back a little on the stick. Whoa! Hold it . . . back a little . . . hold it . . . hold it . . . now back slow. That's it. Okay, you're down."

And with sudden relief you feel the wheels touch ground. When the plane finally stops, when the door has been handed down to the ground, when you're finally out of the frosting cabin, standing in hot, bright sunlight, you are terribly tired. And that's all you are.

28

But later that night excitement suddenly breaks loose, runs riot through the base. The first reduction of their data indicates, NACA says, that your speed exceeded the .94 Mach number you reported for the flight. It's closer to .99, may have been more than that.

"Looks like the next flight will do it," Frost says excitedly over the phone.

"When?" you ask, your weariness suddenly gone.

"Early next week," Frost says.

Then Ridley calls. "Got pretty close." His voice laughs into the telephone. "You're sure that's all you saw on that Mach meter, Chuck? .94?"

"Hell, yes!" you insist. "I thought that's all the faster I'd gone."

"That so?"

"Now listen, Jack." You can see him grinning now.

"Like to see the look on the old man's face when he gets the flight report," he interrupts.

"Me too." You have to laugh yourself.

"What you going to do tonight?"

"I think I'd better take Glennis out for dinner."

"Good deal," Ridley answers. "Give her a kiss for me. I'll see you tomorrow."

You say, "All right."

"Now, listen," Ridley adds. "Just take it easy over the week end, son. If you're not in shape to make that flight, I'm sure Pard Hoover will be glad to make it for you."

"I'll be there," you tell him bluntly and put down the phone.

Then you take Glennis out to celebrate. There's a place called Pancho's Fly Inn, a dude ranch for thirsty pilots near the base. It's got a landing strip and a bar, both fully lighted all night long. It's a good place to hang your hat. You don't get plastered or anything like that. But you do have a few martinis, Glennis and you, a big steak dinner and a few more drinks. It seems like a good idea at eleven o'clock or so to check out a couple of horses and take Glennis for a ride.

"Great idea," Glennis agrees.

"Now look," Pancho says. "I've got strict orders to take good care of you tonight—never mind from who." She smiles and winks at Glennis. "Stand up. Let's see you walk."

"Hell," you answer disgustedly, "I can walk all right." And you obligingly walk in a circle around your chair. "Get the horses, Pancho. You're not old enough to mother me."

"For that last favor you can have all the horses in the corral. Two nags for Captain Yeager," she calls out over the noise in the crowded bar.

"Nice ones," you add.

"With flowing manes," Glennis insists. "What's my horse's name?"

"Dobbin, probably, an old sway-backed mare."

"You should be in the shape my horses are in," Pancho says dryly, watching you walk to the door.

The horses are good, the night air clean and fresh. It's a little cool, but you ride with Glennis into the desert and back again, a wild ride and a fast one, chasing each other through the dark, laughing and shouting, raising a little hell.

"Race you back to the corral," you say.

"You're taken." Glennis is off and away before you know it and you really ride to catch up with her. You pass her finally in a wild gallop headed for the ranch.

"Better sit down, Roy," Glennis calls. "Your seat is showing."

"Yeee-whoo!" you shout and ride hell-bent for the corral. There's only one thing wrong. It's after midnight now. At twelve o'clock somebody always shuts the gate. Now knowing the time, you sort of plan to cowboy through, shine your fanny a little, have some fun. But you ride your horse right smack into the gate. The horse bolts, throws you off and runs away. Glennis comes laughing up to say, "Well, look at Hoppy! Only man in the world the horse can ride."

You laugh it off, but the fact is that it hurts like hell. In the morning it's not much better. You don't know what to do. If you turn in to the base hospital and they find the least thing wrong, they'll ground you. Hoover will make the next flight. The next one is all you want. It's something you've sweated and worked for all these months. It's something you have to do.

So you sneak away that afternoon to visit a doctor in Rosamund, leave his office feeling worse than ever. You've got two broken ribs. You could kick yourself now for being such a fool. But you're not going to let it matter. Nobody has to know it, you tell yourself. You'll do it anyway, make the next flight. It might hurt some but it can't do any harm as long as you don't have to pull too many g's.

The rest of that week end is plain hell. It isn't the broken ribs, although they're painful sometimes. It's the fact that you know you're taking a chance you have no right to take.

"What's the matter?" Glennis asks, watching you sit or try to stand. "Did you hurt yourself on that crazy ride?"

"Just stiff," you tell her.

"You're sure that's all it is?"

"That's all it is."

"You're getting old, Pop," she says. And later, when Ridley drops in she says, "The old man's a little lame today. He tried to take off with a horse. But the horse didn't like it, wouldn't get off the ground."

"That so?" Ridley inspects you carefully as he sits casually down. "Heard something about the gate being closed."

"Just trying to open it for Glennis," you tell him.

"He's considerate," Glennis says primly. But she watches Jack as Jack sits watching you.

"How you feeling?" Ridley asks.

"Feel pretty good," you tell him. "Let's go for a swim."

After a moment Ridley says, "No, don't think I will. I'll take a beer though."

"Sit still, honey," you say as Glennis moves to leave her chair. "I'll get the beer." And you manage to make it out to the kitchen without flinching as you move.

"Listen, sweetheart!" Glennis comes into the kitchen behind you and closes the door. "If there's anything wrong with you, I want to know it." She stands right up to you, a look in her eyes of anger, concern and fear. "You'd better tell Jack if there is. You'd better at least tell me."

"It's just my aching back." You smile and kiss her cheek.

"That vertebra you cracked?" She's worried again.

"No." You could kick yourself for forgetting that. "It's a little bit lower down. You know how I landed, honey, right on my butt."

"You're sure that's all it is?"

"Scout's honor." You hand her Ridley's beer. "Take that to Jack."

"All right," she says, not meaning it. "Our hero," she tells Jack in the other room, "had a bad prat fall. He says that's all that hurts. Here's your beer."

"Thanks," Ridley says. "Too bad he didn't land on his head, wouldn't have bothered him so much." And he studies you carefully again as you come walking back into the room, sit down as casually as you can.

Jack goes home at last. You go to bed. And half the night you lie there thinking about the project and the plane, about yourself and Glennis and the boys. Seen from one side, the problem is a simple one. You've got two broken ribs, no business making that next flight in the plane. You know this. All your training has been to make you the conscious member of a team. If you can't depend on yourself, you have no right to put yourself in a spot where others have to depend on you.

Yet you're pretty sure, think you can fly the airplane without any more risk than there usually is to you and the plane, the project and the crew. And there's something else—this isn't just another flight. You're sure of that. It's something you feel you've earned, the right to make the first supersonic flight. It isn't that you're competing with Hoover. Hell, he's a friend. If you can't make it, there's nobody else you'd rather see fly the airplane. But you think you can. By God, you're going to try.

You'll wait until you get into the plane, you decide that night. That's the worst of it, that crawling into the cockpit of the X-1 while it's in the air. If you can do that, you can fly the thing. If you feel you can't, you'll tell them before the drop. There won't be much chance then of anything happening to the airplane or to you.

Next day you have to convince yourself again, repeat the whole argument as you fall asleep on Sunday night. You have to convince Glennis, too, that you're all right. She doesn't believe it. You don't know whether she knows you're going to hit Mach 1 on the next flight or not. But she knows that something is going to happen. And she knows something's wrong.

"Well, how's the horseman?" she greets you on the morning of the flight.

"Pretty fair."

"You look like they hung you for rustling last night and forgot to cut the body down."

"I had a dream," you tell her, "pretty good one. We finished the project. We all got promoted. I bought a new car, a house in town. We took a trip back East together."

"We did?" Glennis is not doing anything now, just looking at you.

"How's your timing?" she asks. "I mean, is all this going to happen soon, this dream you had?"

"Pretty soon."

"Like today, maybe?"

"Well, I don't know."

"I'm going to get dressed," she says. "You fry the eggs. I'll drive you to the base today."

You've got to make it, you think, as you hear her waking up the boys. It is half-past five in the morning. An hour later you're both at the base.

29

Monday, October 14, 1947. It is twelve minutes after six o'clock in the morning. Light creeps along the gray hills that rim the big air base. On tower, water tank and roofs, bright red lamps wink their warning in the chilly air. Smoke puffs from scattered stacks, curls lazily down and drifts away. An airplane lands, the sound of its engine dying suddenly. And the red rim of the sun slides into the early morning sky. Through the dry field along the road up to the base, a lone jack rabbit runs, darting from tuft to barren tuft of dull gray grass.

Now the sky lightens. But in hangars, shops and offices the lights still burn for men who have worked through the night. It is too early still for shifts to change. The few cars that leave the highway drive up to the guarded gate, pause and then nose their way into the parking lot along one hangar wall, bring from desert towns only the handful of men assigned to work with the X-1—pilots and crewman, mechanics and engineers. But there is movement now all over the sprawling base.

A big fuel truck goes rumbling through one quiet street. Somewhere an engine coughs and comes to life. An Air Police jeep, its long whiplike antenna trembling in air, rolls slowly around the restricted security area. Here and there men walk from barracks down to the hangar now. It is daylight. Low in the east, the sun sits like a red disk on the desert's edge. Grass turns slowly yellow, the dry lake a reddish brown. The distant hills are strangely blue.

"What time will you fly, Chuck?" Glennis asks you as you stop the car.

"Come back a little before ten o'clock." You turn to kiss her. "Be careful driving on that road."

"I will."

"Leave early enough so you won't have to rush."

"All right."

"So long, son." You muss Donald's hair. "You take care of your mom."

You leave the car and carefully close and lock its door, smile briefly, stand for a moment watching as Glennis drives away, then turning, walk back into the project again, step into excitement as you enter the hangar in which the X-1 sits.

Crewmen have already gone to work. Stripped of its access doors, surrounded by tools, racks, ladders and working gear, the ship is alive with men again, spotted with trouble lights. Their long black cords lie tangled on the concrete floor.

"Jack," you call to the crew chief from the tail of the ship. "Let's have a look back here."

Ridley comes in. "Did you get shampoo to bathe the windshield with?" he wants to know.

"Anybody get that Drene?" You turn to the crew chief.

"We got it," Jack says.

"Think it will keep the glass from frosting, Chuck?"

"Why not?" you answer Ridley. "It's worked before."

"Okay." He nods. "Now remember—" Ridley leads you away, together you leave the ship, walk to the office, talking as you go—"you play around with the stabilizer setting before you make the high-speed run. We know you'll lose some elevator control. So find out where you get the most longitudinal control with the stabilizer. Try it at different settings and at different speeds above .85 or .86."

"All right," you agree. "What did they say in Dayton about the last flight report we made?"

Ridley shrugs. "Weren't too impressed. Told us we could try. But they don't think we'll get away with it."

You're in the office now and Frost comes in. "Hey, Chuck," he asks, "where did you hitch your horse?"

"Yeah, how about that?" Ridley joins him. "Understand you go anywhere on that nag."

"Yeager and his wonder horse!" Frost strikes a pose.

"He'd have done better to ride the gate," Ridley suggests.

"Why didn't you let the horse get off and open the gate?"

"Sure," Ridley agrees with Frost as you sit carefully down on a desk. "Those horses have all been trained."

Hoover and Bob Cardenas now come drifting in. "How's the Lone Ranger?" Hoover asks.

"Got you a present." Cardenas grins. He offers a package wrapped in brown paper, tied with a piece of string.

"Thanks, Bob." You take the package, untie the string as the others watch. Wrapped in the paper you find a big raw carrot, a pair of glasses, an old length of rope.

"All cowboys," Hoover says, "use rope."

"You can use that one," Ridley suggests again, "to tie yourself on the horse."

"The glasses and that carrot there are from the rest of the crew," Cardenas says. "I bought the rope."

"Well," Ridley comments, "that's something else you can use—might help you to see corral gates and all those little things it's hard to find at night."

"Why, thanks a whole lot," you answer finally. "One thing about you guys, you're real sincere." All three break into sudden laughter as you put on the glasses, bite into the carrot and pick up the rope. "Drop over tonight," you say. "Come one at a time. Be nice to have you hanging around the place."

There is more laughter, another joke or two until Ridley finally says, "Well, let's go get some food and then we'll all get down to work."

You breakfast together in the service club, go through the line, pick up a cup of coffee, walk to a table and sit down.

"Not hungry?" Frost asks as he takes a chair.

"Had breakfast at home."

"Jack tell you about that stabilizer setting yet?"

"We were talking about it when you guys came into the office with that lousy gag."

Ridley comes up, unloads his tray and begins to talk even before he's had time to begin to eat. "Now listen," Ridley points at you—and the horseplay is over. Even at breakfast you start preparing for the flight. There's little excitement now and no display. But you're confident, every one of you, and you move, talk, think and feel with the conviction that something is going to happen. You each know it is. Your confidence is obvious to everyone.

There you sit, the X-1 crew, and the rest of the men on the project all come drifting in. You have this air of expectancy together and it's apparent now to everyone else who walks through the chow line and sits down to eat. Now the whole base begins to sense that something is in the air, that something is going to happen with the carefully guarded plane you fly. Everyone looks at you knowing this, or you think they do. And a sudden feeling of separation from the rest of the base draws the crew into an even tighter group than you've been before. So that when you leave at last, walk back to the office to begin the job of preparing the full flight plan, the first excitement touches each one of you. The first small rise in tension has begun. The hot morning moves along and you move through its fixed routine. But each of your moves is made with a heightened purpose now and with increased intensity. It's as if each of your muscles knows and your nerves that this is the day—this is the flight. And tension imperceptibly mounts from minute to minute as take-off time comes near.

The flight plan meanwhile is altered, changed, then changed again. The briefing goes on, as in the big hangar and out on the concrete ramp, the X-1 and the B-29 are cautiously checked and readied to fly. You ride in your ship as you always do, from the hangar out to the pit, reciting as always its systems to yourself. And at the pit the action finally begins again at three minutes after eight o'clock.

There's the business of carefully mating the planes, of nosing the B-29 into the lox tank and evaporator. There's the connecting of hoses, the loading of nitrogen gas and fuel and lox. You sit in the cockpit again, check out the landing gear, make certain the domes are spilled, then leave to put your parachute in the cabin of the B-29. Now there's the ride with Ridley back to your room, the struggle into your flying clothes, the briefing with Williams and Beeler and their cautious talk, the endless repeating of phrases formed to protect the ship, "unless you're absolutely certain," or "under no circumstances will you" and "you'd better be sure." Their whole point is that you won't accelerate the ship beyond .96 unless you're certain you can handle it.

You study the card, go over it all with Ridley as you walk back to the planes. "Well, Jack?" you ask.

"Hell, Chuck, it's just another flight, just one more in the series and that's all it is."

"You think we'll do it?"

"Yeah, we might," he says. "We might just do it, Chuck." Then, looking up, "Here's that good-looking wife of yours."

"Hi, Jack," she calls to Ridley.

"Glennis." Ridley smiles, waves a brief greeting and walks tactfully on alone.

"I'm glad you're still here." Glennis is out of breath from running now. Her cheeks are flushed. "I brought something you might want."

"What's that?"

She kisses you suddenly and as suddenly steps back. "I'll wait in the car. Don't be too long."

Half-turned away now, you both pause, each waiting for the other to say "Chuck" or Glennis." "How about dinner tonight?" You manage to grin at her.

"I'd love it. But no more horses."

"Damn that horse!" You manage to laugh. "That's all I've heard today. Don't think I'll ever live it down. Well—" There's another pause—"I'll see you later, honey."

You turn then and walk carefully away from her. And everything moves at once as you come up to the planes again. Pilots and crew go scrambling into the bomber's hatch. The last thick hose is disconnected from the X-1 now. Somebody shouts, "Let's go!" And the yellow bull-dozer, already hooked to the tail of the B-29, backs easily away.

Still on the ground, you run in under the moving bomber's wing, make the last-minute check of cabin and instruments, of switches and of valves, make sure both helmet and mask are wedged in tight and can't fall out. In the last twenty seconds then you turn and run, half-crouched, those two ribs suddenly knifing your chest as you duck under the bomber's belly, force your way into the open hatch.

"Here he is now," Ridley calls to Cardenas.

"Tell him," Cardenas says, "he's just in time." He fires the engines. The bomber trembles as if with your own impatience to get off the ground. It is two minutes after ten o'clock. The sun stands high now in the bright blue sky.

"Muroc Tower," Cardenas calls. His voice is matter-of-fact and calm. "Air Force eight-zero-zero, taxi instructions."

"B-29, eight-zero-zero," the metallic-sounding voice of the tower operator answers. "Cleared runway six. Winds out of the east at seven miles an hour."

"We cleared to roll?"

"Roger, cleared to line up and roll."

"She's all yours, Major," the B-29 flight engineer reports.

"All right, Swindel?"

"Roger," the engineer calls back, "she is all yours."

"Rolling," Cardenas says. The bomber moves slowly off and begins to roll and the take-off chant of the scanners sounds again as they report the left and right gear moving up, left flap and right flap moving up, fifteen degrees on left and right. "Left gear full up, left flap full up," the left scanner calls out. "One and two look clean on the take-off, sir."

"Right gear full up, right flap full up," the right scanner echoes. "Three and four look good on the take-off."

"Roger," the engineer comes on again.

You are off the ground and climbing to altitude now, a

little more nervous, excited, a little more scared than you've been before.

"B-29, eight-zero-zero to Muroc Tower," Cardenas calls. "How do you read me? Over."

"Loud and clear," the tower says.

And you sit on the box and briefly wonder how it will be, how it will feel, just what will happen twenty minutes from now as the bomber climbs to drop you out. The whole of the project moves back through you mind. Recalling each flight, each strange new incident, failure and flaw, you try to remember all you've learned since the sixth of July—three months and a week ago—when you first sat in class and listened to Frost. Thank God, you think, I've never had fire in the plane!

"Scanners from engineer," Swindel says quietly, "five thousand feet."

You reach out then, nudge Ridley, who sits on the deck. "Let's go, Jack. Let's get in the thing and get it over with."

Glad of the chance to move again, to have work to do, you follow him back into the bomb bay, jump on the ladder, shaking it down.

But the moment you drop into that cold wind blast and roar, the fear you've ignored sweeps through your mind. You've got to bend down, double up, twist now and squirm from the ladder's platform into the seat. You hesitate, then suddenly move. A few moments later you're settled down, helmet and mask adjusted, breathing oxygen again. You peck on the canopy. Ridley lowers the door, comes down the ladder to fight it into its place. With radio plugged in and working, with the first instrument check to make, you have enough at the moment to fill your mind. Fear dies again, is almost gone.

With eyes accustomed now to darkness within the plane, you make the first check of the cockpit from landing gear handle on your left to cabin pressure valve in the door on your right. The routine is taut and dramatic now, each movement weighed with the purpose of this flight. "To investigate effects of increased Mach number," the flight report will say. But in a few minutes you will fly at the speed of sound, smash through the wall, invade a region of speed in which no other man has ever lived. You know you will. The certainly shoots from nerve to nerve. Your heart beats faster, muscles tighten with each fresh impulse the thought transmits. Faster than sound! You'll be the first! But all the while you're going through the routine check—gear handle up; jettison valves closed; domes spilled, bleed pressure normal...

Faster than sound, you think again, Mach 1 in minutes now... Battery switch on, rocket chamber switches off; emergency cut-out botton on—In just a few minutes you'll drop out... Oxygen breathing pressure good; voltage up and cabin pressure set at *pressurized*—And what if something should go wrong? But nothing will... Your bail-out bottle is firmly secured, attached to your mask.

"Check list competed," you report. "Everything okay."

"Roger."

"B-29, eight-zero-zero." Cardenas drones identification into the air. "Air Force two-zero-one. Hoover, are you guys on the way up?"

"Yeah, boy."

"Okay, we're just closing 15,000 feet. About twenty south of the lake. Making a right turn now and heading south."

"Roger."

"You over El Mirage, Cardenas?" Frost comes on the air.

"Coming to the southern end of the lake at 16,000 feet."

"I'll be with you soon."

It is all just as it's been on every other flight. The bomber climbs in its spiral over the dry lake bed, the chase planes shoot to altitude in opening phase of the carefully timed and familiar plan.

"Air Force two-zero-one, where are you, B-29?"

"I am coming around—"

"Okay, I see you now, buddy. Coming up to you."

Hoover flies on ahead. Frost in the low chase plane hangs on your tail. There's the sweating again, the fear, the last minute check of the cockpit check already made, the dry run through the predrop check you've still to make.

"Eight-zero-zero," Cardenas says briefly, "five-minute warning."

"Okay, Cardenas, loading the first stage now."

"Ridley?" you call when the first-stage pressure has coming up. "Clear to disconnect nitrogen hose and pilot's breathing oxygen."

"Roger."

"Four minutes."

"Roger, Cardenas. Pressurizing fuel tank."

"Nitrogen hose disconnected," Ridley says. "Pilot's breathing oxygen disconnected."

"Roger, Jack."

"NACA radar to Air Force eight-zero-zero, how do you read?"

"Loud and clear. Three minutes."

"Pressurizing lox tank," you report. "All pressurized."

"Yeager, this is Frost. I'm in position now to check your jettison."

"Roger. Fuel jettison is on."

"Fuel jettison okay."

"Switch off."

"Shutoff okay."

"Two minutes," Cardenas warns.

"Lox jettison switch on. Switch off."

"Lox jettison and shutoff are okay."

"Was that two minutes, B-29?"

"Roger, that was two minutes."

Down on the field meanwhile men wander curiously to doors and windows and look vainly up into the sky. Trucks pause and jeeps and private cars, as drivers shade eyes against the midmorning sun, stare into brightness, searching, for even the big B-29 is only a speck in all that sky. The cars move on, then stop again from time to time.

And under the tower a small crowd waits. From hangars and offices, from barracks, shops and sheds, pilots and clerks have come, civilian engineers, mechanics in old fatigues and coveralls. Some are bareheaded and with squinting eyes, some with their cap peaks down, eyes sweeping the wide sky. Others stand looking down, heads bent to listen as the tower operator suddenly goes on the air.

"Muroc Air Force Base to all aircraft," the tower operator says. "All aircraft stay clear of Muroc Dry Lake area. Test in progress. All aircraft on the ground return to parking positions. Repeat—all aircraft stay clear."

The listening men at the base of the tower look up too now at the glaring sky.

"B-29, eight-zero-zero," Cardenas says, "to NACA radar, Muroc Tower, chase aircraft—one minute warning."

"NACA radar to Air Force B-29, eight-zero-zero, you are clear to drop."

"Roger."

"Muroc Tower to Air Force eight-zero-zero, clear to drop."

"Roger, Muroc."

Dry-lipped and hunched down in your seat again, your fingers tight on the control stick and your muscles braced against expected shock, you wait.

"Yeager? This is Ridley. You all set?"

"Hell, yes, let's get it over with."

"Remember those stabilizer settings."

"Roger."

"Eight-zero-zero, here is your count-down. Ten," Cardenas begins, "nine-eight-seven-six-five-four-three-two-one. Drop!"

It is twenty-six minutes after ten o'clock.

30

"After normal pilot entry and subsequent climb," you will later report on the flight, "the X-1 was dropped from the B-29 at 20,000 feet pressure altitude and at 250 mph indicated air speed."

But there is the long, long second until the shackle releases its grip and you feel that separating snap. There is the fall—you float in midair again, float back to your seat. And then you turn the power on. "Firing four," your monologue begins. The plane shoots suddenly ahead. "Four fired okay . . . will fire two . . . two on . . . will cut off four . . . four off . . . will fire three . . . three burning now . . . will shut off two and fire one . . . one on."

Now with two rockets' thrust, the ship leaps suddenly away. "Will fire two again . . . two on . . . will fire four." With full power on, you climb to altitude. On the way up you change the stabilizer from its predrop setting of one degree nose down, moving it now in careful increments of one-quarter to one-third of a degree at .83, at .88 and .92 Mach numbers as you climb. The stabilizer powers effective at all speeds. At 35,000 feet you cut two cylinders off. Still racing up, you level off at a speed of .92 Mach number, reporting a sudden drop in lox line pressure at 40,000 feet.

"How much of a drop?" somebody asks.

"About 40 psi . . . got a rich mixture . . . chamber pressures down . . . now going up again . . . pressures all normal . . . will fire three again . . . three on . . . acceleration good . . . have had mild buffet . . . usual instability." The Mach needle passes .96. "Say, Ridley," you call him, "make a note here . . . elevator effectiveness regained."

"Roger. Noted."

The Mach needle moves to .98. You report rapid acceleration now and at .98 Mach the needle suddenly fluctuates and then goes off the scale. But there is no jolt, no buffet, no shock. "Ridley!" you call sharply, trying to tell him what you can't say on the restricted air. "Make another note. There's something wrong with this Machmeter. It's gone screwy!"

"If it is, we'll fix it," Ridley answers, letting you know he understands. "Personally, I think you're seeing things."

"I guess I am, Jack . . . will shut down again . . . am shutting off . . . shut off . . . still going upstairs like a bat . . . have jettisoned fuel and lox . . . about 30 per cent of each remaining . . . still going up . . ."

And you will later state in your written report of this, the ninth powered flight, "Acceleration was rapid and speed increased to .98 Mach." The needle of the Machmeter fluctuated at this reading momentarily, then passed off the scale. Assuming that the off-scale reading remained linear, it is estimated that 1.05 Mach was attained at this time. Approximately 30 per cent of fuel and lox remained when this speed was reached and the motor turned off.

"While the usual light buffet and instability character-istics were encountered in the .88–.90 Mach range," your report will continue, "and elevator effectiveness was very greatly decreased at .94 Mach, stability about all three axes was excellent as speed increased and elevator effectiveness was regained above .97 Mach. In short, airplane control and stability were completely normal as 1.0 Mach was attained and passed."

And you will privately and publicly insist that if the Machmeter hadn't been in the cockpit of the plane, you'd never have noticed the smashing of that barrier they used to call "the brick wall in the sky."

But still in the airplane now, you have no time to be surprised at this. "Have shut off now," you call to Muroc Tower, to NACA, to Frost in his F-80, to Ridley in the big B-29. And flying still at tremendous speed, the ship glides on to 45,000 feet. There you perform a one g stall with gear and flaps up. Then, at last, you enter the long glide back to the dry lake bed on which you'll land.

"As speed decreased after turning off the motor," you will note in your report, "the various phenomena occurred in reverse sequence at the usual speeds." That is, in the same sequence, but reversed as your speed drops, the Mach needle falls back on the scale, fluctuates and drops to .98. You lose stability again at .94, encounter buffeting at .90—and sudden weariness as you come in to land.

You can see to land this time. Cold as the cockpit is, the windshield isn't frosted now. "Before this flight," your written report will finally end, "the interior of the windshield was treated with Drene shampoo in the manner developed during the war, and no frosting occurred."

And at twenty minutes before eleven o'clock, just fourteen minutes after the drop was made, your wheels touch down, the X-1 rolls across the runway and comes quietly to rest. Stiff with cold, fatigued more than you've ever been, you release the door, slip off your chute and harness, helmet and mask, unhook your radio. All switches off, domes spilled, you leave the ship, climb out with the crewmen's help and wearily ride away. The hot sunlight begins to warm your flying clothes. All feeling is lost for the moment in your lassitude.

"How did it go?" the jeep driver wants to know.

"Okay, I guess. No trouble. Everything worked pretty well." You ask him then to drive you to the building in which you've got a room. Still tired, you walk inside. You change your clothes. Then you pick up the telephone and call the NACA office half a block away. "I'm tired," you say. "I'd like to delay the briefing on this flight. I want to go home and get some sleep." You walk back out to the jeep, climb stiffly in, sit without saying anything except, "Drop me off at the parking lot. My wife—" You're suddenly anxious to see Glennis now. She's waiting there.

Yet when you leave the jeep, walk to your car, pull open the door and sit beside Glennis on the seat, you can say only, "I'm tired, honey. Let's go home."

It's not that you have no feeling about the flight. You

have too much. But it's buried under the restraint that years of flying have imposed. Emotion, whether it's pleasure, pain or grief—you have none. That is, you cut it off. There can be no display of this. You feel it, yes. But it stays within you, locked in the grip you've learned to keep on the things you feel until their strength is broken. You can release them then in deceptive gestures, carefully controlled, so that grief becomes a quiet word and ride some wild and dangerous act.

That's why, when Frost comes suddenly running up to the car, you want to leave. But Glennis has stopped. Frost grabs the handle and opens the door. "Congratulations, you son of a gun!" he shouts, half-pulling you out of the car as he shakes your hand and, in the same moment, pounds your back.

"What happened?" Glennis asks as Frost still pounds away.

"Oh—" You look at the ground, then smile at her— "we made it on this flight."

"You didn't!"

"By God, he did!" Frost shouts. "And he didn't tell you, Glennis?"

"No, not a word. He just said, 'Let's go home,' as if nothing had happened."

"Go home? Why, you son of a gun!" Frost shouts again, still pounding you on the back. "You were going to leave? This guy has no nerves, Glennis. He didn't say anything at all?"

"Oh yes, he said he wanted to go home." Glennis begins to smile.

"You son of a gun!" Frost shakes his head now as he pumps your hand.

From tower and hangar meanwhile the news has spread to barracks, shops and offices. It is no secret now, this news that is too good to keep. The base switchboard is jammed. Long-distance calls are made and wires are sent from border to border and from coast to coast—to Larry Bell, laughing and swearing back in Buffalo, to Colonel Boyd in Dayton, to John Stack at the Langley lab, to RMI in Pompton Lakes. All through the states the news is flashed. All through this dusty Air Force base.

So that even while you stand quietly beside the excited Frost, the public-address system at Muroc suddenly begins to boom. "Attention all personnel! The Bell X-1—" The voice blares in the streets, in hangars, offices and shops—"piloted by Captain Charles E. Yeager—" The voice rolls from the base out into open fields, out over ramp and concrete strip and dry lake bed—"has just completed the first supersonic flight—" In small rooms and in large the voice reverberates—"achieving a speed in excess of Mach 1—" It is an exciting voice, excited itself now as it wildly concludes—"in a climb to altitude from 35,000 feet!"

"And you," Frost says again, still standing with you in the parking lot, his hand still gripping yours, "were going to sneak away! You son of a gun! Your crazy sun of a gun!"

You leave him then, the pain of those broken ribs like a knife in your chest as you stoop to re-enter the car.

31

But the excitement dies away at last and in the morning it is gone. There is only a sense of accomplishment, a deep awareness of the thing you've done as you go back to work again, back to the routine job of flying the X-1. It hasn't made any difference, that single flight. You're still in the Air Force, still a working pilot assigned to Fighter Test. And the old man's voice still sounds from time to time in the back of your mind—"And if you're assigned to this project, do you understand the role you will play in the history of aviation? Do you realize the tremendous amount of personal publicity to which you will be exposed? Do you think it will have a negative effect on you . . . interfere with your performance as a pilot? Would you be able to go on with your routine duty? Go right on flying as a regularly assigned pilot? Would you continue to be stable under the pressure imposed by fame?"

You said you would. You think you can. As time goes on and the rewards come in, you really try. You make thirty flights or more in the X-1 in the next thirteen months. It is odd to think that you log only four hours' time in all those flights. Because so much happens. You exceed the speed of sound a dozen times or more, get up as high as 60,000 feet, a record that's not officially confirmed. You fly the X-1 vertically, both up and down. You win the Mackay Trophy, an Oak Leaf cluster to the DFC. You share in the 1947 Collier Trophy with Larry Bell and John Stack of NACA for the first supersonic flight.

It is for the combination of scientific research and

aircraft design and construction with military planning, evaluation and use that the Collier Trophy is awarded. But you have the feeling that some sort of medal ought to be struck for your wife. Your own compensation for whatever risks there are is adequate. It isn't the money—just a captain's pay and the flight pay you certainly earn. But there is the experience itself of climbing each time through the darkening sky into the rich, deep blue of altitude eleven miles or more above the earth. There is the wonderful ease with which the airplane flies, the sense of accomplishment with which you land, and the recognition in which you share.

Yet for Glennis there is nothing but waiting, only the fear that touches every aspect of her life. You leave in the morning. She can never be certain you'll come home at night. All pilots' wives feel this from time to time. Glennis lives with it every moment of the day. And her fear is heightened by the nature of the planes you fly. It isn't only the X-1. As the project settles down you're assigned to all experimental aircraft that come to the base. On a given day you may fly three or four different planes. You're not really certain of all procedures all the time. You sit in one strange cockpit after another, think out each procedure for each of the planes you fly. But you're never at ease in any one of them. After a while this tells on you. You live under constant strain. Your wife does, too. There is some release for you in the action and in the end of every flight. There is none for her. You are often away. On Friday you may leave Muroc for Dayton or England, Okinawa or New York. You might be back on Monday. You might not. Glennis sits waiting. She never gets away. There is no real escape for her. Then in the summer of 1948 she's pregnant again. This time it worries her.

You've been through the sound barrier several times. There's been some talk about the effect of flight at the speed of sound on pilots who experience this. The baby Glennis is carrying will be the first "supersonic" baby, the first human being conceived whose father has been exposed to the dustless light of altitude and to buffeting, shock and turbulence that takes place as you fly beyond

Mach 1 and come back through the pull-out to subsonic speeds again. There might be, Glennis hears, some negative effect. The baby might be a mutation, some sort of freak.

"Just remember—" She tries to laugh it off at first— "it's on your side of the family, not mine." But the new fear grows in her mind. "I don't know," she says sadly one night, "it was fun looking forward to Mickey and Don. But this time, Chuck, I'm scared."

Watching her then from day to day, you're worried, too. This isn't something you really understand. You don't connect her sickness with her fear. You know only that each day she's a little more tired, a little more depressed. You don't know why. With Mickey and Don on your hands, you don't know what to do. Neither does Glennis. "It isn't fair to the boys," she says, ashamed of being sick, ashamed of having let you down. "And it certainly isn't fair to you."

"Just take it easy," you answer. "It isn't fair to you either. Don't worry about it. Get some rest."

"But I feel so useless." Admitting this depresses her, tires her even more. "Chuck, what in the world are we going to do?"

Her mother and father come to look after Glennis and the boys. It will all work out, her mother keeps saying.

But it doesn't work out. Glennis never complains. Yet you know how she feels and there is little pleasure in doing anything that takes you away from her.

"Well, honey," you say each morning in apology, "I've got to go."

"I'll be all right," she insists.

"Just take it easy."

"I'm tired of taking it easy."

And at night you hurry home to reassure her, to tell her you're there and that everything is all right.

"I'm not all right," she says quietly. "Honey, what's the matter with me? I don't want to be like this!" She begins to cry a little. "Why?"

And you hold her quietly until she falls asleep. In the morning you have to leave again. The project, your work, whatever you have to do, half-carries you through the day, from day to day and from week to week. So that before you know it, the first year at Muroc has gone by. The second is on its way. There's little time in which to wonder where the time has gone. There is too much to do.

You fly the X-1 on most of its scheduled flights, exploring speed and altitude, exploring the plane itself. The flights, dramatic at first, each one a separate event, merge in your mind to become a single experience of wearying intensity and of seemingly endless speed through minutes that seem at times to be as long as months. And as you fly, you learn.

Normal flight characteristics associated with high Mach numbers are light buffet, lateral and longitudinal instability, decreased elevator effectiveness. But as you become increasingly familiar with the plane you notice more.

The X-1 is right-wing heavy throughout the transonic range and up to above Mach 1. From .87 Mach number the buffeting increases and there is a nose-down trim change. At .90 Mach buffeting becomes severe and the nose-down trim change is reversed. At .94 this trim change is again reversed. As speed increases, in other words, the nose becomes heavy, then light, then heavy again, and buffeting becomes increasingly severe. At .94, meanwhile, the elevator and rudder begin to lose effectiveness; there is little response. But at .95 buffeting begins to decrease and at .96 it disappears. The stabilizer remains effective at all times, the ailerons, too. At .98 or .99 Mach number the plane smooths suddenly out to normal flying characteristics. As you go on from there up past Mach 1, the needle momentarily stops, then jumps from .99 up to 1.06, for example, or 1.05.

You cannot always do what you want to do with the X-1. It will not always yaw to the left when you think it will, or roll or stall. But buffeting in the transonic range is less severe as you increase the altitude at which you fly. At Mach numbers in excess of 1, you can make gentle turns and climbs. Its flight characteristics do not change very much.

Neither does anything else. The cylinders often fail to

ignite. Sometimes the solenoid fails to release the shackle
holding the X-1 into the B-29, or the shackle sticks,
delaying your drop for seconds that seem like endless
time. There is always fear. And sometimes there is fire in
the plane.

Fire—that is the worst of all. On the nineteenth flight
the engine howls, begins to sound suddenly like a blazing
hot kerosene stove with too much oil in the pan. The
fire-warning light is off. But the cabin suddenly fills with
smoke. You don't know what will happen next. The sight of
that smoke just freezes you. If there weren't so many
things to be done, you'd lose your head.

Three of the four cylinders won't fire. You run on the
fourth until the fuel is gone, nervously reach .70 Mach
number, nervously glide down and land. It happens again
on the next flight. The engine rumbles again. The fire-
warning light comes on this time. You jettison fuels and
land. There is fire again on the flight after that, loose
chamber igniters the probably cause. The damage is slight,
except to the pilot's peace of mind. Because the minute
you first smell smoke, the moment that big red warning
light comes on, you don't know what to do, what to
expect. For the first time you are really consciously frightened in the plane. You don't know whether to shut off fuel,
or whether to jettison or not. You want fuel out of the
ship. But if a jettisoning line has burned in two, the aft
end of the plane will fill with fuel when you hit the switch.
There will be just that much more fire in the plane. Yet
you know that if the fuel stays anywhere in the ship, it
might explode. The liquid oxygen, too. The ship will blow
up and you'll blow with it. You just don't know what to do.

"Ridley!" you're calling all this while. And you're
calling Hoover, too. "Can you see anything? Got a fire
warning here! Smell smoke! What can you see? Can you
see anything at all?"

"Pretty far back behind you," Ridley says. "I can't see
anything at all."

"I see nothing," Hoover says.

So you try to think back through the systems of the
ship. You analyze all your instruments, guess what's been

happening, trouble-shoot the thing yourself. And at last you take a good tight grip and flip the jettison switch, expecting the plane to blow apart. You just hump up, pull up in your seat and wait for the blast that will scatter the plane in a million pieces and spatter you through the air. And nothing happens.

"Probably had a little fire," Hoover says calmly then. He's come up on your tail. "Couple of holes burned in your cowling. But there's nothing burning back there now."

Yet the fire-warning light still flashes and you're still all hunched up, ready to blow right out of the cockpit, to go right out through the metal skin.

"No fire," Ridley reports. He's on your tail now, too. The fuel and lox have been jettisoned. You begin to relax. But it's a long, long time until you feel at ease again. When you go home that night you're still half-scared. And Glennis is worried all over again at the way you look. It's one of those nights when you know you're going to dream. You try to sleep on the couch in the living room. The nightmare begins. She hears you, anyway.

"No, Chuck," Glennis says. Awake, you find her at your side again. "Only a dream, darling, just a dream." But there's no strength in her now as she holds your arm. You carry her back to bed and she seems terribly light. For a long, long time you sit in the darkness beside her, calming her fear, doing your best to calm your own.

"How's the baby growing?" you ask her.

"Don't," she begs.

"There's nothing to worry about," you say. "It'll be a girl this time."

"Please, honey."

"She'll look like you. Your side of the family, all right?"

"Oh, God," she says, almost beginning to cry again. "I hope it is."

"It will be, Glennis." You hold her hands. "You'll see. We'll have a fat little girl. She'll look like you."

"Not if she's very fat, she won't."

"Well, don't you worry. If she's as good-looking as her mother is, she can be fat."

"I'm not very good-looking now."

"Right now you've got the prettiest look on your face I've ever seen."

"Chuck," she asks you suddenly. "What happened today?"

"Oh, nothing," you answer. "Same old thing."

"I'll bet it was."

"Bet you a brand-new dress you'll have a girl," you say insistently. She smiles then and begins to relax. And after a while you both fall quietly asleep. At eight in the morning you're back at the base again. At nine you fly, if not in the X-1, in the next ship that's scheduled for test flight. The weeks go on, the months. There is no change.

Then, in December of 1948, a new rumor comes along.

32

No one will really say now why the United States Air Force authorized the belated ground take-off of the X-1 from the strip at Muroc early in 1949. Accepted by the Air Force and flown through the sound barrier, the ship has performed the purpose for which it was designed and built. There is considerable risk in taking the heavily loaded plane straight up from ground. Yet this is what you are going to do.

"In connection with the proposed ground take-off of the X-1," Larry Bell wrote to General Donald Putt at the Pentagon in December of 1948, "I am enclosing herewith for your information a copy of proposed procedure that has been prepared by Dick Frost in conjunction with all of our engineers concerned with this project.

"We recommend," Bell concluded briefly, "that these procedures be followed and if you desire, we will be glad to ask Mr. Frost to go out to assist in the preparation for this flight."

The length of the proposed procedure alone indicates the seriousness with which Sandstrom, Emmons, Wheeler, Smith and Frost considered the ground take-off. Five pages of single-spaced typing accompanied Bell's letter to General Putt.

"It is our understanding," the engineers began, "that the Air Matériel Command plans to perform a ground take-off of the Bell X-1 airplane in the near future. While the airplane was designed initially to take off under its own power, the margins of safety were necessarily lower than those customary in fighter take-offs. Because of this and other considerations, the air-launch flight plan was subsequently adopted and has proved very satisfactory, as you know. However, it appears that the AMC has reason for performing at least one ground take-off, and we therefore feel morally obligated to recommend the safest procedure for this flight."

What then are the reasons for performing this flight? No one seriously plans to risk pilot and plane in a few seconds of exciting play, no matter what it might prove. No one has said, "You will on such and such a date, *et cetera*." Yet this is what will be done—the decision has been made to take the X-1 off the ground. For flying is still one of the most competitive and exciting ways in which a man can earn his daily bread. And the men who were originally attracted to the risk-and-instinct-defying business of flight were adventurous men, contemptuous of fear. In doing each day what had never been done before, they established a tradition for those who followed them. It is a tradition simply stated, difficult to live with. Nothing is impossible. So you take the risk. That's why they put you on flight pay.

That, basically, is why the ground take-off has been proposed, why it will be done, why you're all eager to do this, in spite of the heavy odds.

Five major factors, the engineers have reported, will be involved in taking the X-1 off the ground. These factors are:

I. The effect of high take-off speed on a somewhat overloaded landing gear.
II. The effect of longitudinal acceleration and the high angle of climb on center of gravity location.
III. The effect of normal accelerations less than $+1$ g on propellant supply.
IV. Aerodynamic characteristics of the airplane.
V. Rocket motor characteristics.

With so many risks, so much to be concerned about

in the flight, why has the ground take-off of the airplane been authorized?

"I had something to do with it," Larry Bell will later admit. "To make a world record anytime and to have it credited, it must be approved by an international group of which the National Aeronautical Association is the American member. The NAA never officially recognized the X-1's first sonic flight because it had been made in a plane dropped from another plane. They said, in effect, that to have the X-1 recognized as the first official supersonic airplane, it would have to reach Mach 1 in a flight from ground take-off. So—" Bell shrugs and smiles, remembering again.

But there is still another reason. It never occurred to Larry Bell or to anyone else to go after official recognition by the NAA until a competitor came along. The Navy now had a supersonic plane. Their plane, the Navy said, "Is more than a rocket-powered glider." Its power plant will take it up to altitude from ground, then to Mach 1.

This is the background. That is why the X-1 has to take off from the ground. It is not a decision freely made, but one forced by another competing group. It is a decision informally authorized one night in mid-December, 1948, at the dinner in Washington commemorating the forty-fifth anniversary of the Wright Brothers' first flight.

"Chuck," Bell asks—and General Hoyt Vandenberg is with him now—"what do you think about the Navy taking their plane up from the ground?"

"Hell, Larry," you answer, "anything they can do, we can do, too."

And Bell turns now to Vandenberg. "General?" His eyes sparkle with excitement. "You know the Navy has this plane. They plan to take it off from ground and they say they'll get it up to altitude with fuel enough to hit Mach 1. You know what that means. Those guys will claim a first. But the X-1, as you know, was designed for ground take-off. We ought to do it first. I see no reason why we can't. Neither does anyone else, including Captain Yeager here, who pilots the plane."

"I understand." Vandenberg, Air Force Chief of Staff, touches a finger to his chin. "When—" He is almost grinning to himself—"is this going to happen?"

"When will the Navy do it?" Bell asks.

"No, when will we?"

"How soon," Bell asks, "can you get back to Muroc, Chuck?"

"I'll leave," you answer, "right after chow."

"The day after tomorrow," Bell tells Vandenberg.

The general answers, "Good," as his grin breaks out and he walks suddenly away.

However rich the personal satisfaction might be for any man, it is a decision made without personal reason. It is a decision made for the group. But it is a decision too in which risk lies.

"To minimize condition I (effect of high speed take-off)—" The engineers continue their cautious advice—"the following recommendations are made:

1. The propellant tank should be filled to approximately three-fourths capacity, which will give a gross weight of about 10,000 pounds.
2. All tires, tubes and brake 'biscuits' should be brand-new and in perfect condition.
3. The main wheel tires should be inflated to 110 psi and the nose wheel tire inflated to 90 psi (on the ground).
4. The struts should be filled and inflated per past instructions. (See appendix I.)
5. The take-off should be made relatively early in the day before the runway has been appreciably heated by the sun. (It is assumed that the take-off will be made on Runway No. 6 to the east-northeast so that the entire lake bed will be available for landing run in the event of rejected take-off. Incidentally, in such an event, it is recommended that brake use be kept to a minimum to avoid overloading the nose-wheel strut.)"

You yourself don't think too much about whatever hazards there might be in taking the X-1 off the ground. You're eager to do it. There's another challenge there. It is a familiar situation, one to which you react without concern at first for the details.

But the risks are there and you're glad to know that they're fully recognized by Bell engineers.

"To minimize condition II (the effect of longitudinal acceleration and the high angle of climb on center of gravity location) the following recommendations are made:

1. The center of gravity will travel aft between 2.5 per cent and 4.5 per cent, depending on the longitudinal acceleration and the angle of climb, so in filling the airplane the initial *c.g.* location should be 22 per cent of the mean aerodynamic chord of the wing.

2. To insure this initial *c.g.* location, an actual weight and balance should be performed just before take-off, using the balancing pads provided. Perhaps the best way to do this would be to fill the fuel tank to the desired level with the airplane supported on the balancing pads and a padded contour block under the aft fuselage, and then fill the loxygen tank until the airplane balances. Obviously the airplane must be shielded from wind while doing this, and take-off must be made as quickly as possible thereafter to prevent lox boil-off from having an appreciable effect.

3. Captain Yeager is best qualified to select the initial stabilizer setting and will, of course, be prepared to change it instantly if necessary."

It will be, you know, another one of those things. You'll sit in the cockpit nervously waiting to take off. You'll be scared as hell until you're back down on the ground. You know that, but you'll do it anyway—not for yourself alone. Not for the group. But simply because you're the pilot of this plane. This is your job. And its responsibility is something you accept without any further thought.

"To minimize condition III (the effect of normal accelerations less than $+1$ g on propellant supply)," the engineers continue, "the following recommendations are made:

1. Because normal accelerations less than $+1$ g reduces the propellant head, and thereby reduce motor thrust, the smoothest portion of the runway should be used and atmospheric turbulence must be at a minimum. Take-off early in the day as recommended above will tend to insure the latter condition, but it is recommended that it be checked by take-off of other aircraft immediately before the X-1 flight.
2. After take-off a spiral climb in the manner already perfected by Captain Yeager will insure maintenance of at least 1 g normal acceleration and prevention of difficulty."

That is, if the take-off is successful. You think it will be but you're not really positive. You never are. What, you begin to wonder, if—? There are too many *if*'s to think about—*if* you prang the airplane or *if* you auger in. So that finally you take refuge in the last of them. If there were any chance of that, you tell yourself, they'd never authorize this ground take-off. And yet you half-suspect they would. And that you'd do it anyway.

"To minimize condition IV (aerodynamic characteristics of the airplane)," the engineers go on, "the following recommendations are made:

1. It will be desirable to retract the landing gear very rapidly after attaining the height of several hundred feet and before indicated air speed has exceeded 250 mph. However, flap retractions should be relatively slow in order to avoid sudden change in CL. [Lift

Coefficient.] Therefore, the orifices in the flap and landing gear actuating cylinders should be modified until considered satisfactory by actual ground test. These orifices are drilled in the tube fittings screwed into these actuators and should be changed one drill size per test until a satisfactory speed is achieved. (See Appendix II.)

2. In the event of a forced landing immediately after take-off, the landing gear should be extended in contrast to the normal procedure of making a belly landing.

3. Captain Yeager will undoubtedly wish to keep his climb speed below .85 Mach number in order to maintain control effectiveness and prevent sudden changes in trim."

Reading their careful instructions for the preparation of the airplane, you gradually begin to realize what it is you've let yourself in for on this flight. And all you want is to get it over with. It is the same old feeling of impatience and of eagerness. It's not that you don't know what fear is. You do. But you can't run away. You are eager not so much to do it as you are to get it done, to have it over with, an accomplished fact. The plane isn't ready now, however, and there is more advice.

"To minimize condition V (rocket motor characteristics) the following recommendations are made:

1. It should be possible by the use of brakes to keep the airplane from moving under the thrust of at least three cylinders and probably with all four cylinders firing; therefore, the motor should be started with the brakes locked in order to assure proper operation of igniters and cylinders before action begins.

2. Cylinders No. 2 and 4 should be started first in order to avoid any possible yaw resulting from thrust alignment."

With all four cylinders on, you ought to go up like the proverbial bat out of hell and you probably will—if you go up at all. What if you don't?

In concluding, the Bell engineers recommend that:

1. The gyros be vented overboard and the cabin be vented to atmosphere through both the normal and emergency pressure relief valves.
2. The spiral climb mentioned above should be made to the right so that if for any reason the windshield should become obscured, the cabin door can be jettisoned, thus affording the full vision of the ground through the door opening.
3. After performance of this flight, the tires and tubes should be replaced. The manufacturer originally recommended tire and tube replacement after every two take-offs because of the possibility of undetectable ply separation during take-off run.

"If this ground take-off is performed as planned," say the engineers at last, "it will be a truly spectacular sight...." And you agree. But what will the ground observers see? And how will it feel to you in the cockpit of the plane?

It is something everyone wonders about as the ship is prepared for its ground take-off.

"Ought to be quite a ride, Chuck," Ridley quietly observes. "You're going from dead rest straight up in the air. Be quite a sensation."

"Why?" Glennis demands insistently. "Why do you have to do it? Why does it always have to be you?" Flat on her back and sick, Glennis is eight and a half months pregnant now. "Why?" she begs you again.

Why? You can't explain it to Glennis. Feeling as guilty as you do, you don't know what to say. "Because," you begin patiently, sitting down on the edge of her bed.

"What are you going to prove this time?"

"Nothing," you admit and guiltily stare at the back of her head as she turns in helpless anger, even more helpless fear, away from you.

"Then why take the chance?" she asks, not looking back.

"If we don't," you begin, "the Navy—" But you stop short, facing again the sudden impossibility of explaining to Glennis, who lies there wondering if this time you'll auger in, if she'll ever get up and walk again, if her baby is going to be some kind of freak. "Honey." You touch her arm.

"Oh, darling." She turns back to you now. "I'm terribly sorry to be such a fool." And her arms go around your neck. "Of course you have to. Don't pay any attention to me."

You try to tell her then what lies in the minds of all the men who have helped to build and to fly this plane, how important it is to all of them that you make this flight. But there's not much you can say. You can't explain why each of you is what he is, how you all came together to do this thing, to fly the first airplane to reach the speed of sound, the wonderful defiance with which this flight is being made.

"It's something," you finish abruptly, "we've got to do."

"I know." She suddenly smiles. "Good luck."

Three days later, on January 3, 1949, the baby is born, a fat and healthy little girl. Her name is Sharon.

And two days later, on January 5, the plane is finally ready for the ground take-off. Early that morning, you riding its wing, the crew chief mounted on its tail, the little X-1 is hauled by a yellow tractor down to the edge of the lake. The rest of the crew rides on ahead in a battered weapons carrier, its black- and yellow-checkered flag moving ahead like an advancing guidon against the unseen enemy—Bridgeman, the Navy and their Douglas *Skyrocket*.

Even at rest the X-1 seems again this morning to be almost alive and borne on air. Confident and yet professionally diffident, amused and yet concerned, the crewmen disperse themselves around the ship and wait. Crouching on heels, they grin up into the sky, nod heads, turn grinning to you and smile at one another.

"Well." You enter the cockpit. "Here we go." And the *we* is superfluous. The men who, waiting, watch you enter the ship, all have a part in this. It may be the last bold gesture you will all make together. It is a gesture that you feel compelled to make.

Because—The hell with the Navy! Rockets two and four cut in at once with their double blast. Now you fire one and three, and then, releasing the brakes, slip from the first imperceptible movement into a sudden rush across a bare one hundred and twenty feet of ground. Less than a second later the ship is airborne, shooting up with an exhaust velocity of over a mile a second. In one hundred seconds from the time the first rocket is fired, you're up to 23,000 feet. Some of the crewmen have not yet risen from their heels as you jettison fuel and lox and glide back in to land again. The crewmen move now as suddenly as the ship had moved a few short minutes ago, some leaping up with laughter, some men swearing with delight. You yourself, as the wheels touch down and the X-1 rolls across the runway to a stop, are still digesting the sensation of that sudden climb.

Unlatching the door from within, you reach from the cockpit now to shake the hands that wildly reach for yours.

"God damn!" somebody shouts exultantly. "The hell with the Navy!"

Relieved of your weight as the crewmen lift you out, the nose of the X-1 bobs gently up and down. The ship sits quietly at rest again. But the wild and excited men all rush you, laughing, off to celebrate. And Glennis, still in the hospital, waits nervously for you—or for someone else to call.

33

Glennis is better, happier now and more at ease, a little more certain each time you fly the X-1 that it's no more dangerous than any other plane. That isn't true, of course. On one flight in the X-1 you went into a high-speed stall at 63,000 feet, fell more than 20,000 feet before recovering. But the illusion of safety in the plane is something you both try to build against the obvious risk with which you go each day to work.

And gradually your life begins to settle down again. You have a new house in the Wherry project a mile or two from the base, and the new car you promised Glennis— it's a pale-green Model A, not much of a car to look at. There is, in fact, something absurd in parking this thirty-year-old coupé to pilot the X-1. But there's a car at home for Glennis now, more freedom for her, less time in which to worry about the *if* with which she continues to live.

The project meanwhile goes on, long after the X-1 has been grounded, sent to the Smithsonian Institution in Washington, veteran of more than a hundred dangerous flights. For there are new planes now and your job is still the same. Each morning you get up and fly, each night go home to sleep, sometimes to dream. But hitting Mach 1 has become a common experience in which other pilots begin to share. Ridley has flown the X-1, and Colonel Ascani and Colonel Boyd. The plane has been flown, too, by Captain Jim FitzGerald, dead now, by Major Gus Lindquist, Colonel Frank Everest and a respectable handful of other Air Force pilots. Her sister ship, the X-1 Number 2, has been flown in their careful and exploratory

251

way by NACA's civilian pilots—by Howard Lilly, dead now, by Herbert Hoover, first civilian pilot to follow you through the barrier—a smaller handful, a few more.

As for the X-1 Number 3, that one blew up. It was totally destroyed during a loading operation at the base. But there have been other planes designed and built to continue the search—each new airplane a new experiment as carefully tested and cautiously built as the X-1 was to carry its pilot and a quarter-ton or more of instruments at faster speeds and higher altitudes—each flight a new departure into the high and wide unknown—each fact recorded, filmed, radioed or telemetered back to ground to extend from day to day the limits of the known world.

There's the Bell X-2, all stainless steel with sharp-edged swept wings. Powered by a Curtiss-Wright rocket engine, the plane exploded over Lake Ontario in the Spring of 1953, killing its pilot "Skip" Ziegler and a crewman in the mothering B-29. Bell promptly built a second version of the ship. And there's the Douglas X-3, Northrop's tail-less X-4, and Bell X-5 with an adjustable wing whose sweep can be varied in flight from 20 to 60 degrees. There are others, too—the XB-51, the delta wing XF-92, and those less radical, almost operational ships, the B-47s, B-51's, F-91's and XF-92's that come to the base for endless tests. You fly them all and even the slowest of these planes is sonic now. Somebody, somewhere, hits Mach 1 in something almost every day. And Pancho Barnes, who used to offer a meal on the house and all you could drink to any pilot who reached Mach 1 and lowered the sonic boom, politely withdraws her offer as you finished your fourteenth free filet.

"It's not only you, Chuck," she complains. "It's everybody else. I'll be feeding the whole damn Air Force one of these days."

"Pancho," you admit, "you've got a point. Let's have another beer." Then after thinking a moment you grin at her. "I'll tell you what. Why not let the offer stand to the first guy who hits Mach 2?"

"Mach 2? How fast is that?" she wants to know.

"Oh, 1,600 miles an hour—twice the speed of sound."

"Sounds like a good risk." Pancho laughs. "Let's let it stand at that. But I don't know why you should be interested," she goes on. "You'll be so old by then you won't be able to chew a steak. It'll be some twenty-year-old kid with an appetite like a horse."

"Like to lay a little side money?"

"Just a minute," Pancho says. "I've got a funny feeling I've just been had. What do you know that I don't know?"

"Nothing," you grunt. "Here's to the next one, Pancho. Just tell the chef not to make the steak so rare."

"Go on." Pancho pretends disgust. "Get out of here." She picks up your empty glass and walks indignantly away.

And you go back to work again, back to the same old job of flying airplanes, your hands a little more weathered now from the pressures under which you fly, a few more lines around your eyes. Your hair begins to thin out a little. And maybe your reactions aren't as fast as they were. But the tension of 1947 and '48 has leveled off. The children are growing now. Glennis has even decided she ought to have another one.

"What will it be this time?" Ridley wonders.

You predict, "Another girl."

"Don't be so sure," Glennis says. "The odds are two to one."

"And, boy, they're really odd. Mickey, Don!" you call out as the boys come racing through the front door, run into the kitchen, slip back through the hall and out of the house again.

"What?" A cowboy hat on his head and a big cap pistol in his hand, Mickey leans through the door and grins.

"You kids aren't making half enough noise for cowboys," Glennis says. "Whoop it up a little more."

"Bang!" Mickey says, raising his pistol with both hands. Pulled suddenly from outside, he abruptly disappears and the door slams shut again. "I don't want to be an Indian," Mickey wails outside and Sharon comes crying into the house.

"They won't play with me!" she sobs.

"Come on, honey, up here on Daddy's lap."

"But I want to play with Mickey!" she protests.

The door flies open again. Don, followed by Mickey, comes running in, slides into the dining room, runs through the kitchen into the hall. Still together, the boys race through the living room once more and out again.

"I'll be an Indian!" Sharon cries as she slips away from you to follow them.

"Well," Don says, "you've got to lay down then when you're shot." And he shouts, "Bang!"

"Boy—" Glennis shakes her head—"what am I going to do with four like that?" And a few days later—in October of 1951—Susie is born.

"Two of a kind," you tell Jack as you pass out the cigars.

"Not bad for a beginner," Ridley says. "One more, Chuck, and you'll have a full house."

You tell him wryly that you've got a full house now and you go back to work again, to plane after plane in which you fly at speeds impossible to reach, incredible a year ago. And the routine of your work at Muroc, its name now changed to Edwards Air Force Base, is broken only by equally routine trips all over the world. You fly to England, Germany, Dayton, Ohio, and Washington D. C. You fly to Okinawa to test the first captured MiG, down to Los Angeles to make a speech. And you come to feel after a while like a puppet hung on the end of somebody else's string. Life isn't yours any more to live quietly at home. Fame, if that's what it is that continually takes you away, is nothing but interference with the things you really want to do.

It's not that you're the best pilot in the world. The Air Force has hundreds of pilots as well-qualified as you are to do all the things you have to do, and to make the speeches about them, too. You're no better pilot than any of the other men who've been trained to test-fly experimental ships. It's just that you flew the X-1 on its ninth powered flight. It might have been Bob Hoover, Jack Ridley, somebody else. But you were there in the cockpit of the plane on October 14, 1947. There are times when you honestly wish it had been someone else. When you see your family for the first time in weeks, leave them again for Mexico, or for Butte, Spokane, New York, Chicago or Hollywood. When you'd rather be flying, hunting, fishing or anywhere else in the world, but you're cramped instead at another banquet table, facing another microphone. When Don asks, "Will you be home for my birthday, Dad?" and all you can tell him is, "I hope so, son."

It's no pleasure, this being a showpiece. Because all the while you have to go on with your primary duty. No matter what's happened, you're just another pilot in competition with everyone else assigned to the base. You have to do just as good a job as anyone else can do. You have to do better, in fact. Publicity has given you a reputation, credited you with testing ability no pilot can possibly deserve. Half of it is just plain rumor and the other half isn't true. But you have to fly with that reputation, compete with it, just as you have to compete with everyone else. And you have to be ready to jump into a plane and scoot off to dinner whenever the whistle blows.

So that after a while combat, the war in Korea, seems like the last refuge, the easiest spot in the world. "Jack," you tell Ridley one night, "I've had enough of this. I'd like to go to Korea, to get back in a fighter squadron again."

"You would?" Ridley asks. "Why?"

"If Glennis would let me."

"Well, she's not about to. Are you, Glennis?"

"Judas Priest!" Glennis says flatly. "That's all I need. Something else to worry about."

You know you won't go but you try to explain the way you feel. "I'd like to go," you begin, but you don't know what to say. It isn't the danger, the killing, the excitement of combat. You've had enough of that to last the rest of your life. But during the war you lived in your squadron with rich and wonderful simplicity, enjoyed companionship you've never found since then except with Ridley himself and with a few others during the early weeks of the project here.

"I'm tired," you finally begin. "Except for you, Jack, I've got to compete with every pilot here. I've even got to outfly myself. I have no real complaint. These pilots are all nice guys. As far as the Air Force is concerned, we've got a team out here. But it's not like a squadron is. And you fly too damn many different planes."

"We all do," Ridley agrees.

"Yeah, but we don't all drag our tails from one end of the country to the other all year long, and in between trips sit down and try to fly four or five different, completely different airplanes every day. Sometimes I sit in the cockpit of an old F-80, something I know well and I've flown before, and I have to go through the whole damn system to remember it again. The new ships are even worse. You sit there and think it out. But you're never positive. You never know that plane as well as you should, as well as you'd know it if it was the only plane you had to fly. I don't think I've been completely relaxed in an airplane in the last five years."

"Who has?" Jack says. "Those days are gone forever, Chuck. Flying will never be the fun it was for any of us. Remember the first airplane you ever flew? A light little single-engine, fabric-covered trainer. All you had to do was keep it level and keep it up. And you only wore enough to keep you warm.

"Then they started adding things to your equipment and to the plane—helmet and gloves and flying boots aren't enough for the pilot any more. You've got a G suit now, a pressure suit and an oxygen mask. You've got to have something to keep you afloat if you hit the water, and something to keep you dry. There's a suit to keep you warm at one altitude and a suit to cool you off at another. Year after year, Chuck, it's gotten to be a more nerve-racking business. It's enough to make you sick at your stomach sometimes. If they ever develop an oxygen mask you can throw up in, we'll probably all get sick more often than we do."

"Some conversation," Glennis interrupts to say.

"Well, Glennis," Ridley goes on, "unfortunately it's true. Look at what's happened to airplanes." He shakes his head. "That little propeller-driven, gasoline-powered, fabric-covered monoplane that was fun to fly is a thing of the past, as far as military aviation is concerned. We find ourselves in sometimes doubtful control today of something that's apt to become a missile before we know it. Look at the planes we fly—air-conditioned, heated for one altitude, cooled for another. And the higher and faster we go, the colder the airplane has to be on the skin. But the pilot has to work in reasonable warmth. Otherwise his protective clothing would hold him helpless in his seat.

"And he can't sit helplessly there while the airplane flies itself. The pilot is surrounded by instruments that tell him what to do. On radio alone he's got half-a-dozen channels he ought to monitor. He may have four or five different radar systems. He's almost got to be an engineer. The plane has a complex electrical system, an intricate hydraulic system and, on top of that, a number of automatic devices, servo mechanisms that work faster than any pilot can. But he's never certain that they're right. The whole airplane is, in fact, essentially a closed loop servo and there's no room for the pilot in the loop, however necessary his brain might be. His body is always in the way; it's a drag, the weakest instrument on which he depends for his life.

"Maybe," Ridley finally suggests, "that's why we're all so damn uncomfortable sometimes. Maybe that's why you feel the way you do."

"You may be right," you admit. "All I know is that I'm tired tonight."

"Hang on for a while, Chuck," Ridley tells you then. "The X-1A is coming out."

"The X-1A? What kind of ship is that, Jack?" Glennis wants to know.

"Be like old home week," Ridley says. "Just like the X-1 but just about twice as fast."

"Well—" Glennis moves restlessly in her chair—"here we all go again."

"Don't worry about it, Glennis," Ridley says. "It'll be just like old times."

"That," she says sadly, "is just exactly what I mean."

Epilogue, September, 1953

34

Immediately behind one of the two big hangars at Edwards Air Force Base there is a small building, a long, one-story frame structure with a sloping roof. This is "the office," local field headquarters of the Bell Aircraft company.

Entering, you find yourself in a narrow corridor running the length of the whole east wall. The doors that open off this hall are all marked with neatly lettered signs. *Test Methods Section, Administration, Engineering Files, Instrumentation Data and Analysis, Flight Test Engineering, Design and Structure, Blueprints*. Each door leads into a different office. Working in any one of them you will almost always find some of the men who build, who service and maintain or fly the company's experimental ships.

And here you will still find today some of the men who long ago, in the old conventional days of piston-engine, high-octane-powered and propeller-driven flight, researched, designed, constructed, tested, guessed about and finally flew the Bell X-1. In those old days they were all young. But they are old men now, some over forty, almost forty-five.

"It's a good thing we were all young," one of them, Wendell Moore, remembers. Still a young-looking thirty-five, a power plant engineer on the X-1, he has the same job today on a new ship, the X-1A. "Some things we did," he says, "only because we didn't know they couldn't be done."

You're in the hangar now. It is 1953, and the impossible is still carefully being done. Tucked in one corner of

259

the hangar, dwarfed by a wingless rocket, a four-motored experimental jet bomber, and half-a-dozen other ships of varying size, sits the squat little X-1A, successor to the X-1. It looks like the same fat little airplane, low on the ground, heavy on its small tires, wingless almost and still like a hummingbird, its sender foil extended to explore the thin, unreadied air through which it speeds.

The skin of the X-1A is unpainted, though, like stainless steel. But wires, tubing, pumps and valves, the veins and nerves with which she flies, are still bright-colored within her pale-green belly, just as vivid against her gleaming skin.

It is, you know, essentially the same ship, although important changes have been made. The cockpit sits high up on the nose for better visibility. The whole of her fuselage for three feet or more behind the pilot's seat is lox tank now—Dick Frost's idea. He got rid of the heavy sphere, making this section of the plane itself a drum-shaped tank. This new plane carries more lox, flies for whole minutes longer than the original X-1.

The turbine pump has been developed, too, to force the fuel and lox back to the rocket motor—the pump for which Bob Stanley had no time to wait. The old dangerous and heavy nitrogen-gas-pressure system is obsolete. And the ship no longer uses water-alcohol for fuel. Hydrogen peroxide, considered too dangerous in 1947, has taken its place.

But the X-1A looks like the same airplane and seems again too small and slight to carry a pilot, all her fuel and recording equipment at more than the speed of sound. Again you stand, your mind forgetting details of thickness, weight and size. And you're impressed by the airplane's smallness and ungainly grace.

Standing alone for a moment as the Bell ground crew works rapidly to ready the ship, you see in your mind the whole of the project's past, the preparation and the flights, the fear and pleasure in each drop. Ten, nine, eight, seven—it's an old routine by now. You've done it so often that the count-down now begins sometimes at five. The drop is the same. But flights are longer now and at faster speeds. For whole years lie between your first flight in the X-1 and your last, the fifth or sixth in the X-1A. Six whole years in which the project has grown and everything has changed. Yet everything is basically the same.

In a few minutes the X-1A will be towed from its hangar, filled with propellants, taxied down to the end of the runway, lashed to the ground and fired by some of the same men who were here six years ago. One of the same engineers will supervise the same sort of crew as they go through what is essentially the same routine, although more complicated now than it was in 1947. And you will sit as before in the crowded cockpit of the plane, checkout its power plant and its controls. Just to make certain that when the plane is in the air, the rockets will fire, the X-1A will fly.

"Well, Chuck," Moore says, "let's go. They're going to haul her out."

When you see the ship again she's sitting in the same old gentle fog of liquid oxygen, the whole midsection of her belly that is lox tank now, smoking white and frosting in the desert air. Surrounding her, the same familiar crew of men, the same vehicles all work against the same old risk.

"Remember the old days, Chuck?" Moore asks.

Yes, you can remember the old days. Everything seemed more simple then and probably was. There were fewer fire trucks and fewer guards. The beryllium copper wrench with which Moore approaches the ship now was a thing unheard of in the early days. You used ordinary steel tools until it occurred to someone that with liquid oxygen you needed only a little spark and the whole damn ship would blow up on the ground. No, there weren't so many restrictions, so many little things you had to do. You were all younger then, a little more eager and a little more secure. Why is it suddenly not the wonderful thing it was—this project and this ship?

Maybe—you answer the question Moore has stirred in your mind—it's just because six years ago you didn't know the little bit more you know today. It was all new then and all exciting. Each day's discovery merely increased the mystery of the day to come. Now it has almost become a grind. You'd rather be back in the car with Mickey and Don. In a great many ways you'd rather go fishing than go through the whole routine of preparing for another flight.

"Chuck," Moore calls then, waving you over to the ship.

Indifference gone, your interest fresh again, you walk through misty lox back into the present, into the project. And later the same old eagerness is in your mind as you drive with Mickey and Don to the edge of the tie-down area to which the ship is being towed.

"You boys stay in the car," you tell your sons.

"Can we watch?" Mickey wants to know.

"Yes, you can watch. But stay in the car."

"All right," Don says.

"Mickey," you tell him, "watch the tail. That's where you'll see the flame."

"Will it burn?"

"Sure, it'll burn but there won't be anything back there that can catch fire."

"Will it make noise?"

"Yeah, it'll make a lot of noise."

"More than a jet?" Don wants to know.

"Much more than a jet," you tell him.

"Gee!" Don says and Mickey echoes him.

You leave them then, a little regretfully, walk slowly away. By the time you reach the ship she's been nosed in to face the hangar a few hundred yards away and tied securely down to steel hooks set in the apron on which she stands. Fire trucks surround the plane, their hoses unleashed and running again. There's a sound truck, too. Crewmen, observers and engineers wear headsets and a microphone so that each can talk to the others, listen to everything that's said. It will all be recorded on tape run in the big sound truck so that after it's over you'll be able to hear whatever happened, whatever might be said. You'll even be able to see it all. The base photographer has set up a motion-picture camera. He runs meanwhile from one point to another taking hurried stills. It will all be a matter of record this time, you tell yourself, no matter what.

Yes, everything is different now, you think again, as you climb into the familiar cockpit of the little ship. Moore is at the cabin door, not Frost. You suddenly remember Frost and the other crewmen who are gone. Everything's changed. Your own job is different now; it is more complex. The ship has been visually examined and inspected for leaks. Now you begin the long list of items to be checked, a hundred and ninety-seven, to be exact, a list so long that each man holds in his hand a mimeographed write-up, reading as he works. And each marks off each item as it's checked.

But once the long list is completed there is only the same old blasting roar as you fire the number-four rocket first, then number two. You cut off four, then fire three and cut off two, then fire one and cut off three. And with number-one chamber running, you turn on three again, add two and four, the familiar roar increasing behind your back, blasting away from the stubby tail in a long bright flame that boils on the concrete apron, skids into desert sand and stone. Then for a moment you see this with your young sons' eyes, hear the loud blast as if for the first time. And for that moment fresh awareness of the power and purpose of this little ship sinks into your mind.

Fuel almost gone, you cut off number-four chamber now, then two and three. But something is wrong. You can't shut off number one. Moore finally reaches in and hits the panic button, an emergency cut-off that releases all fuel in the tanks. The rocket quits. You leave the plane.

Flat-voiced in the sudden silence, Moore says, "Well, we had a complete check-out on that one, Chuck. Even the panic button. You ever hit that before?"

"No," you admit, "don't think we ever did. Boy, there's just too much junk in that cockpit. Can't we get some throat mikes, get rid of all those wires?"

"Is that all that's bothering you? I guess we can," Moore says. And together you walk away from the ship.

The group around the plane is dispersing now. Firemen still wash down the ramp as the X-1A stands quietly at rest. But the sound truck moves off. The camera is swiftly dismounted and packed away. Observers walk to their cars and leave. It begins suddenly to rain.

"There's Iwanoski," Moore says. "I want to talk to him. He ought to know what happened to that thing."

"See you." You wave and walk back to the car.

"Boy," Mickey says, "I bet it gets hot in there!"

"No, son," you answer, "as a matter of fact, it's pretty cold."

"I told you so," Don says.

"Well, Don, you've seen the thing before," you tell him quietly.

"He doesn't know anything," Don says.

And Mickey answers, "Yes, I do."

Back in the office five or ten minutes later—the small room crowded with six or seven men—you sit wherever you can and talk it out. Cross-legged on Moore's desk, you watch him drink milk from a paper cup. Mickey and Don have found the well in Moore's desk and in the big desk facing his. You can hear them crawling through their tunnel, whispering, laughing between themselves.

"Don," you say quietly, "Mickey, behave yourselves."

With a sudden scramble the two boys simultaneously pop up from different ends of their hiding place. "We are," Don says and Mickey echoes him.

The men in the room laugh loudly and the talk goes on. "Suppose we can get those old headphones out of there, get rid of all those wires, Wendell?" you ask Moore.

"We can do that," Moore says between sips of milk.

Sartore, listening, says nothing. He's waiting for a long-distance call from Buffalo. You talk for a moment about the weather, then fall silent, each of you wondering what happened to the rocket chamber that wouldn't quit.

"Must have been a valve," Moore says suddenly.

"Where's Iwanoski?" Sartore asks. "He ought to know."

As if he'd been waiting for his cue, lean, hawk-faced Iwanoski comes abruptly into the room. "I got it," he says. He holds in his hand a cylindrical object smaller than a spool of thread, no bigger around than a dime. This is the valve that stuck, and it is passed from hand to hand, each man examining its small defect.

"Ha," you say.

"What would have happened if that thing had stuck while you were up in the air?" somebody asks.

"Yeager," Moore says, "would have really had a ride. Let's get some lunch."

And it is established once again in the fall of 1953, after six years of flight, precaution and development, that the plane you fly is still a dangerous plane. Anything can happen on the ground or in the air.

35

Two months later, on 12 December, 1953, you make another routine flight in the X-1A.

Airborne, spiraling slowly to launch altitude, you go carefully through the long check list, one necessary item at a time. The B-29 cautiously circles above the sprawling base. To right and to left the chase planes fly. Ridley waiting on one side, Murray waiting on the other. In the bomber above you, down on the ground below, the men assigned to the project—pilots, technicians and engineers—move once more through the strict procedure that precedes the drop.

"Item thirty-five."

"Roger."

"One and one-quarter degrees nose down."

"Roger. Item three-six-*a*."

"Building first stage. Items three-six-*a* and three-six-*b* are complete."

"Roger, Chuck." The voice is DeYoreo's, crew chief riding in the B-29. You know one another so well now you no longer need to use last names on the interphones and over the air. "Items *c* and *d* now being completed."

"Charlie, you have good lox top-off now," Murray reports from the chase plane on your left.

"Roger. Item *c*," DeYoreo goes on.

"Lox shut-off valve coming open," you answer. "Now it is open."

"This is Bell One, Russ." DeYoreo calls Major Harold Russell, piloting the B-29. "Approximately four minutes to drop."

266

"Roger, four minutes to drop."

"Lox top-off procedure being terminated, Charlie," DeYoreo continues. "Item three-seven-*a*."

"*A* is complete."

"*A* is complete and *b* is complete. Item three-eight."

"Three-eight is complete. Bell One to Bell Two." DeYoreo calls Garth Dill back in the bomb bay of the B-29. "Garth, can you disconnect the lox top-off source, please?"

"Right," Dill answers, "Bell Two to Bell One. The lox top-off fitting is disconnected and stowed."

"Roger, Garth. Go ahead with item forty."

"Three-nine complete," you chime in, "going to forty."

"Yeager," the Bell truck calls from the ground, "there is no wind on the lake."

"Okay, mate."

"Charlie, this is Russ," the bomber pilot calls. "I would like to drop in about one minute, if I can. We would be in a good position."

"Take just a second, Russ. Item forty complete, Sil," you tell DeYoreo. "I have about 3,900 pounds."

"Item four-two," he answers.

"Four-two coming on. Four-two complete."

"Roger, forty-three complete and forty-four."

"Okay, chase pilots. This is Yeager. Lox jettison valve is coming open."

"Good jettison," Murray and Ridley call in.

"This is DeYoreo, Yeager. Okay four-six."

"Four-seven is complete," you answer.

"Ready for four-nine."

"Four-nine is complete."

"Fifty—is five-zero complete, Charlie?"

"I will get it on the count-down. I am all clear to drop now." Without thinking about it any more, you hunch down in the seat, dry-lipped again, your body braced against the routine shock, your fingers tight as always on the stick.

"Okay," Ridley's voice begins. "Building speed, Charlie. Thirty-two thousand feet now, 210 miles an hour. When I kick you out you will probably be about ten miles north of

Victorville on a heading of 280 degrees. Building up speed now . . . got two-fifteen . . . got two-forty . . . now two-forty-five. Okay, Charlie. You give me the word for the count-down."

"Okay, Russ, start your count-down slowly."

"Roger, starting count-down, staring from five down to zero. Five—four—three—two—one. Okay," he tells the co-pilot, "drop her, Danny."

The co-pilot pulls the release as he says, "Drop!"

And your monologue begins as you drop out again. "Drop is okay . . . firing four . . . four on—"

"No light, Chuck," Ridley interrupts.

"Is it on now?"

"Yes, it is on now," Ridley says.

"Will fire two . . . fired two."

"Bell truck, Yeager," the ground calls now. "What cylinders are on?"

"Four and two are on . . . three coming on now . . . start . . . cylinder seconds on two-fifty right now . . . cylinder seconds back to ninety-seven right now."

"Bell truck, we have your time, Chuck."

"Okay. Push over."

"Bell truck, twenty seconds."

Dropped at 30,000 feet, you climb on three cylinders to 45,000 feet and cut in Number one. From there you go up with full power on in an arc to 70,000 feet. Up there you level off. You're pushing the thermal barrier now. The heat on the skin of the X-1A is a scorching heat. But it's cold in the cockpit of the plane. Things happen so fast—you're flying at such tremendous speed—you've got so much to do that you don't reallly know what happened. And looking back later on you don't really care to remember.

"Visibility in the X-1A is better than it was in the original X-1," you will admit. "I don't know whether that was any help at all. I saw things I'd rather not have seen . . . the wings buffeting with the shock waves on them . . . a rather rough flight . . . certainly wasn't a gravy ride. I was busy with that airplane. . . ."

Approaching 1,700 miles an hour, design speed of the

airplane, the X-1A is hit by violent shocks. You reach a maximum speed of 1,650 miles an hour—*twice the speed of sound!* Your fuel exhausted then, you pull out through the same violent buffeting and shock into the transonic range again. Then, suddenly, you lose control of the ship. You're not flying the airplane any more. There is no correlation now between what you do and what the X-1A does as it hurtles along, still up at 70,000 feet. You're in the airplane and that's all—just going with it for the ride. And now you're really scared. This is the end. You're going to get clobbered now. You know you are. It's over, the whole damn thing. You're dead.

"Got him in sight, Kit?" Ridley calls Murray as if from yesterday.

"No," Murray answers from the past. "He's going out of sight—too small."

The voices have no reality in this lost moment of your life. You're taking a beating now and you're badly mauled. You can see stars. Your mind is half-blank, your body suddenly useless as the X-1A begins to tumble through the sky. There is something terrible about the helplessness with which you fall. There's nothing to hold to and you have no strength. There is only your weight, knocked one way and another as the plane drops tumbling through air. The whole inner lining of its pressurized cockpit is shattered as you're knocked around, and its skin where you touch it is still scorching hot. Then, as the airplane rolls, yaws and pitches through a ten-mile fall, you suddenly lose consciousness. You don't know what hit you or where.

It is like dying really because you've given up. Without even knowing how or why, you've reached a point where there is nothing you can do, no move you have strength enough to make. For the first time in your life you've lost control, not just of your plane, but of your hands. You swear, you pray, and nobody hears a word, not even you. Because you're knocked out cold. In fifty-one seconds you fall 51,000 feet.

Then you come slowly back to life again. "Yeager?" you hear. "Chuck!" Ridley is calling insistently. "Where are you, Charlie?"

The plane has righted itself and is now in a graceful, slow and gentle glide. "I'm . . . I'm down—" You hear yourself gasping hoarsely, trying to talk. "I'm down . . . to 25,000 . . . over Tehachapi. Don't know . . . whether I can . . . get back . . . base or not. . . ."

"At 25,000, Chuck?" Ridley demands, his voice even more insistent now.

"I'm—I'm—" you begin to babble again. "Christ."

"What say, Chuck?" Ridley demands again.

"I say—" you begin to come to your senses now. "Don't know . . . if I tore up anything or not—" looking around you now—"But—Christ!"

"This is Murray, Chuck. Tell us where you are, if you can. Where are you, Chuck?"

"I think—" You're still gasping—"I can get back to the base . . . okay, Jack. Boy!" Your head has suddenly begun to pound. "I'm not going to do that any more!"

"Murray, Chuck—tell us where you are!"

"I'm—" You still can't get your breath. "Tell you in a minute . . . got 1,800 pounds source pressure . . . don't think you'll have to run a structure demonstration on this damn thing."

"Chuck from Murray. If you can give me altitude and heading, I'll try to check from outside."

"Be down at 18,000 feet. I'm about—be over the base at 15,000 feet in a minute."

"Yes, sir!" Murray says it as if to say *at last*.

"Those guys were so right," you comment. "Source pressure is still fifteen seconds. I'm getting okay now—got all the oscillograph data switches off—camera off. It's okay."

"Bell truck, Charlie—jettison and vent your tanks."

"I have already jettisoned. Now I am venting lox and fuel. Leaving hydrogen peroxide alone."

"Bell truck, Roger."

"I cut it—got in real bad trouble up there."

"This is Murray, Chuck. I have you."

"Does everything look okay on the airplane?" you ask him.

"I am still catching up to you."

"Going to do a 360 degrees here to the left," you advise him.

"I do not have you," Murray complains. "That's a T-33!"

"I am right over the end of the diagonal runway, right over the north-south runway at the three-and-a-half-mile marker. I am going to make a right-hand pattern—gear coming down. Source pressure still at 1,650. Gear down and locked. Got me in sight yet, Kit?"

"Negative."

"Come down to 12,000 feet on a right-hand down-wind leg over the end of the east-west runway in the south end of the lake."

"All right," Murray says. "I see him now."

"Got him, Kit?" Ridley asks.

"Yes," Murray answers.

"Flaps coming down," you report. "Source pressure still 1,600. I am a little fogged up—not too bad."

"No!" Murray calls out suddenly. "I don't have you, Chuck! That isn't him either!" he complains again.

"I'm on the base leg," you tell him. "I'll be landing on thirty-five right in a minute."

Your voice is still flat with your fatigue, and down on the ground small knots of worried spectators stand watching your approach.

"Kit," Major Thompson suddenly calls to Murray, "swing to the right, sharp! Clear down on the edge of the lake bed!" His voice is taut. "This is Tommy!"

"I'll be down over the south track there in a minute," you tell them wearily now, "down to 7,000 feet."

"Roger," Murray answers.

"Going to land a little long," you say. "I would appreciate it if you'd get there and get . . . this thing off—this pressure suit. I'm hurting."

"On the final, Kit!" Major Thompson calls.

"Just over the edge of the lake right now, Kit," you tell Murray. "Got about two-twenty indicated."

"Kit!" Major Thompsons calls. "He's right in front of you! Down below you to the right, Kit!"

"Fifteen-fifty," you continue. "Everything's all right. By God! I told you that counter went around twice!"

And Murray, behind you at last in his F-86, begins to talk you in. "Coming off fifty . . . thirty . . . twenty . . . twenty . . . twenty . . . five . . . two . . . holding about two-and-a-half . . . one. Looks good, mighty fine."

"You know," you admit as your wheels touch down again, "if I'd had an ejection seat, you wouldn't still see me in this thing. If there'd been any way to get out, I'd have gotten out."

"Chuck," the Bell truck asks as you roll across the lake bed, "did your suit blow on you?"

"No, it never did. I opened the—uh—it got up to about 43,000 and I opened the windshield defroster and it went back down. I think I busted the canopy with my head."

"Bell truck to Yeager—wow!"

36

Battered and bruised, you sit down later to think it over. Has it been worth it, whatever you've done? And where will you go from here?

"What do you think?" you ask Larry Bell.

"Chuck," Bell says carefully, "I think the record will show that this airplane—all the X-1's, I should say—is probably the most valuable research airplane the government has ever had. It's had quite a career, that airplane has. And so have you.

"In terms of its performance the X-1 could easily be painted as the most dangerous airplane in the world. Yet it's never killed anyone. And—you may not agree with me after what happened to you today—I don't think it ever will, not in flight. Not just because it's a good airplane. It's just fate. Isn't that a strange situation?" He looks from you to Ridley and to all the others in the room. "You can be clobbered in a hundred-mile-an-hour airplane. But fifteen or twenty men have flown the X-1 beyond the speed of sound. There have been no changes in its original design. It's the same air frame that came off Bob Wood's drawing board. And it's been a phenomenal ship. Why, it's gone faster than any man, child or beast, I guess, and it's gone higher, too."

Bell shakes his head. "Now as for what happened this morning, I don't know. At that altitude there isn't much air. You cut off all four engine cylinders at one time. Maybe the rapid loss of power made the ship lose stability in that thin air. Murray had the same trouble at even higher altitude. So, I don't know." He shakes his head

273

again. "Maybe you cut off the power too suddenly in one case, too gently in the other. Maybe we'll have this same thing happen at each multiple of the speed of sound. There may be a multisonic barrier of some sort. We just don't know.

"But—well, that's what this airplane is for, to investigate this kind of problem, this and heat—the thermal barrier—the problems of altitude and speed. So it may be better than it looks." He brightens then. "Anyway, the X-2 will be coming out here in the spring. It's a much better ship than the X-1A, much faster. Maybe then we'll see—"

"I think," you say, "I'll let somebody else take that one up."

"Just listen to the old man," Ridley says. "He wants to retire into a fighter squadron where life's easy and the flyin's fun. Thinks he'll be safer there, the lazy son of a gun."

"My God, Chuck," Bell says, "you're a fixture out here! Nobody will know this place if you take off."

"That's right," Jack says. "Hell, you'll be homesick. Are you sure you feel—"

You feel a sense of achievement. It was a challenge to start with but you've accomplished a job. You're glad of that. You're in a good position now. That's certainly true enough. They give you a medal here and a trophy there. But you don't fool yourself.

You were all losing out. In peacetime, military pilots have always been looked down on, especially Air Force pilots in Flight Test. You were nothing a few years back but old diehards who couldn't get by on the outside. All you did for a living—well, you went out and pranged a few airplanes now and then. That's what everybody thought.

But this project opened a few closed eyes. It gave Air Force test pilots prestige they'd never had before. All men who fly respect you now for what you've done together, for what they know you'll go on to do. That, in addition to its assigned objective, is what this project accomplished.

"Hell," you say finally, "I'm no better pilot than the rest of you guys are who've been trained for this sort of thing. Just lucky to be in the X-1 at the right time." You touch the bruises on your face and suddenly grin. "To me, the biggest achievement for all of us is the fact that we've gotten something back that was somehow lost to military pilots. I can go out of here not knowing more than any company test pilot knows about flying a ship. But I'm rated higher than any civilian is. That's true for all of us. And seeing the shape the world is in right now, some day that might be worth whatever the project cost.

"As for leaving this place? Hell, I don't know—it's kind of hard to express. I'd like to get back into the old fighter grind and rest up. You fly one airplane and you're with good friends. That's the way I was trained and I'll go back to it at the drop of a hat."

"Looks to me," Ridley says, "like you're going back to it at the drop of an airplane."

And there is laughter now. "You're damn right, Jack," you admit, laughing with all the others.

But that's not all, you think, as the laughter runs on. It will be a good thing for your family. You'll get out of experimental testing, get into a squadron, go over to Europe again sometime. It will be nice for Glennis, who's had a pretty tough row to hoe, nine years of it. Nine years straight, with no breaks.

That night at Pancho's you propose four toasts. "To Glennis to begin with because—well, she knows why." You kiss her suddenly and drink. "Let's drink to the airplane now," you say, "the best damn ship I ever flew." You all drink then to the X-1 and to the X-1A. "Pancho," you call out when your drink is gone. "Fill 'em again, I've got another one. This is to Jack and to all the rest of you guys."

"Whose tab does this go on?" Pancho interrupts to ask.

"*Whose tab?*" you ask indignantly. "Haven't I got a little bet with you? Didn't you put up a meal and all we could drink against Mach 2?"

"All *we* could drink?" Pancho is just as indignant now as you are. "Hell, Chuck, didn't you leave a couple of squadrons back at the base? Can't I send something over to the guards? And besides—" Pancho begins to smile—"I said the first pilot to hit Mach 2. And it seems to me I paid off to Scott Crossfield a little while ago."

"Boy, look at her try to wriggle out of this one!"

"A deal," Pancho says flatly, "is a deal. Give Yeager another drink," she tells the bartender now. "This *one* is on the house."

"Okay," you finally submit. "I've only got one more toast to propose. Here's to the lucky son of a gun they assign to pilot the X-2!"

And Glennis says quietly, "Here's to the pilot's children—and his wife."

BANTAM
SHOP·AT·HOME
C·A·T·A·L·O·G

Special Offer
Buy a Bantam Book
for only 50¢.

Now you can have Bantam's catalog filled with hundreds of titles plus take advantage of our unique and exciting bonus book offer. A special offer which gives you the opportunity to purchase a Bantam book for only 50¢. Here's how!

By ordering any five books at the regular price per order, you can also choose any other single book listed (up to a $4.95 value) for just 50¢. Some restrictions do apply, but for further details why not send for Bantam's catalog of titles today!

Just send us your name and address and we will send you a catalog!